Also by Alistair Cooke:

A GENERATION ON TRIAL:
U.S.A. v. Alger Hiss (1950; 1952)

ONE MAN'S AMERICA (1952)

CHRISTMAS EVE (1952)

These are Borzoi Books
published in New York by Alfred A. Knopf

TALK ABOUT AMERICA

T·A·L·K ABOUT AMERICA

ALISTAIR COOKE

ALFRED ★ A ★ KNOPF

NEW YORK 1969

CONTENTS

To the American Reader   1

PROLOGUE

1   *Politics and the Human Animal*   5

I INSTITUTIONS

2   *The Cranberry Caper*   13
3   *The Father*   20
4   *A Tiny Claim to Fame*   28
5   *A Town Meeting*   32
6   *Beizbol*   42
7   *The Summer Bachelor*   48
8   *The Iceman Goeth*   55

II PROBLEMS AND STEREOTYPES

9   *The European's America*   63
10   *The Generation Problem: The Twenties*   71
11   *The Well-Dressed American, Man!*   77
12   *The American Neurosis: Instant Health*   84
13   *LBJ*   90
14   *Wanted: An American Profile*   97
15   *The World Gone to Pot?*   104

III PEOPLE AND PLACES

16   *Give California Back to the English*   113

17 *HLM:RIP*   120
18 *The Road to Churchill Downs*   128
19 *The Colonel of the Plains*   138
20 *Alcatraz*   145
21 *Marshall*   153
22 *The Submariners*   162
23 *The Palm Beach Story*   168
24 *Glenn in Orbit*   175
25 *Our Father Which Art in Heaven*   181
26 *A Lonely Man*   188
27 *A Ruined Woman*   194
28 *Robert Frost*   202
29 *The Non-Assassination of John F. Kennedy*   209

IV POLITICS

30 *The Business of America?*   219
31 *The Invisible Rulers*   225
32 *The Frontiersman*   232
33 *Topic A: 1954—The Court and the Negro*   239
34 *Topic A: 1963—The Deep South*   247
35 *Topic A: 1965—Watts*   253

V THE VIEW FROM THE WEST

36 *The Western Myth*   261
37 *John McLaren's Folly*   268
38 *The New Californian*   276
39 *California: A Foretaste of Tomorrow*   283
40 *A Bad Night in Los Angeles*   290

EPILOGUE

41 *Vietnam*   301

TO THE AMERICAN READER
———————————————————✳

Sixteen years ago, I put together a collection of the weekly radio talks I had been broadcasting from the United States for the B.B.C. since the last day of March 1946. The broadcast series was known, and still is, as "Letter from America." The book was called, in this country, *One Man's America*. What to call this second, and larger, collection? Much has happened to the smiling face of America in the meanwhile, and for a time I was tempted to call this volume *Another Man's Poison*. Some people say we are on the verge of the Second Civil War. And it may be so. But even on the darkest days, cheerfulness kept breaking in. I am not by nature a "Whither America?" man.

This may annoy people abroad, and cantankerous immigrants, who accept the ups and downs of their own way of life but like to picture the United States as a different order of society: one big crass tragedy. America, it may be news to the learned, is a part of the human condition and within its borders there is still a vast variety of interest, amusement, goodness, evil, humor, absurdity, and all the other human attributes. These are what anybody's letters touch on, and these talks were always conceived as a little link between the writer and a sympathetic listener an ocean away in a room or an automobile. If the reader should want to know further about their "purpose" I hope that the Prologue will meet the case.

They are printed in a roughly chronological order except where a topic is timeless enough to fit in anywhere. I have again run together talks on the same theme. Mostly they are printed as they were given except where the printed page demands a little more attention to readable syntax. The three talks about the Negroes carry the dates when they were given, because by so doing they show the great changes in our attitude toward the so-called Negro revolution.

I have done, I suppose, dozens of talks on Vietnam, but on reflection I decided that the one here included as an epilogue (it was given on March 24, 1968, and was the thousandth in the series) will suffice to say the best that I can contribute about that disastrous episode in American history.

Most Americans, in spite of the evangelism of bloodshot politicians, live their lives without any feeling of "national destiny" and without seeing their country as the big, brutal world power of the nasty cartoons. My aim is still what it was when these talks began: to run up and down the human scale that unites a Lancashireman to a Texan and a German to a Siamese. I was staggered to discover, only four years ago, that these "Letters" are heard on every continent but this one. I have been welcomed, and heartened, by friendly families in Switzerland and Kenya and Hong Kong and Sydney and Singapore and remote islands in the Caribbean. I am glad I never knew this sooner. I might have discovered a "mission" as an interpreter. It is now too late. People are sufficiently alike in Leeds and Los Angeles and Bangkok to embrace their similarities, and sufficiently different to shout, "*Vive la différence!*"

Courage, men. The human beings may yet defeat the politicians.

A. C.

New York City, June 30, 1968

PROLOGUE

1

POLITICS AND THE
HUMAN ANIMAL

As sometimes happens, I was chided the other morning,[1] in a letter from an indignant correspondent in England, for having given a talk about the complexities of American football when I might better have given a sermon about the complications of the Middle East. Men were dying, he reminded me. Empires were tottering. A tyrant was squeezing the lifeblood from Britain's lifeline in the Suez Canal. In a word, I was fiddling while London, Cairo, and Washington burned.

If I believed this, I should be embarrassed to talk at all about one country to another. But in all these talks I have gone along on the original theory that people are permanently curious about how other people live, and that all the politicians and propagandists in the world working three shifts a day cannot forever impose their line on two people sitting alone in a room. They are the only proper audience for a letter. I grant my correspondent that there are vast heavings and resettlings of power around the world; that there is a ferment in Asia and Africa; that there is a periodic flow of bad blood across the Atlantic; that the rich grow richer and the poor poorer with consequences that could end in world

[1] During the height of the Suez crisis.

famine and revolution. I can only reply that I still feel no embarrassment in maintaining, in a warlike time, a civil tongue.

If this sounds impertinent in our present troubles, let me repeat a few sentences I wrote as the preface to a collection of these talks that was put out some years ago: "Politics will undoubtedly bedevil us all till the day we die, but . . . even the prospect of early annihilation should not keep us from making the most of our days on this unhappy planet. In the best of times, our days are numbered, anyway. And it would be a crime against Nature for any generation to take the world crisis so solemnly that it put off enjoying those things for which we were presumably designed in the first place, and which the gravest statesmen and the hoarsest politicians hope to make available to all men in the end: I mean the opportunity to do good work, to fall in love, to enjoy friends, to sit under trees, to read, to hit a ball and bounce the baby."

Am I saying that the world is too much with us, and is incurable anyway, and that we should gather roses while we may? I am saying no such thing. I *am* saying that when the nations rage furiously together we should not be misled by their hullabaloo into thinking that the world's anxieties, however grave, are the fundamental things in life and that all else is a bauble. It happens, merely, to be my daily chore to sit and watch and listen to the chief actors on the political stage, domestic and foreign, and I am struck by many things. By the ease with which a nation does something from instinct and justifies it by reason. By the careerism and vanity that dogs the ambition of most politicians and statesmen. But I am struck most of all by the absence of humor, which as much as any other solvent could relax the protagonists in any quarrel, however international, and halt them in their race to murder each other from the highest motives. Most of the chief dele-

gates to the United Nations are hard-working men, but because they are trying to handle the world's conflicts they are
not thereby or necessarily the most serious men around. Some
of them are certainly the solemnest men around.

And however splendid the United Nations Charter may
be, there is nothing inherently noble about the United Nations
delegations. I suggest that my critic is making this sort of
mistake. He is mistaking the label on the can for the contents.
Most first-rate comedians are in private life more serious than
most politicians and all of them are melancholy men. And
what may be essential to one's self-respect may not be essential to a friendship, whether at the other end of a loudspeaker
or at the other end of a room.

I have, for instance, a close friend, a merry, kindly, and
simple man, very able in his special field of finance. I feel
agreeable in his presence and I admire his human qualities.
At the shabbiest period in recent American history, when the
fear of domestic Communists was most paranoid, this friend
was a strong, even a devout, McCarthyite. He used to load my
morning mail with the transcripts of all the testimony before
the Senate Subcommittee on Government Operations, over
which the late Senator Joseph McCarthy presided with—by
my lights—such indignity and malevolence. Of course, Mc-
Carthyism was a fundamental issue of the time, not only an
American political issue but fundamental to any man's notions
of justice and decency. You might guess, therefore, that my
friend's admiration for McCarthy marked the parting of the
ways for us. Well, it was an embarrassment, but not to our
affection or continuing association. Of course, if by some convulsion of history (a sudden depression, say, and twenty million unemployed) McCarthy had become an American
dictator, my friend and I would probably have said goodbye
and retreated to opposite sides of the barricades. Nobody has

sharpened this point better, in my view, than the late Justice Holmes when he said that the purpose of civilized argument between friends is to arrive at the point where you agree that someday it might be necessary to shoot each other. Until that day is unavoidable "the democratic process" both in public and in private is no more but no less than an acceptance of the notion that in important issues you may be wrong.

My first mentor in journalism in this country was a man who had no use for democracy at all, except in this crucial belief. "Democracy," he once wrote, "is the theory that the common people know what they want, and deserve to get it good and hard." But he also wrote, "What I admire most in any man is a serene spirit . . . when he fights he fights in the manner of a gentleman fighting a duel, not in that of a longshoreman cleaning out a waterfront saloon." We had a tacit understanding that while I allowed him to shoot off his face about the fraudulence and guile of Franklin Roosevelt, I should then be allowed to go off and vote for him. This division never interfered with a friendship that was amiable at all times.

I believe this to be not only a sane approach to politics but essential to all the things that lie outside politics.

I hope that the blood pressure of my critic is still holding. Politics, I grant, is of great importance to us all, since it affects our survival and the future we plan for ourselves and for all the countries that lie outside our own. It is admirable, though not, I believe, compulsory, for people to take an interest in politics. But first things first. How much politics is there in the greatest novels? In Flaubert, Dickens, or Dostoevsky? How much in the greatest poetry? In Shakespeare, Yeats, John Donne, or whoever? Surely nobody will deny that poets and novelists, poets especially, deal with human experience at its most intense and most profound. Was Thomas

Hardy indifferent to the great issues of his time because he chose to look steadily and long at the life of a few Dorset villages? Is the poetry of Robert Frost trivial because it deals with a bit of pasture or the death of a hired man? Frost, by the way, had his own recipe for the end of the world. It would not come, he thought, in the shock of avenging armies but either by lust or by hate.

> Some say the world will end in fire,
> Some say in ice.
> From what I've tasted of desire
> I hold with those who favor fire.
> But if it had to perish twice,
> I think I know enough of hate
> To say that for destruction ice
> Is also great
> And would suffice.

You may say that a first-rate poet, because he is a rare bird, rarer than a first-rate politician, has earned a special exemption from the obligations of politics. Not because of his special gift, he hasn't. That would be like saying that all wars should be fought by the poor and the ungifted. And although a mere journalist cannot achieve the intensity or profundity of a good poet, he still has the obligation to see things as he sees them and not as he would like to, or as somebody else says he should. If paying tribute to Caesar is not his main business in life, he must pay his citizen's due and get on with what really interests him.

What do you suppose the Secretary General of the United Nations turns to when he goes home at night? Mr. Hammarskjold is, he likes to say, "the curator of the secrets and prejudices of seventy-nine nations." That should be enough to fill the waking hours of any conscientious man. But it evidently is not. When he steps off the high wire of his diplomatic circus and comes down to earth, does he agonize all over again about Suez or the Congo or the seizure of Hungary? He settles to the permanent things. He reads Eliot and Robert Lowell and André Gide and his favorite novelists —Mark Twain, Hemingway, Stephen Crane—and most of all the man whose high seriousness and perfect accommodation of his style to the thing he wants to say make him, in Hammarskjold's opinion, the modern master of serious English prose. James Thurber.

So let us take our stand on the Middle East or the presidential election or any other burning issue, and in the process perhaps lose a friend or shoot a friend, or agree to differ and do neither. Then let us get down to life and living.

I INSTITUTIONS

2

THE CRANBERRY CAPER

Many wise men, from the Greeks to the president of the Olympic Games committee, have deplored international athletics, the Olympic Games most of all, as an almost ideal method of stimulating international ill will. But offhand I can't recall anybody's deploring national holidays. Certainly I have never heard an American belittle, or as we now say downgrade, the festival of Thanksgiving. Other local and national orgies—Mother's Day (an invention of the florists and telegraph companies), Love-a-Dog-Week (an invention of breeders), and Income Tax Day (invented by Wisconsin) —they abide our criticism. Thanksgiving Day is free and sacred. And even to pry into its origins is not considered a patriotic thing to do. This may be because the most ardent patriotic celebrations are usually based in a myth. Thanksgiving is based in the strong belief, too holy to examine, that the first Americans fell in love with what they saw here and have been grateful, on the last Thursday in November, ever since.

Well, we all know that the Pilgrims settled on Cape Cod and subsequently called the place Plymouth. But only a weasel will want to remind us that those stout and forbidding puritans, whose character now seems so fitted to the bare seacoast and the cranberry bogs of Massachusetts—only a mean and scratchy person like me will reflect that these emigrants never had any intention of landing in what we now call New England. They were headed for Virginia, "where nature hath in store fowl, venison and fish, and the fruitfulest soil, without your toil. Three harvests more, all greater than you wish, and the ambitious vine crowns with his purple mass the cedar reaching high to kiss the sky, the cypress, pine and useful sassafras."

This, need I say, was written by a man who never went there. And in this sense Michael Drayton is the first of the American real-estate promoters. He wrote this come-on fifteen years before the exiles in Leyden joined their grumbling brethren in England and sailed out of Plymouth for what Drayton promised them was "Virginia, earth's only paradise." We all know, but don't like to say, that the Pilgrims were in several minds and many more quarrels aboard the *Mayflower;* and that, having missed the coast of Virginia, some of them wanted to follow Henry Hudson's course and come on to New York; that they were blown a couple of hundred miles to the north and east, realized it, turned south again, ran into more squalls and finally hove to off Cape Cod and made the best of it. They thanked God, who had brought them "over the vast and furious ocean, again to set their feet on the firm and stable earth." But they had no sooner done applauding His mercies than they reflected that "they had now no friends to welcome them, nor inns to entertain or refresh them, no houses or much less towns to repair to. Beside, what could they see but a hideous and desolate wilderness, full of wild beasts and wild men; for which way soever they turned their eyes they could have little solace or content, in respect of any outward objects." This advertising

copy has been allowed to lapse from the handouts of the
Massachusetts tourist board. It was written by William Bradford, a Yorkshireman, who did make the journey and who,
thinking back to Drayton's promises of the luscious fruits of
this delicious land, must have pondered bitterly on the wisdom of W. C. Field's advice: "Never give a sucker an even
break."

Well, what could they do? They could go home again,
and the honest Bradford says that "it was muttered by some
that if they got not a place in time they would turn them
around and leave their goods ashore, and leave them." There
was nothing to sustain them except the gloriously English
thought that they were English and that, therefore, however
miserable the physical prospect, it might be good for their
characters. Bradford cautioned them that if only they stayed
alive and begat original Cape Codders their children would
say: "Our fathers were Englishmen which came over this
great ocean, and were ready to perish in the wilderness, but
they cried unto the Lord, and He heard their voice and looked
on their adversity, etcetera." The delicious "etcetera" is Bradford's, not mine, and surely reveals a man racked with
strong emotion. However, there is no doubt that they stayed.
And that's how Thanksgiving, and cranberry sauce, and smog,
the martini, and the Bomb were born.

The accepted myth of Thanksgiving dates it either from
the moment the Pilgrims touched the weatherbeaten shore
and fell on their knees or, more plausibly, from a great feast
they threw after the first harvest. Both of these legends, I am
sorry to say, are of doubtful truth. For the puritans didn't approve of any sort of feasting or merrymaking, and it is a fact
that the day they got off the boat and resigned themselves to
digging the foundations of a colony was Christmas Day. All
merrymaking and even sacred celebrations were forbidden

on the dour grounds, reported by Bradford, that "what day soever our Lord was born, most certainly it was not the 25th of December."

Yet people have a habit of holding on the more tenaciously to historical celebrations for which there is the least historical proof. Some time or other, in the middle nineteenth century, somebody thought it would be a charming thing to declare one day in every year as a day of national Thanksgiving. Abraham Lincoln was the first president to put out a national proclamation to that effect, two hundred and forty-three years, by the way, after the thing itself. He was not warmly or widely taken up on it, but by the end of the century a good many states had their own Thanksgiving Day, on different dates. The problem now was to get them to recognize the same day. The moment a state acquires its own festival, any interference by the federal government is called tyranny, or censorship, and—in our time—"creeping socialism." Within living memory, Thanksgiving has settled on the last Thursday in November. And once this day was well established as an immovable American feast, Franklin Delano Roosevelt was on hand to move it. He was a great tickler of sacred cows not bred on his own pastures; and having failed to set up a new Supreme Court, he was miffed and thought of moving Thanksgiving back a week. This proved, what many patriots had long suspected, that Roosevelt was hankering after the restoration of the monarchy, and in a blaze of republicanism several governors put out their own counterproclamations. The row rumbled through the following year until Congress decided to put an end to it, as it had done just ten years earlier after another long wrangle, with an Act of Congress. In 1931, "The Star-Spangled Banner," a long and unsingable song, was declared to be the American national anthem. In 1941, the last Thursday in November was enacted as the true, the official and unchangeable and only day of Thanksgiving.

In the intervening years nothing blasphemous had happened to Thanksgiving until the Secretary of Health, Education, and Welfare heard that his health department, formally known as the Pure Food and Drug Administration, had discovered in two bags of cranberries traces—brace yourselves, men—of aminotriazole, a weed killer that had been distilled into its poisonous essence and forcibly fed to rats. Guess what? Of course, they got cancer.

It is possible that strangers to American folkways will feel at this point that they are losing the plot. Well, if the Pilgrims had landed in Virginia, chances are we should never have heard of aminotriazole, or better, of cranberries. But the Pilgrims, I think we have now made it plain, landed on Cape Cod. And just as people who own only one suit must go on brushing it lovingly, so the poor people of Cape Cod, who have hardly any crops to call their own, must make a pride of their cranberry bogs. When Bradford and his crew arrived, photography was not even in its infancy. So we have no picture, which I for one should relish, of the Yorkshiremen tasting their first cranberry and putting on their Charles Laughton face. But it was the link between them and starvation. It was what God had ordained for them, and being God-fearing men they found it good and tasty. Saving hellfire and brimstone, they had better. And ever since, it has been an unchallengeable American doctrine that cranberry sauce, a pink goo with overtones of sugared tomatoes, is a delectable necessity of the Thanksgiving board and that turkey is uneatable without it. I ought to say that American turkeys, which are bred now by a special process to have four breasts and weigh anything up to seventy pounds, are magnificent. But, you will have gathered, my testimony on cranberry sauce falls short of absolute objectivity. There are some things in every country that you must be born to to endure; and another hundred years of general satisfaction with Americans and America could not reconcile this expatriate to cranberry sauce, peanut butter, and drum majorettes.

There are some nations, the Syrians and Greeks among them, that manage to get along very well without defiling their lamb with mint sauce, or worse yet mint jelly. But who eats turkey without cranberry sauce? Certainly not any self-respecting American family on the last Thursday in November. Hence the terrible panic that overcame the country in 1959, when it was suspected that the acrid element, which Bradford and his men so manfully put up with (they died, by the way), was aminotriazole. The Pure Food and Drug Administration sent out a general warning. Those two lethal shipments might infect the seven million pounds of cranberries that had been preserved for consumption on Thanksgiving Day. Well, the Secretary of H., E., and W. went tearing through the whole sample and found that the two suspect bags were the only threats to the national survival. The other six hundred and ninety-nine million, nine hundred and ninety-nine thousand, and ninety-eight pounds were declared safe for human consumption. Safe, but no tastier. Now the American housewife was free to purchase the sacred berry and prepare it according to the subtle recipe dictated by Fanny Farmer, the Republic's Mrs. Beeton. If you must, here is the secret of cranberry sauce, which will load every plate in the nation and be served in little frozen gobs on plastic trays on every airplane. Here it is, set down a century ago with all the elaborate and loving Fanny Farmer flourishes:

"Three cups of cranberries, one and a quarter cups of sugar, one cup of boiling water. Pick over and wash cranberries. Cook with sugar and water ten minutes. Skim, cool, serve six."

Tension, as the newspapers say, mounted high when a reporter at the White House asked the President's press secretary if the President and Mrs. Eisenhower were going to take the risk of serving cranberry sauce with their Thanksgiving dinner. Mr. Hagerty, who can be high on dudgeon, said in high dudgeon that he didn't know and he didn't care. Would he care to find out? He said he most certainly did care and had no intention of finding out.

Mr. Hagerty, I think, was right. There are limits, or ought to be, to the prurience of the press. It is not for us to poke into the White House kitchen and check on the patriotism of the President of the United States. Let us leave it there.

P. S. The Eisenhowers served apple sauce.

3

THE FATHER

A simple way to turn an honest dime in a small company of Americans is to ask them on a bet how many national holidays are observed throughout the United States. They will usually count to no less than five: the birthdays of Washington and Lincoln, Independence Day, Thanksgiving Day, and Labor Day. There are in fact only three. Labor Day, invented in New York as a trades-union celebration, is not among them. Nor is the birthday of Lincoln. Only thirty-two states of the Union pause on the 12th of February to commemorate the most impressive life in the American experience. It was natural, however, that the defeated South should have taken a sour view of Lincoln for many decades after his death; and to this day, from Virginia round the whole bend of the South, through Louisiana and Texas, his birthday is officially disregarded. Once you cross the Texas line and enter New Mexico, you can begin to honor Lincoln again.

This leaves, therefore, only one American in history whom the entire country delights to honor. On every 22nd of February, the offices and factories close down. The hundred and seventy elevators that serve the sixty thousand wage slaves who work every day in the little plot of Manhattan ground known as Radio City—they run not at all, and the wind whistles through the shafts. Over the Post Office Building, looking out on a tropical sea in San Juan, Puerto Rico, an American flag is run up and languishes in the hot air. And five thousand miles to the north and west, in a forest lookout tower in the snow-capped Cascade Mountains, another flag goes up and slaps against a frozen pole. Over every public building in this country and its territories and possessions the flags are raised, and the schools are closed.

There is a Fifth Avenue dress house that always, on this day, takes away its early spring models and loops its windows with purple draperies, beneath which, in a pool of light thrown by a single high spot, stands a lump of cool white marble: the bust of a big-faced man with a big aquiline nose, a considerable chin, an eighteenth-century wig, and the drooping eyelid that novelists prescribe for what they call a patrician gaze. It is of course an effigy of George Washington, to whom once a year all sorts of men pay all kinds of tribute. Even the *Wall Street Journal* is not published on the sacred birthday, though the day before I see there was inserted a chaste two-column advertisement for a jewel firm. Its copy consisted of a single sentence: "If, to please the people, we offer what we ourselves disapprove, how can we afterward defend our work?" An oddly moral remark, you might think, for a jeweler. But the quotation was from none other than the father of his country.

Washington towers over the generations of notable Americans as Shakespeare towers over the literature of England. He is acceptable to everybody for at least one of the same reasons: we don't know too much about him, or what we have learned we have idealized, so every man can construct a Washington in the image he likes best. From time to time, most recently in the 1920's, snide authors come along to try and show that Washington was a promoter of stock companies, an exploiter of mines and timber, a man "who knew more profanity than Scripture . . . had no belief in the wisdom of the common people but regarded them as inflammatory dolts." But these scandals never seem to take. They get the same reception that they had from Calvin Coolidge when he was asked in the White House what effect a particularly scurrilous biography of the first President would have on his reputation. Coolidge swiveled round in his desk chair and biliously looked out the window at the soaring Washington monument, which is raised over the capital like the sword of the Archangel Gabriel. "He's still there," said Coolidge.

At this late date, it would be almost tasteless to compose a picture of Washington as a great if frail human being. Every nation has to have one or two blameless legends, and Americans feel as uncomfortable today to hear that Washington was a land grabber as an Englishman would be to hear that King Alfred was a cannibal or the late Queen Mary a secret drinker. Washington's birthday is as close to a secular Christmas as any Christian country dare come this side of blasphemy. I hasten to throw in quickly that the United States, though founded in the main by Christian men, was not set up as a Christian nation, since its creators had had their fill of the established church that hounded their forebears. It may explain why, when Americans are sorely troubled, they turn for official inspiration not to the Koran or the Bible but to the colonial scriptures, to the sayings of the Founding Fathers, most of all to the speeches of Washington.

There is today a pronouncement of his that they linger over with a great yearning. It is regularly reprinted and blazoned in newspaper editorials on any 22nd of February that Americans feel about to be tricked into a European war or seduced into an alliance. It is a passage from Washington's so-called Farewell Address, which he gave as he took leave of the presidency. It reads today rather like a commentary of General de Gaulle on the "special relationship" between Britain and the United States. This is it: "A passionate attachment of one nation for another produces a variety of evils. Sympathy for the favorite nation, facilitating the illusion of an imaginary common interest in cases where no real common interest exists . . . betrays the former into a participation in the quarrels of the latter, without adequate inducement or justification."

It does not quite have the swing of "Tell me where is fancy bred" or "My luve's like a red, red rose." So down the centuries Americans have tended to shorten this unmemorable, and unlearnable, passage into a snappy single phrase: "no entangling alliances." When it is pointed out that this is a misquotation, that the phrase actually came from the lips of Thomas Jefferson, the sensible retort is that, anyway, that's what old George meant to say.

Now that we have the effigy and its legend pretty well established, let us come down to the man himself.

His family came from England and he was born in Virginia in 1732. His father was what you might describe as a substantial small squire, a status that made him possibly a grander figure in the Southern colonies than he would have been in the old country. Almost anybody who owned land in Virginia led a life which was a curious combination of a farmhand and an aristocrat. (I am aware that grooms, gillies, and the like were all, until the First World War, elements of the aristocratic system—"all part of the same show," as a Prime Minister of England eloquently put it; but except in the rituals of blood sports their habits were not interchangeable.) Washington learned all that could be learned about the farming and management of his father's estate, which had passed to him from a half-brother who died young. He raised cattle, he was out in the fields growing tobacco, he shot wild turkey and ate it on the bone. He had taught himself a lot of mathematics and on his surveying trips he was always adding to his land. He rode by day and often by night, he brushed up against the Indians from time to time, and a scalp was as natural, I imagine, as a cow flop.

He served in the French and Indian Wars as a general's aide and had horses shot out from under him and acquired an enviable, though local, reputation for a blank refusal to panic. Then quite suddenly his health failed him and he resigned his commission and retreated, for what he thought would be the rest of his life, to a fine stretch of land overlooking the Potomac River where he had built an elegant and charming white house with a little Wren tower, a Colonial façade, and a long portico supported by slender columns. (It is now a national shrine and, along with the Spanish mission at Santa Barbara, California, used to be one of the two handsomest colonial relics in America. But both of them have been refaced and at close quarters look like something out of Disney.)

He was in his bearing and looks and manners an eighteenth-century British soldier and landowner; and if he could be resurrected he would undoubtedly alarm a great many Americans by sounding and seeming more British than the British. He had, for instance, very decided ideas about the relations of one class with another. In the towns, at any rate. In the country it was another thing: he was with many conditions of men who were "part of the same show." Not only did he not slap backs, he made a point on becoming President of not shaking hands. He thought it was unbecoming for the President of a great state to touch the flesh of his subjects.

The Senate used to bristle over this characteristic, and when he was inaugurated as President in New York—an early and transient capital—he came down the Hudson in a great barge and he clattered to the ceremony in full-dress uniform with a flourish of outriders. As he took the oath of office, the impressive silence was cracked only by the growl of a Senator from Massachusetts saying to his neighbor: "I fear that we may have exchanged George the Third for George the First."

You would think, then, that there was little in this reserved and lordly man to provoke the famous compliment that was spoken on his death: "First in war, first in peace, first in the hearts of his countrymen." Six feet three or four (the tape measures vary), imperious, self-sufficient, contemptuous of jolly human relations, his sword at his side, a big face serene to the point of complacency but pitted with smallpox, a frosty eyebrow under which rolled a sleepy blue eye, which, however, was said to rouse itself a little at the sight of a pretty woman—I think he must have been one of those people, not always appealing, whose greatness was simply the triumph of character over the flesh. Perhaps he was British enough by instinct to rise at the same qualities in his country's rulers. He had been, remember, a militiaman in the British army and had been the victim of some very overbearing officers. Not unnaturally he came to attribute arrogance to the land of their birth. He detested the strict and pettifogging restrictions on American trade that were soon to cause a war, and to cause, in fact, the United States of America. He organized the resistance in Virginia to the English Stamp Act and the Tobacco Act. He was a Virginia delegate to the first meeting of the colonies which met to decide, and did decide, to fight the mother country. He was chosen, not at that time by the mark of his obvious superiority but by a political deal, as the commander in chief of the rather miserable army that undertook to defend the American continent against the British.

How did it come about that in five short years he was able to break through the strong chrysalis of a Virginia gentleman and take wings and become a name which in its day combined the authority of Napoleon with the magic of Franklin Roosevelt? The answer seems to lie not in any personal charm but in his iron resolution to keep the American army united when it was all but ready to fall apart from incompetence, indifference, corruption, and starvation. What an army it was! For every trained soldier there were three half-trained, and ten mechanics, farmers, illiterates, half of them pressed into service or bought into service, deserting in droves, buying their way out when the going was rough.

According to Jefferson and other reliables, he often failed in the field and was not, in the military sense, a great general. But for eight years, and through many defeats and constant betrayal, he was as cool as an icicle and as impressive as God. He believed in his men long after they had ceased to believe in themselves. He fought with and for them even when the Congress thought of calling off the war. And in the famous winter of 1777 he was lucky to rescue from two thrashings by the British the ragged remnant of an army, so puny and bedraggled that the word went to Britain that the war was almost won. He pulled together a few thousand men, many times outnumbered by the crack troops of the enemy, and he camped in a rolling, bare valley in Pennsylvania. Less than half his men had arms, most of them had neither shoes nor shirts. The Congress took flight into the mountains of Pennsylvania and there was great rejoicing in London. During that winter, it is not too much to say, whatever was mortal in Washington was absorbed and elevated into the legend. He lost men from disease, desertion, treachery, and very many simply starved to death. Congress was so out of sympathy with this bitter-ender that it reorganized the War Department without his say-so. But he kept his camp at Valley Forge through the racking winter. And in the spring the French lined up with the rebels, and the rebellion held.

So Valley Forge was no victory. It was a pitiful siege. But it explains the veneration in which Washington came to be held, then and ever after, for of all the battles of the war Valley Forge was the proudest. It was the heart of the Revolution, the thing itself. No great general has ever been remembered so exclusively by such a defeat or by such a homely place name.

When he died, Napoleon was observed to bow his head, and in the English Channel the British fleet fired a salute of twenty guns.

4

A TINY CLAIM TO FAME

If Lincoln saved the Union by bringing to heel the rebel part of it, George Washington built the Union by means that offend nobody; and consequently, his is the only American birthday that is a true national holiday, proclaimed in all the states of the Union and in the territories of Puerto Rico, the Canal Zone, Guam, the Virgin Islands, and the District of Columbia.

A year or two ago I introduced a sketch of the all-American Father with some such downright statement. I was wrong. On the last day of January, in 1955, I was again mulling over the virtues of General and President Washington and making another try at distilling the juices of Old George on paper. Since my piece might be heard by zealous parsons and retired librarians, who love to pore through encyclopedias and challenge a hectic reporter grabbing his facts from memory against a deadline, I thought I had better make quite certain that Washington, alone among all eminent Americans, rated a universal celebration for his birthday in every state and territory of the Union. I consulted the fine print of the most current almanac, and this is what I read:

"February 22nd. Washington's birthday. A legal holiday in all states and territories except Idaho."

I could think of no good reason why Idaho should stand out so mulishly against the rest of the Union in refusing to honor the man who brought into being not only the United States of America but, in a sense, the federated state of Idaho. Now Idaho is famous for many good things. It lies amid some of the most spectacular mountain country of the Far Northwest. Its Coeur d'Alene country, in particular, is a region of twinkling alpine lakes and skimming bluebirds and mountaintops that glisten with legions of arrowheads which are, in fact, the dark-green tips of the noble Douglas fir tree. Idaho is known wherever the human animal in this land settles to a plate of meat and two veg.: renowned for the fluffy monster that is the favorite baking potato of the American housewife. The state is famous also as the native land of a resourceful and gallant Indian woman, one Sacajawea, who met and guided Lewis and Clark, the first white men in that territory, on their way to the source of the Columbia River. She helped them map her country and find their way unharmed to the Pacific Ocean.

When George Washington was alive, Idaho was not even habitable or known country. But in the intervening years, surely the Idahoans must have heard of him. Who, then, held out against the unanimity of the nation? Who was the plotter who for one hundred and sixty-three years had kept the patriotic Idahoans from enjoying a right proclaimed by law in the other forty-seven, as it then was, states of the Union? The President of the United States may proclaim a national holiday, but it is up to each state to dispose of his proclamation or approve it.

So, on that 31st of January, I sat down and wrote to the

chief executive of the sovereign state of Idaho the following letter:

"My Dear Governor: In preparing one of my weekly *Letters from America*, a series of broadcasts done by me in New York and transmitted thereafter throughout the British Isles, Europe, Africa, and Asia on the overseas services of the British Broadcasting Corporation, I came across the puzzling and grievous fact that the state of Idaho is the only one in the Union that does not recognize the birthday of George Washington as a legal holiday. This is an oversight, or aberration, I simply hate to have to mention to my listeners in a talk which, three weeks from now, I hope to devote to the immortal memory of the father of his country. There is time yet to correct this evident misstatement, one so gross that I fear its circulation around the British Isles alone, not to mention Switzerland, Kenya, and Hong Kong, will dreadfully dim the luster of the great state of Idaho. Will you, dear Governor, be so kind as to state the contrary fact and give me, if you can, a hint as to how this ridiculous error came into being? Sincerely and anxiously yours . . ."

Five days later I received, by special delivery, a splendid letter bearing the embossed seal of the state of Idaho, whose motto, by the way, is *Esto Perpetua*, which under the circumstances might roughly be translated "Let Us Perpetuate This Error." But I found out just in time that it means "Exist Forever." The letter read:

"Dear Mr. Cooke: The question which you present in your letter of January 31st is now before the Legislature, and a Bill is pending and may be law by February 22nd. Perhaps in your broadcast you will be in a position to include Idaho with the other States of this Union. Very truly yours, Robert E. Smylie, Governor." There was a rapidly inscribed P.S. in the Governor's own handwriting, and need I say I have it already preserved in amber alongside a signature of G. Washington himself. The postscript said: "The bill is now before me for signature. It will have my approval, and February 22nd will be a legal holiday in Idaho. R.E.S."

It would be fascinating to know whether any such bill had pended in the legislature much before the Governor wrote that letter. The document gives off a crackling, desperate air, and in my mind's eye I thought I could see the state senators and assemblymen rushing to vote on the bill between the dictation of the Governor's letter and the scribbling of his P.S.

But let us not be mean in this matter. Let us draw a veil over the extempore dialogue, the frothing telephone calls between the Governor's mansion and the speaker of the legislature and the house committee on holidays and memorials and the chairman of the board of Idaho Potato Exporters Inc. The patriotic vote was taken and was ratified. Suffice it to say that there is more rejoicing over one state that repented than over the forty and seven just states that needed no repentance. Every time I squish a hunk of butter into the divine white foam of an Idaho baked potato and chop down its skin, I shall say, "God bless Robert Smylie, sometime Governor of the great state of Idaho"; and of course I shall add, "God Bless George Washington," chopping down trees, as he no doubt is, in the Elysian gardens.

5

A TOWN MEETING

Once every four years the small and beautiful state of New Hampshire takes on the sort of self-importance that annually afflicts Indianapolis for its speed races, Kentucky for its derby, Holland, Michigan, for its tulip festival. New Hampshire holds the first of the presidential primaries to show who has a chance, and who has none, to become President of the United States.

New Hampshire has fewer inhabitants than the city of Boston. It has fewer voters than a New York City suburb. Less than a hundred thousand people vote in the primary. But because it is the first "beauty contest" on the calendar, the rest of the country pays exaggerated respect to its verdict, although it is often rendered on the basis of gossip, loyal affection for a New Englander, and a strong prejudice against most out-of-state crusaders. This power of a handful of New England voters to hold the first elimination contest, and to call the turn for steelworkers in Gary, Indiana, and longshoremen in New Orleans, is regularly deplored. But nobody does anything to stop it. And in the past, New Hampshire has snuffed out powerful challengers in a night or given a new lease to candidacies far beyond the reach of their national

appeal. So, on the second Tuesday in March, as the local
politicians are the first to admit, "the average voter in New
Hampshire feels ten feet high."

The state has the misfortune to be known as the Granite
State, which is possibly a legacy from a travel writer of the
late seventeenth century who warned all comers that "beyond
these hills northward is daunting terrible, being full of rocky
hills, as thick as molehills in a meadow, and cloathed with
infinite thick woods." This does not convey the tourist's picture of a land of gurgling streams, forests of white birch,
green slanting meadows, and white wooden houses and rippling hills and a cascade of scarlet maples in the fall. Unhappily, March does nothing to support this view. It is a waste of
wood and rocks and knee-deep snow, and only the highest
sense of duty compels a newspaper reporter to leave the
furnace of his hotel, in the shabby capital city of Concord or
the grim industrial town of Manchester, and go mushing
through the Arctic with the lonely men who will do anything
to get to be President. I must say that once you have been
with a red-nosed Kefauver making signs to a French-speaking
family in a crossroads store, or watched a watery-eyed Taft
pump the frozen mitt of a farmer in a snowbank, you feel
forever after a secret bond with the candidate. And if you
meet him afterward in the glow of the White House you look
at each other like a couple of pick-and-shovel miners who
made it on Nob Hill.

But these soul-saving expeditions come to an end, and on
election night I was driving down to Concord when I came to
a village that was no more than a few wide lanes of white
houses in moon-white fields. There was an old Colonial
church, with leaded windows and a soaring spire, that looked
in the light of a full moon like a snowhouse built by Sir
Christopher Wren. The place was ablaze with light, and

because it was piping cold, and because this was where the natives cast their vote, I decided to feel a pulse or two, to get the earliest possible lowdown on the way the other states would go. I parked my car in among forty or fifty others and pushed the main door and came in on a big hot room where the heating pipes were sizzling against the ceiling. There was some sort of a meeting going on and I was about to tiptoe out. But a big-bosomed lady at the door persuaded me instead to tiptoe in.

It was the entire basement of the church. At the far end of it was a small stage flanked by two flags. One had five gold stars (of the men who had died in the Second War) and two hundred and ten blue stars (of the men who had gone into the service). On the right was the other flag, with thirty-seven stars for the church members who had served. There were three little leaded windows in each wall and between them various prints of old New Hampshire, and up front a lithograph of George Washington. There were, I should guess, a hundred, a hundred and twenty people in there. Farmers in knee boots, leather jackets and plaid shirts, overalls, jeans, snow boots, galoshes. Road men in peaked caps and check shirts. Women in cloth coats and bandannas and hats that had served through two wars. Young girls in ski pants and windbreakers. Tradesmen and a teacher or two in coats and ties. They all sat on rows of folding chairs facing the stage, and some of them were picking their teeth and wiping their mouths and making discreet sucking sounds. Which was no wonder, for midway and against one wall was a big table with a coffee urn the size of a gangster's tombstone, piles of paper plates and tumblers, doughnuts, a big pumpkin pie, and loads of sandwiches wrapped in wax paper. There wasn't much food left now, since everybody had piled in on arrival, before the business started.

The business. It was all set down in a fat little booklet, which had gone out to every family in the town by mail and which now rested on their laps. It was the annual report of the Town of Boscawen (pronounced Boskwine). A handsome print job of a hundred glossy pages, containing an accounting of every nickel spent in the past year, beginning with "Property Tax, current year $76,659.84," going on to $1,172 tax to the railroad and $300 for dog licenses and down to "Ezekiel Webster, $300 for fuel for the grange hall."

What they were doing was nothing less than the annual business of the town meeting, which is called in every big and small town of the six states of New England, and in many places in the Midwest originally settled by New Englanders; so that every man and woman who lives there shall have a voice in how the town's moneys are to be spent.

Shall they build a new hospital? It will go to the vote. Shall the bounty paid to every boy who brings in a dead hedgehog (porcupine, to be exact) be reduced to twenty-five cents or maintained at fifty cents? The porcupine is a pest in these parts and ruins floorboards, sewers, and the family's sleep. There was a tense issue here. Some boys had been fetching in only the tails, which can be ingeniously manufactured. The moral question was whether they ought not to have to turn in also the nose and whiskers. While this was being debated an old bald man in knee boots got up and hurled three logs on the stove in the middle of the room. The temperature had been easing down to a chill eighty-five or so. The old man went out and soon the pipes started sizzling again, and it was back to a comfortable ninety-five. There was a hound dog somewhere which occasionally heckled the proceedings with a long low whine. When it heard a motion passed with a reverberating "Aye" it let loose with a short, high yelp.

Down beneath the stage was a roped-off section in which sat the elected rulers of the people: one old, one middle-aged, one young. They are the selectmen, locally known as the sea-lectmen. They have been since the earliest times the town's executive committee. The old, crusty-faced man was bending over papers. The middle-aged one was cheerful and paunchy and rocked comfortably on the back legs of his chair. The young one had a black hairline as low as Boris Karloff's but was otherwise very spruce and sat up taking notice, no flies on him. (It was his first term.)

There is a precise and well-understood ritual to this homely meeting. At a given signal, a young woman got up and went on the stage and sat down, opened her shorthand book, and poised her pencil. Opposite her was an upright piano, on which was draped a floppy overcoat and a gray hat. And between her and the piano now stood the owner of the hat and coat: Mr. Cecil Grimes, a long-retired schoolteacher, a thin, medium-sized man with his chin jutting high like a prow, not out of defiance but because he evidently saw better at that angle through his steel-rimmed glasses. He champed his lips and the people cleared their throats and stilled a few leaping children, and Mr. Grimes tapped his gavel. He was the moderator, and he would conduct the meeting.

There were some perfunctory questions about various items in the booklet, and these explanatory exchanges gave you a chance to catch up on the agenda. $14,362.09 for road maintenance. That might sound like a lot for a small village but in winter the snow can pile to ten feet and in summer the roads groan and crack with the heat. The snowplows guzzle gasoline and there is the matter of repairing their scoops and brushes after every snowfall.

$4,288 for old-age assistance. $135 for Memorial Day "and other patriotic celebrations—fireworks for Independ-

ence Day, a new flag for Washington's birthday." The flag-
pole in Boscawen had cracked last year and it took $50 to
mend it.

The reckoning went on through eighty pages. Everything the town had bought or disposed of was listed: $67.38
to an asphalt company, 90 cents to a grocery. They kept a
tally of the human sweat. Edward Dunbar must have been a
powerful man; he got $242.65 for unspecified labor. Napo-
leon Dennis—$119.70, labor. Existe Champagne (another
man, by the way)—$151.55, labor. All the way down to the
conscientious C. H. Atkinson, who earned $1.20 as "annual
wage for highway maintenance."

"If there are no more questions," Mr. Grimes was now
saying, "please turn to the first page and make manifest your
pleasure." There were no questions. "Aye?" he asked. There
was a general aye. No nays. Next item.

$2,350 for street lighting, $1,400 for the town library.
Evidently this had all been gone into before. Both items were
ayed into approval. Old crusty-face, the chairman of the selectmen, stood up to ask $7,000 for the town poor and old-
age assistance. A big farmer stood up, holding his cap in his
hand. "How come," he said, "we're asking less than last
year? Are there less old people or what?" Crusty-face said he
didn't want to sound "like a hard-hearted overseer" but "we
have cause for congratulation, the old people have been in
excellent health this year, and we have some money saved. So,
I'm asking only $7,000." Nothing very suspicious there.
They let it go.

$400 was asked for the cemetery. That seemed so low,
compared with the $7,000 to keep the old alive, that it
practically confirmed the chairman's contention. But another
man thought it was a little high. So the gravedigger, a ruddy
cheerful contradiction of all the gravediggers of fiction, got

up and said you had no idea how much work there was
cutting through the long grass, and another thing was "a
pesky new weed" that was covering the tombstones and ob-
scuring the lettering. A ruminating man, who looked as if he
spent time in there peering at old inscriptions, nodded wisely.
And the gravedigger got his $400. They went on to vote
various amounts for sidewalk construction and then launched
into some pretty heavy figures—remember this was a village
—including $600,000, no less, for borrowing on short-term
notes.

Then came a small squabble. The cheerful middle-aged
selectman wanted a sum of money to apply to the deficit of the
hospital down at Concord. It was the only hospital the natives
of Boscawen used. He asked for no more than $324. A tall
man rose, and he must have been a respected citizen, for
everybody stopped whispering and listened to him. "I move,"
he said, "to pass over." He gave no reasons and the selectman
appealed to everybody: "Now look, in every year we send at
least thirty-five of our people to the Concord hospital. Last
year the hospital had to charge off $724 as bad bills from us.
Now I don't see why it isn't a fair proposition to give something for—what we have received." A few heads recognized
the slogan and bowed reverently. The tall man was up again
and hissing slightly. "Did the selectman," he wanted to
know, "feel so indebted before he was elected as one of the
directors of the Concord hospital?" Or was it "a new feeling?" There was a triumphant giggle. The selectman made a
despairing "come now" gesture. But the tall man had his
way. It was passed over. No money, they all agreed, except
for a new hospital.

It was item seven, however, that caused the big hassle.
What was the town going to do about its old covered bridge?
New Englanders, it says in all the guide books, are legiti-

mately proud of their covered bridges, one of the most charming and practical of all New England "inventions." (In fact,
they have them in well-wooded countries everywhere from
Norway to China. There is one in Switzerland that was built
in the early fourteenth century. Germany has hundreds. But
not to be boorish about it, the covered bridge is accepted as a
New England invention in a poetical sense, like the phrase
"American as apple pie," which causes no international stir,
unless you can count the apoplexy that overcomes all Yorkshiremen when they hear the phrase from American lips.) No
question, anyway, covered bridges are a characteristic part of
the New England scene and in the eighteenth century were
built to form the only connecting highways across the long
rivers that divide so much of New Hampshire and Vermont.
They look like big barns spanning a river. They were covered
(I make this elementary point for puzzled city folk) to brace
the side structures against storms and to keep the snow out.
Many a life was saved in the old days when a man made the
covered bridge through a howling storm and rested there for
the night. By a more delicate token, many a marriage was
made there too. In country parts of Vermont they are still
called Kissing Bridges.

But progress, as dumb people are always telling us,
cannot be stopped. Boscawen's bridge, which thousands came
to see and photograph, had had its view blighted by the sight
of a big factory just up the river. Moreover, the practical
utility of the covered bridge had been bypassed by a big
cement-and-steel bridge a mile or two upstream.

The selectmen, however, wanted to raise "a sum of
money" either to preserve the bridge or to dispose of it. They
figured it would cost about $3,000 to keep it safe for foot
passengers for one year. The audience rose to this challenge,
as well they might, for are not New Englanders proud of

their heritage? Not noticeably, it would seem, for there was a cry, rising to a chorus, of "Destroy it!" The chairman, or senior selectman, winced visibly and pointed out that a historical society, "an out-of-state interest," was nibbling for it but —he had to confess—had made no promises. That was enough. They voted 10 for preservation, 45 for disposal. Which brought bounding to his feet a genteel, faintly villainous-looking man—might have been a lawyer.

"One moment," he shouted, and "One moment" in a quiet echo. "There must have been a misunderstanding about the meaning of the word 'dispose.' Surely no one wants to destroy the bridge, to tear it down?"

"Yes, we do, destroy it!" from innumerable people who understood what disposal means.

"Just a minute!" The selectman had a paper in front of him and he rustled it and began to read off the alarming price asked by wrecking companies just to cart it away. Everyone grew patriotic again. Still, $3,000 was a lot of money just to patch it up for one year. The room was buzzing with confusion and dogma. But a gleam appeared in the selectman's eye. He had a very fine ploy up his sleeve, and after coughing and looking out benignly on the crowd he shushed them and said: "It comes down to this. The historical element hasn't said yes, yet, and I'm gonna say that if we don't appropriate some money at this meeting, some child's gonna walk across that bridge one day and fall in the river, or some out-of-towner's gonna break a leg, and we'll have a $30,000 damage suit slapped on us. Now, how about that?"

$3,000, it was suddenly discovered, looked like a bargain. So they voted it, in theory to "preserve the old covered wooden bridge," in fact as an insurance premium against damage suits, and as a bait on which to hook the nibbling "historical element."

When the last gavel had sounded and it was all over, I walked out and nodded to the old selectman. In one day they had set the town's affairs in order and voted their choice for President of the United States. "It's been quite a day," I said.

"Sure has," he said. "That darned bridge and the hospital been sore subjects around here."

"I was thinking," I said, "of Eisenhower."

"Oh that," he said. "Sure. Come back. Anytime, be mighty pleased to see you."

The New England town meeting grew out of the English vestry meeting, but it grew very fast into something else because in the eighteenth century landowners with royal grants were always trying to run the town. It was the majority vote of the town meeting, made up of everyone from the parson to the street sweeper, that handcuffed their power. In 1774, two years before the American Revolution, London caught on a little late to the subversive content of this humble institution. The Parliamentary Act of that year banned it throughout the colonies as a "revolutionary and powerful force." Which it was and can be, wherever the people have the wit to preserve it. For it is the original backbone of local government and local initiative in the United States. To the sophisticated visitor it is now, of course, merely quaint and delightful. To the people who take part in it, though, it is the Parliament of Man.

6

BEIZBOL

One of the most reliable clichés of American newspaper writing is the opening phrase: "The eyes of the nation were focused today on . . ." There is one day of the year when this is true. It is the first Wednesday in October, the opening of what is majestically called the World Series. On that day the champions of the two major leagues play each other to decide which team, by winning the best of seven games, shall be declared to be the world champions at the old Russian game of beizbol.

We never, by the way, seem able to make up our minds whether Russian propaganda is too subtle or too crude. But it was a shrewd move of theirs in 1952 to look into the origins of the American national game and, after a severely scientific survey, conclude that it started in the Ukraine sometime in the Middle Ages. Of course, the best way to meet these objective Russian surveys is to make one of our own. And that is what we're going to do. In fact, it has been done for us—twice. Once by a commission set up in 1908, and again by a learned and curious librarian who had strong reasons to doubt the commission's findings.

In the country south of the Mohawk Valley, in the setting for several of the stories of James Fenimore Cooper, there is a town called—not unnaturally—Cooperstown. It is now a regular port of call on the tourist route because of a museum, sacred to the memory of one Abner Doubleday. He, it says here, was the only true inventor of the national game. The museum has a lot of early relics. It has a homemade baseball supposedly used by the great man himself. It preserves prints of Union soldiers playing baseball in North Carolina during the Civil War. It has bronze plaques bearing the names of retired heroes of the game who have been voted into the so-called "hall of fame" by 75 per cent of the members of the Baseball Writers Association. Tap an American anywhere between the Canadian and Mexican borders and ask him who invented baseball and he will reverently pronounce the name Abner Doubleday.

Let me begin by quoting the official account as it is quite briskly told in the federal guide to New York State: ". . . baseball grew quite informally from Old Cat, a favorite boys' game in Colonial days, played by a thrower, a catcher and a batter. In 1839, Colonel Abner Doubleday, a student in a local military academy, later a major general in the Civil War, limited the number of players to eleven, outlined the first diamond-shaped field and drew up a memorandum of rules for the game which he named 'baseball.' " That is the version confirmed by the investigating commission I referred to after its researches in 1908. It was not, by the way, a government commission, as most baseball fans like to assume. It consisted of a sporting-goods manufacturer, a bunch of baseball managers and one United States Senator who was mad about the game. Even the Encyclopaedia Britannica (a Chicago publication) says about this commission: "It was appointed ostensibly to investigate the origins of the game but really to 'prove' its exclusively American origin."

Well, by 1908, any other inventor of the game who

could challenge the Doubleday legend was dead and gone. Cooperstown, New York, was naturally delighted to be singled out for glory. And the commission's findings passed into the record books and the tablets of sacred Americana. However, there is another name rarely mentioned by baseball scholars, and it is not surprising, because he is a dissenter and a skeptic; once you have picked and immortalized a public hero it is an awful nuisance to discover that he is a fraud. The name of the Doubting Thomas is Robert W. Henderson, a quiet fellow who, true to the requirements of his job as a staff member of the New York Public Library, doesn't like to take things for granted. Down the years he had poked around into the baseball story and by 1939 he was ready to launch a shattering offensive against the legend of Doubleday and Cooperstown. He confirmed, for instance, that Abner Doubleday went up to West Point in 1838, the year before he invented and named baseball at Cooperstown while he was presumably on leave from his military education. But at that time, cadets never got any leave in their second year. Mr. Henderson also doubted that Cadet Doubleday managed to grow into a colonel in one year as a student. Luckily for the legend, the records of that investigating commission were lost in a fire. All that's left is a small file of papers quoting the main witness. He was a resident of Cooperstown bearing the suspicious name of Abner Graves. He laid it down that his namesake invented the game and that the runner was put out by the fielder hitting him with the ball. Since this doesn't happen in baseball, and granting that the man was telling the truth as he had observed it in many a stretcher case, Mr. Henderson began to cast around for a game in which it did happen. He found that it had been the normal practice of an English game for a couple of centuries. He then started to go through the English records.

He found out—what even the Oxford dictionary had overlooked—that the word supposedly coined by Doubleday is first mentioned in 1744 in a letter of Lady Hervey in which she writes about the habits and pastimes of the then Prince of Wales: "The Prince's family divert themselves at baseball, a play all who are, or have been, schoolboys are well acquainted with." Jane Austen in one of her novels writes about a heroine who "had nothing by nature heroic about her . . . she preferred cricket, baseball, riding on horseback . . . to books." Mr. Henderson began to pile up a mountain of documentary evidence from English literature, mainly from notebooks and journals and the like, to show that baseball—and so called—was a very popular children's game in England in the early eighteenth century. In the same year as Lady Hervey's letter there appeared a children's book of games, one letter of the alphabet for one game. B stood for baseball, and it has a picture of the player at the plate, a pitcher, a catcher, and two posts for bases. The book was a best seller and was reprinted twice in America. And in 1828, when Abner Doubleday (if he ever existed) was nine years old, the *Boy's Own Book*, published in London, had a whole chapter about the game and illustrated it with a picture of a diamond, with bases at each corner. Many a rearguard Doubleday man will concede that perhaps Abner did not invent the game but certainly invented the diamond. Not old Abner. Colonel Jane Austen, maybe, but not General Abner.

What came out of Mr. Henderson's subversive labors was that a game called baseball, which looks very much like a rudimentary version of today's American game, was played everywhere in England in the eighteenth century; and that it was called "baseball" in the southern counties, "rounders" in the West country, and "feeder" in metropolitan London.

From all this there emerges the solid, objective, and

bitter truth that baseball was invented not in the Ukraine, and not in Cooperstown, New York, but in England; was at first an amusement of the landed and leisured gentry of the southern counties; and that they called it baseball. Now since such people, when they emigrated to America at all, shunned the rude and pious New England shore and joined the more congenial Virginia colony, they brought over the game and the name. It developed several varieties here; and six years before Abner Doubleday, that charlatan, invented it, it was being played throughout the tidewater South and later in New England. In Philadelphia there was a full-fledged club.

All right, say the desperate Doubleday partisans, forced back now into the Catskills like guerrillas, so Abner may not have invented the game or the name but he surely drew up the rules of the modern game. Well, they too must have been lost in the fire. Because the only documentary record of a complete set of rules, on which the contemporary game is based, is one printed in 1845 by the Knickerbocker Baseball Club of New York. And this version of the game grew into modern baseball through the accident, if we may so call it, of the Civil War. There were over fifty clubs enrolled and competing in a national association as early as 1850. The invincible champions of that year, who never seem to have lost a game, were the renowned Excelsiors of Brooklyn. All these clubs were composed of amateurs. It is not too much to deduce that baseball followed the precedent of other sports, blood sports especially, that now belong to the honest working man, whether in the Ukraine or elsewhere. They start out as the amusement of the rich and leisured until one day the squire finds himself in a tough spot and there is an onlooking groom, stableboy, or gillie with a mean left-handed curve ball.

Well, the club games stopped with the Civil War. But the Union armies spread the Knickerbocker game through the border states and the South and played everywhere behind the lines. By the time the war was over, and the survivors went home in all directions, the only possible competitor to the New York game, played with a hard ball, was a softball game, played by small boys and Bostonians, who invented it (and let's not go into that).

The New York game was, then, the core of modern professional baseball. Amateur baseball may be the glory of the high schools but in the colleges it is rapidly on the wane. Baseball has suffered from the usual afflictions of an easy-going amateur diversion that turns into a high-pressure professional business. It has a very complicated system of buying and selling, of contracts and franchises. Twice in its modern history tremendous financial scandals have almost destroyed its reputation. But let us confess that in its present form it would alarm and astonish Jane Austen and the Prince of Wales, as well as the rude outfielders of the Ukraine. It is *the* characteristic American athletic spectacle and combines in its marvelous standard of fielding and the cunning flight of the ball through the air all the invisible (I mean subtle) skill of cricket and all the very visible competitive frenzy of the English national game, which I take to be association football.

A baseball stadium is a far cry from the fields and the lowly vacant lots of its origins. And baseball bears almost no resemblance to the game which Americans make a point of deriding and ignoring: cricket. If the Atlantic alliance is to hold on the playing fields, we shall have to act on the suggestion of the late Robert Benchley, who bravely suggested that it would be better to abolish cricket and baseball and "start all over again with a game that both countries can play—preferably baseball."

7

THE SUMMER BACHELOR

An American telephoned me the other day to ask me what was meant by "flanneled fools." I had to explain to him that in Britain the summer game is played in flannels. He jumped, wrongly, to the conclusion that boxing was the British summer pastime and that everybody got fitted out for it in long skiing underwear. I introduced him gently to some of the mysteries of cricket, not the least of which is why grown men stand around for most of the day doing nothing at all in temperatures of fifty degrees. I tried to keep my exposition to simple words, but when you are talking about transatlantic weather the simplest words are the most deceiving. I remember once picking up the Paris edition of the New York *Herald Tribune* and looking up to the left-hand corner of the front page to see how the people were faring in the Manhattan midsummer. It prints the weather reports of London, Paris, and New York, and the newspaper naturally has to take on trust the language of the weather bureau of origin. It said, "London, fair, 71 degrees, continued hot; Paris, 78, warm; New York, clear, high 83, seasonably cool."

This could serve as a text for the British export drive, which falters always on the presumption that an American means the same thing as an Englishman when he talks of a "light suit." In Britain, it appears to mean light in color. Here it means lightweight. If this is understood, the golden rule for the textile exporter will then be clear: it is to coax the American buyer into purchasing large quantities of the raw material in Britain—as sheep, if you like—and then let him use it and cut it according to his habits and his needs. For British clothes in America will make a man feel uncomfortable outdoors in summer and indoors in winter. It is possible for a North European to feel at home here anytime up to Christmas. He could keep his old habits and his regular suits and feel he was still in a temperate climate. The New Year transports him to the pole, and in a temperature of one above (above zero, that is) the word "cold" will take on a sharper meaning for a Londoner, say, who has never in his or his forebears' lifetime known anything colder than nine degrees. Summer here is, however, the bigger problem for the Briton. He is rightly aware that New York is named after old York but he goes on to the fatal assumption that the trip from one to the other involves a direct east-to-west passage of three thousand miles. What he rarely knows is that he has also gone eight hundred miles south, that old York is located on a level with the tundra of Labrador, whereas New York is at the precise latitude of Corfu.

This clash between the romantic legend of our sameness and the facts of life is what sparks the Englishman's shock. He discovers that the changeover from winter to summer life is brutally abrupt, and that to adjust to the violent swing of the thermometer he has to acquire habits more suited to a fieldhand in a banana republic than to the gentle vagaries of a London heat wave. (I recall another London headline: "75 Again Today! No Relief in Sight.") He will discover that New York is more of a summer furnace than a summer festival. He will learn that it has created unfamiliar local institutions. He will soon hear about the summer bachelor, the forgotten man of American folklore.

To appreciate the pathos and charm of the summer bachelor, you have to learn the stages by which a normally jogging and contented husband becomes one. Last week, then, the family took off for our summer house at the end of Long Island. (This is a custom not restricted to what used to be called the upper middle class. The continental mainland of the United States sweats abominably from May to October and any humane husband who is not fettered to the marriage bed will rent a shack anywhere in the mountains, by a lake or the seashore, as far as possible from Chicago, St. Louis, Pittsburgh, or a score of other infernos.) The induction into summer bachelorhood is almost as violent as the season that causes it. One day you are living in a normal house or apartment, with carpets, grocery deliveries, timed meals, friends, and everything; and the next you'd think the Russians were coming. You wife is out of bed like a rocket. She beats around the house like a beaver. "Excuse me," she says, as I am in the middle of a shrewd sentence on the typewriter, and up comes the carpet. Up come all the carpets. At ten a.m. the kitchen doorbell buzzes and a huge man in an apron clomps in and, with the aid of three helpers, lugs the carpets away to be stored.

There is a clatter of china in the kitchen. All the civilized eating utensils are going into boxes and cocoons of tissue paper. My wife breaks in again and lifts a warning finger. She indicates one shelf and one drawer. "There you are," she says. For the next three months or more I am to use two cracked kitchen plates, a chipped saucer, drink my coffee out of a premature Coronation mug (Edward VIII) and stir it with a spoon bought fifty years ago by her mother, a relentless Southerner. It looks like a petrified alligator, and that is what it's meant to look like. It says on it, "A present from Jacksonville, Florida."

Now there is a noise not unlike the furious exhaust that sets in in the tenser moments of science-horror movies ("The radioisotope, Fleming, throw the safety rod, man!"). It is a team of vacuum cleaners. I stumble into the living room, for it is in darkness. The curtains have come down and four shades have gone up, two white ones on the outside, two green ones inside. The nifty satin upholstery on the sofa is obscured by a dingy slipcover. So are all the upholstered chairs. The lamps are swathed in bedsheets, giving them the appearance of Arab sentinels. A screen is being pulled across the open entrance to the living room, and my wife gives the annual order: "Stay out of here, remember!" (I have no theories about American wives. They are, so far as I'm concerned, wives.) A mountain of laundry is piling up in the hall. There is a tearing sound coming from the clothes closets —the winter clothes are being entombed in plastic hangers and all the clothes give off a characteristic smell. It used to be mothballs. You used to hear them rattle around in the night. Now they tinkle, for they roll up and down small perforated tins with hooks on them that hang on the racks. The closets are squirted with some noxious chemical, and the ones that contain the winter suits are dynamited with bombs of DDT. This may all sound very drastic. Alas, our insidious summer enemy is a beast unknown to a true temperate climate—the buffalo moth—and if you ignore him, you are apt to confront an interesting wardrobe in the fall, of garments that might have served as targets on a rifle range.

So now, the blankets are entombed, the sheets changed, rooms closed off, refrigerator defrosted and denuded of food (it looks neater that way, to my wife at least, when she returns in October). I am permitted to run the refrigerator sometime later and it will soon contain cans of beer, a moldy tomato, a box of crackers, and some limes and lemons. Just before the family leaves, she issues the battle orders for the summer campaign: "Always put the garbage out before you go to bed, never start on a new bottle of milk before you've finished the old one. Never go out and leave the windows open. Keep the shades drawn in the living room. Right?" Very good, General, and goodbye.

The winter cycle is completed the summers that the children go to camp. There is a special fuss to be made with duffel bags and blankets and swimming shorts and two blankets and name tapes. And you all go off to Grand Central Station and align your brood with one of the many regiments of children lined up and waiting for the call to their track and their train. And again you hear one of the most powerful folk songs of America. A stationmaster stands by a large board and he looks at a card in his hand that lists all the names of the camps and the platforms of their outgoing trains. Nine thirty strikes. And he warms up his baritone and chants: "Indian Summer—track nineteen. Shining Mountain—seventeen. Pine Grove—twenty-one. Camp Wawokeewe—nine. High Wind—fifteen. Meadow Lark—eighteen. Thunderbolt —twenty-nine."

It is over. They are gone. You leap to a telephone and locate another displaced person. You bathe and shave and hear yourself singing forgotten songs of liberation. This first evening is unusually high-spirited. The drinks flow free and so does the coarse interchange of remarks about family life. You decide that your companion is a fine man you have tended to underestimate. Then you go home and recall with a start that you are on your own again. You hear your shoes crackle on the dust of the desert that is the long, dark hall. You peek into

the living room and switch on a light. The standing lamp by
the switch is a dim figure indeed. Its shade has been wrapped
around with a fez of crinkly white paper, and it stands there
like Lawrence of Arabia in ambush. You duck out and into
the bedroom. The silence is chilling. You get a beer and read
a little, or stay up and watch the late show, and then the late
late show. At three you turn in, and at eight you feel terrible.
Each weekend, you suffer the troop trains of the New Haven
or Long Island Railroad and limp raggedly into the bosom of
your family. On Monday it starts again.

At this point a suspicion will have crossed your mind
that has certainly crossed the mind of the summer bachelor.
Indeed, George Axelrod made a play about it and called it
The Seven Year Itch. The title itself suggests a clinical thesis
and we will leave it with its author. For most men it does not
take seven years to recall that New York contains, among its
martyred and lonely millions, an old girl friend, or some
agreeable but impeccable social worker, or some other honest
female whose devotion to her work denies her the blissful
exile your wife is now embarked on. Peter Arno captured and
immortalized this suspicion—of yours—in a cartoon that
showed a portly gent, one of those waggish Blimps with the
spotted bow tie, marching smartly down Park Avenue with a
very trig young woman on his arm. Coming up the avenue,
and just level with him, is a majestic matron of about his age.
"Why, George Fitzgerald," she cries, "what*ever* keeps you
in town?"

I will not blemish a family program with any other
comment than the thought that one of the most profound of
all American idioms is that priceless old catch-phrase: "I love
my wife but oh you kid." I bring up this touchy subject
because an accident of technology is, I think, about to produce a sociological revolution in the United States. And I

know that you expect me to keep you up with sociological revolutions. The cause of this one is the air conditioner. In the old summer days, the summer bachelor went at weekends from the oven of his apartment to undressed days and what he thought of as cool nights. Now he leaves the ice-cool paradise of his apartment for the hot days and the dank nights and the midges and bugs of the country.

Two days ago, a Wednesday, I pressed the elevator button of my apartment house and as the door slid back it revealed the capacious frame of a neighbor of mine from the twelfth floor. He is a retired old gentleman, a notable fisherman and a solid but saucy character. I asked him what kept *him* in town in midweek. "Are you kidding?" he said. "It's like the basin of the Ganges out there. I retreated to this wonderful apartment. And you know what? My wife showed up this morning. God damn!"

"If this goes on," I said, "it's going to play the devil with fishing."

"Fishing nothing," he said. "It's going to play hell with marriage."

8

THE ICEMAN GOETH

One of the best American journalists of our time—and one who, like many of the best, started as a sports reporter and moved on to higher and deeper things—has put the case against the double-dome commentator with awful finality. "Of all the fantastic fog-shapes," he wrote, "that have risen off the swamp of human confusion since the big war, the most futile and at the same time the most pretentious is the deep-thinking, hair-trigger columnist or commentator who knows all the answers just offhand and can settle great affairs with absolute finality three days or even six days a week."

I am reading this sentence, and wincing at it, in a week when it would be possible, and in some journals compulsory, to write about the deepening morass of Vietnam, and the threat of turbulence again in all the American cities where the poor watch the television ads, and are given a heady, though preposterous, glimpse of the high life among the carefree whites. A commentator these days is almost under contract to speculate from time to time about the future of Man with a capital M. I resist this clause. Man has an incurable habit of not fulfilling the prophecies of his fellow men. And if you don't believe it all you have to do is to look back to the prophetic literature of twenty, thirty, or forty years ago and see what the seers of the time were threatening us with. When I was a college student the absolutely taken-for-granted advanced thought of the day foresaw that very soon the world would have to see the inevitability of what they called "eugenic or selective breeding." The idea is that you pick a girl whose parents are intelligent, highly bred, and successful and you mate her with a whiz kid possessing a dizzy high I.Q. and what you get is a procession of children of superior intelligence, character, breeding, and sensitivity. It's astonishing that the advocates of this silly theory—the Count Keyserlings and the Schmalhausens and the cut-rate Bernard Shaws and such—didn't look around and see how often the intelligent and well-bred produce a shifty moron or a hopeless misfit; whereas a cretin has been known to marry a syphilitic and produce a Beethoven.

We don't hear so much, if anything, any more about selective breeding of humans. But we do hear a great deal about the unique generation of today's young, their uncanny capacity to develop inner freedom, to smash the restraints and hypocrisies of two thousand years of something called the Establishment (a fine phrase often used to belittle anybody who is in a regular job he likes), and, in general, to have learned the secrets of the human soul for the first time. "Discovering your identity" is a byword of the American student. I have still to learn if it means much more than the old slang phrase of the twenties: "Be yourself."

It is odd, though, is it not, that the one prophet who now seems to have had a more accurate vision than anyone else is the man who at the time appeared to be proposing the most far-fetched future for the human race? I mean H. G. Wells. An atom bomb and satellites whizzing between the planets seemed like the fantasies of a madman. Yet these things came true, and selective breeding is another faded delusion of the intelligentsia. To be fair, I think it faded the day that Bernard Shaw, being invited by Isadora Duncan to mate his towering intellect with her gorgeous body and spawn a genius, sent her a postcard saying: "But suppose it had your brain and my body."

This all comes up because a certain Pierre Dupuy, the commissioner general of Canada's world's fair, christened it last week with a solemn sentence, of a kind which, you will have gathered, I find depressing not for what it contains but for the picture it suggests of the man who said it: "Whether he knows it or not, whether it pleases him or not, Man is swept up in a huge wave of change, which is transforming before his very eyes continents and peoples." I'm sure he's right, but while we are tightening our seatbelts to prevent being swept up and deposited on Mars or Venus, I should simply like to note a very small wave of change that has broken, and that nobody at all predicted in 1939.

In that year a building went up in Manhattan called the Premium Ice Plant. It was not by a long shot the first of its kind but it has turned out to be the last. It was on East 13th Street, and it was designed to produce 425 tons of ice a day. Except in its ice-making capacity, it was nothing revolutionary. It was, if we'd only known it, the last link with a long and ingenious American tradition that begins with the Indians putting their perishables into earthenware jars in caves, proceeds with the shipping of natural ice from New York to the West Indies at the very beginning of the nineteenth century, and after innumerable tinkerings here and abroad achieved its most dramatic usefulness in the middle of the American Civil War. In the year 1863, there appeared crossing the American continent the novelty of a refrigeration car —not a mechanically refrigerated car, but an insulated railroad carriage packed with natural ice and attached to a train traveling west to California. It took aboard a load of fruits and vegetables, turned round and retraced the continental journey in burning weather, and delivered to Washington and the Northern armies the first load of fresh produce from three thousand miles away. It was one reason why the North, which had captured the railheads, won the war.

Well, back to the Premium Ice Plant. It came about (not to go back to the Stone Age) because in this climate of drastic extremes you have to find a way of keeping food fresh. They found this out very early in the settlement of this country. The Indians used subterranean springs to cool their food and caves to bury it in. The colonials dug deep wells or storage cellars, of thick stone walls, that never saw the sun. A little later on, they used to cut ice from the winter ponds and store it in insulated stone houses to use in the summer. The North sold it to the South, where ice was a rarity. In 1805, a bright fellow in Massachusetts laid the groundwork of a fortune by shipping ice to the West Indies and South America and all the way to India. By the 1880's mechanical refrigeration, to preserve fruits and other perishables in cold storage, became pretty much routine. By the 1930's the home refrigerator was getting to be standard. But even then farms, country cottages, and most working-class houses and all tenements relied on what they called an icebox. (It is still, by the way, the hangover American name for what the English now call a "fridge.") It was a wooden cupboard, usually lined with lead or some other insulator, into which a couple of times a week you hefted a load of ice, delivered at the back door by —— the iceman.

There is a catch in my voice as I say that word. For the iceman was not only a public servant. He is a legendary figure in American folklore. And a most romantic one, for reasons I

hope I don't have to spell out in tasteless detail. He was, shall
we say, the most reliable male visitor to the ordinary home.
He came when the husband was away at work. Put two and
two together and you have the groundwork for a whole raft of
jokes that gave great pleasure to the audiences for burlesque
and vaudeville. The basic jokes were elementary indeed, like
that about the new husband, a lineman stranded in a storm
atop a telegraph pole, whose workmate asks him if he isn't
worried for the safety of his bride. "Oh, she's all right," he
says, "she's safe at home with the iceman."

The imagined antics of the iceman made him, in fact,
the American Don Juan. Even when I first came to this
country, in the thirties, he was so much taken for granted, so
generally accepted as the all-American bounder, that you
could not find a mention of him in the classic studies of
American humor, which, alas, tend to be written by a scholar
so busy fixing his telescope on the old backwoodsman, the
lying buffalo hunter, the Arkansas traveler, and other comic
types who've been in their graves a hundred years that he
rarely bothers to look up and enjoy the types who infest our
own contemporary life. I am indulging some of the same
myopia myself, for here am I celebrating the iceman just as
he is finally dead and doomed. The Premium Ice Plant, on
13th Street, was just officially condemned as a victim of
progress, of the universal presence in the home of a machine
that makes its own ice. The iceman has gone forever, to be
buried alongside soap flakes and the soda fountain and other
victims of the home freezer. The presiding judge, a poetic
character, shed a quiet tear as he pronounced this liturgy:
"The ice wagon, the hitching of horses, the iceman hauling
ice, his hawking cries reverberating from tenement to tenement, his unsung virtues, his mythical escapades, are now
part of the soul of yesteryear." I guess the iceman's place in

American mythology has now been taken by the free-lance photographer, by Alfie, a free-wheeler in more ways than one and a devil with the women.

In saying farewell to him, let us recall an epitaph he would be proud of. There is a story about a small boy who every night used to kneel down in his father's presence and pray for all the senior members of his family in turn. "God bless Grandpa," he used to chant, "God bless Grandma, God bless Mom, God bless Dad." One night he began with a slight variation. "Goodbye, Grandpa," he said, "God bless Grandma, God bless Mom, God bless Dad." Next day Grandpa dropped dead. A little while later, he was saying, "Goodbye, Grandma, God bless Mom, God bless Dad." And the next day Grandma was no more. Dad, to put it mildly, was sorely troubled in spirit, and pretty scared. A few months later to his horror, he heard his son praying, "Goodbye, Dad, God bless Mom."

Next morning, the father tracked his way to his office with extreme caution. He avoided the buses and the subway, he walked with a catlike tread, he watched out at every intersection for the traffic, he worked all day with painful circumspection and tiptoed home at twilight and fell exhausted in his chair. He broke into a sweat. "Holy Smoke!" he said. "What a day *I've* had."

"You think *you've* had a day," said his wife. "Guess what happened to me? The iceman walked in here and fell down dead."

II PROBLEMS AND STEREOTYPES

9

THE EUROPEAN'S
AMERICA

It is the fall. The fall of the year, an American institution now so well known, and even respected, in Europe that you no doubt expect me to take off, as I annually do, about the scarlet maples pouring like a fire through New England, the brilliant light everywhere, the thin milky trails of woodsmoke that rise into a bottomless blue sky. Well, once you've created a stereotype it is time to demolish it. The fall has refinements, even perils, that the autumn in other countries does not share. Once you've learned the big clichés of a country, which are true and which are not, it is the off-beat clichés that really fix the place in your mind, and make it like no other, and may even endear it to you, years later in another country far away. Let me illustrate.

The other morning, just after breakfast, a lady by the name of Miss Frieda Sims was going her rounds on the twenty-seventh floor of a New York hotel. Miss Sims is a floor supervisor and she was looking to see which rooms were vacant, which ones the maids could get into to clean up, which rooms needed to have the breakfast tables removed. She unlocked room number 2752, peeked in and saw the happy disorder of breakfast dishes. She went in to wheel the table out, but she came out in a hurry with no table, and she was screaming.

This sounds like the beginning of one of those classic American crimes, like Miss Lizzie Borden going into the kitchen on a very hot morning to get a cup of coffee. And it goes on promisingly enough, because the next incident involves the hotel's security force, which came running and verified Miss Sims's report. She had stopped screaming by now and she was able to stammer out that there was somebody in there. It wasn't a guest, not like any guest she had ever seen. It was an owl, just a common or garden American barn owl (*Strix flammea* to the initiated), which looks rather like an African woodcarving or the top of a totem pole. It seems the owl was just cruising by the hotel at a twenty-seven-story altitude (there's the New York touch), saw the open window, glanced in at the breakfast dishes and decided to make a landing on the remains of a melon and a couple of shirred eggs. The commissars of the security force (what, before the iron curtain, we just used to call house dicks) evidently made the bird secure. They threw a blanket over it. Then they telephoned the SPCA, which seems a contradictory thing to do, since they were busy smothering the owl. However, a Mr. Norton soon came up from the Society with his equipment, a pair of thick gloves; for you should know that the American barn owl has a four-foot wingspread, a curved beak, and what the New York *Herald Tribune* (which gets its reporters into the damnedest places) described with relish as "razor-sharp talons."

Mr. Norton put his gloves on, embraced the owl with professional tenderness, took it off into the park and set it free. This fugitive from the world of freedom got tangled up in twentieth-century civilization, but within half an hour a man put his hand in the air and the bird flew away in one swoop back to the primitive world from which we all originally came. There is a technical snag to this fable. An eye surgeon tells me that no owl, however wise, could look into a hotel room after breakfast. The owl, it seems, is a kind of hotel dick in its own right and can look into hotel rooms only at night. I see that Audubon noted this over a hundred years ago. "Owls," he wrote, "seem to us a dull and stupid race, principally because we only notice them during the day, which nature requires them to spend in sleep, the structure of their eyes compelling them to avoid the light and seek concealment in hollow trees, in caves and obscure retreats."

What started out as a children's story, then, full of sweetness and light, is in fact a near-tragedy. This bird was lost and plunging through a blinding world of light and saw a barn, an obscure retreat, which turned out—pitifully—to be room 2752 of a New York skyscraper.

This is the kind of story that could only happen in the fall. There is, indeed, a special anxiety that overtakes bird lovers then, when the great migrations to the South begin. Many fine species have not yet heard about the invention of the skyscraper, and some ordinary birds are even wildly attracted to it. The starlings, for instance. It is a happy fall during which flocks of starlings don't smash into the Empire State Building, which is four times the height of the tallest California redwood and higher than any building anywhere, even—I'm afraid—in the Soviet Union.[1] These accidents have a poignant appeal to anyone who, in the fall, has to work in a city and who knows that beyond the city limits lies a world

---

[1] When the jet airplane came in, there was a more perilous hazard from the starlings. In several crashes, it came out that they had been sucked into the engines.

crammed with color and beauty and old habits that unfortunately play no part in the European picture of that detested
"American way of life."

The day before the barn owl flew into the hotel, I was
reading a piece in an American magazine by Mr. Cyril Connolly, a writer with whom I feel a strong sympathy and never
more than in this piece, which was about the widespread
Americanizing of Europe. What are those influences which
many Europeans think of as all America has to offer, and
which they wish had stayed on this side of the Atlantic?
Connolly lists them: "jazz, gangster stories, bad films, tales
of violence, science fiction." I could add some others, especially the compulsion to break up the relics of London as an
eighteenth-century country town and riddle them with chro-
mium-plated fronts and dingy "American" snack bars and
amusement arcades and the tattiest attempts at modern
"American" architecture. Not to mention the Cockney's sur-
render to what he imagines is American slang, the frantic
imitation be-bop, the transatlantic zoot-suiter. The point is
that these influences, picked up I suppose from the movies,
are almost always bad imitations of crummy originals. What
is alarming, and what the European seems unaware of, is that
they are often planted firmly in a solid English background,
in the sort of place they would not be found in the American
background. They do not have chrome cocktail bars along
the noble stretch of North Street, in Litchfield, Connecticut, or
snack bars at the bottom of Zion Canyon. Along the new
motor parkways of New York and New England they do not
even allow the petrol companies to build their own pumps.
The stations, like the overpasses, must conform to a design
sanctioned by the commissioner of parks or highways and be
made of the local stone. And the fences that bind the parkways are the same for a hundred miles or more and are made

from a pine that fits the landscape. It is an unexpected and admirable thing about the development of the automobile age in America that Americans have developed a sense of style as watchful as that of the men who gave us the urban style of eighteenth-century London and the country style of eighteenth-century New England.[2]

I sometimes think that a European deploring the horror of Pittsburgh and Detroit and St. Louis and "your Midwest cities" is not really criticizing the Midwest or American cities but the nineteenth-century city anywhere. But it is also a fact that though American towns may, and do, seethe with the random horrors that are now so faithfully transplanted to British towns, it is almost easier over here to get away from them. My European visitors are always surprised to discover how much virgin forest there appears to be on the edge of town. Theoretically, there are only two big stands of the forest primeval in this country, one in the Cascade Mountains and the other in the Bitterroots, both far out on the northwest Pacific Coast. But I'm thinking of long-settled country. I have taken Englishmen in a car fifteen minutes from where I am talking to you and once beyond the George Washington Bridge they are weaving around great rocks and little woods as dense as the New Forest. A half hour from Times Square (all right, then, two hours in the rush hour) they can be in something that looks like Fenimore Cooper country, and it is not hard to imagine on dark nights an Indian slipping through the trees, slinking across the six-lane divided highway and standing as aghast at the lights of Manhattan as I am when I see what the "developers" have done to Regency Mayfair.

For nearly two centuries now, there has been a contin-

[2] The billboard lobby and the freeways are now doing their damnedest to date this compliment.

uous argument, sometimes amiable, sometimes bloodthirsty, about which country was influencing the other the most. Until about fifty years ago, the example was all one way, and the way was east to west. But it has been changing very fast. Every world power leaves indelible imprints even on countries that pretend to hate it. And as Europe comes to admit, which it soon will have to, that the United States is now the ranking world power, its customs and gadgets and manners and literature and ways of doing business will powerfully influence the young. They may reject them later on, as Europe pulls itself around and asserts again, as I don't doubt it will want to, its own pride and independence.

But in the meantime, Britain still retains an advantage which will not pass over to America, I think, for a long time to come. It is this: Americans who have not been in Europe tend to imagine what is best about her, Europeans who have not been in America tend to imagine what is worst. Ask a few simple Americans what Britain means—ask a schoolgirl, a farmer, a shopkeeper, an elevator man (I have just tried it) what comes to mind when you say "Britain"—and they will say something like: "Oh, old buildings, more easygoing than us, I guess, beautiful countryside, tea in the afternoon, Shakespeare"; and, as my elevator man added, "And I understand they are very dignified, very strict, they tell me, in their law courts."

This may sound very naïve to you. But it picks up a flattering myth and not, like the other way around, a libelous one. My own daughter, fourteen years old, swings violently between wanting to go to England and being afraid to. Why does she want to go? Because she imagines the place peopled with Mr. Pickwick and Romeo and Juliet and Robin Hood, not to mention Laurence Olivier; and because she is crazy about the tables that Sheraton designed and the chairs and desks of Hepplewhite and imagines that every little house in England would throw out anything less graceful. She has, indeed, heard rude things about the cooking. But I tell her that this is steadily improving. I tell her also that it is true about the parklike countryside and the fat cattle and the sheep as big as buffaloes in Scotland, and it is due as much as anything to the fact that the grass pack of English dairyland is five times as dense as the proud grass pack of Iowa. She thinks the English countryside must be heaven. (By the way, she takes entirely for granted the stupendous beauty of the Tetons and the desert and Yosemite, which leave Englishmen feeling that they have come face to face with their Maker.)

And why *doesn't* she want to go to England? Well, she explains, wriggling nervously, "Everyone would expect me to be on my best behavior, they are so polite and—everything."

This is quite a reputation the British have built up. And the other tourist countries of Europe are not far behind. We read here about the exquisite care the French take over their food, and the dedicated way they tread on their grapes, and the devotion they bring to their public buildings. We do not hear about the really garish modern housing that begins to sprout in the Parisian suburbs, or about the alarming incapacity of the French for self-government. We read about the ruthlessness of the Mafia as it goes about its business in New York or New Orleans but not about its stranglehold on the enslaved slum of Sicily. From Italy we read rather about the preciousness of a new Roman "find" in Tuscany or about the charm of the Appian Way, not about the clutter of billboards that disfigures it.

It will surely be a great day when you ask an Englishman what comes to mind at the mention of the word "America" and he replies: "The white villages of New England and the eighteenth-century houses, the neighborly warmth of the

Midwesterners, the contributions of American scholarship, the buffet meals that young American housewives whip up, the style and color of so many American homes, the outdoor life of California, the God-given glory of Bryce Canyon and the man-made marvel of Hoover Dam."

10

THE GENERATION PROBLEM: THE TWENTIES

More years ago than I can bother to add up I was taking a walk through a forest of birches in northeastern Germany, in Silesia to be exact. I was teaching English at a school in a small country town and walking with me on this afternoon was a wiry boy with a stoop and a damp nose, and spiky hair and glasses so thick that coming on him today in a thicket by the light of a full moon you'd think he was an invader from Mars slouching in incognito. Roughly, you could say he was an intellectual, or working up to one. He had a fierce, dogmatic manner and a steady gleam in his eye. I didn't know him well but I respected his seriousness and his sincerity. Unhappily, he was a disciple of an Austrian who was being much talked about, who was also serious and sincere and up to no good. The master's name was Adolf Hitler.

We were living then in the twilight, though we didn't know it, of German liberalism. It was a melancholy time, not because of what was to come but because of what was already there: a depression so all-embracing that it blighted the whole of life. The school principal would invite you to coffee and cakes, and he'd have to ask you to share the cost. In the big cities, when you took the most modest meal, the waiters were

under orders to seat nobody against the windows if they
fronted on the street. The sight of a slice of meat on a plate
was enough to draw a crowd of glassy-eyed adults and children with black pouches under their eyes and bellies like
balloons. They would press their faces up against the window
and move their lips in that wordless, dumb way of fish in an
aquarium. Then there would be a piping of whistles in the
street, the big striding cops would come lunging in, and the
wretched pack would panic and break away.

I tell you this not to wring your withers but by way of
doing justice to an idealistic fourteen-year-old who saw, much
sooner than was good for him, that the sensible, decent Social
Democrats in the Reichstag were fiddling with the best intentions while Germany was burning to ashes. As we walked
through the woods, this boy lectured me on the inevitability,
the need, of Hitler. The man was not much more than a name
to me, though I had—in an idle tourist moment—gone off
around the Braune Haus in Munich and been pretty much
amused by the uniforms, and the operatic solemnity, and the
fat, unloved secretaries who bowed before a Hitler portrait as
before the cross. Some of the boys used to scribble swastikas
on the toilet walls, and every Monday morning the headmas-
ter hauled them up and punished them. I told this boy he had
a right to his opinion but Hitler, in my view, was a fraud. I
said fraud because I'd just then learned the German word—
betrug. He was furious at this and sulked for a half-mile or
so. Then, glaring straight ahead, he said doggedly that he
thought Hitler was "the only solution for the generation
problem."

I didn't know what he was talking about. I thought it
must be one of those jaw-breaking German compound nouns.
"How do you stand, then," he said, "on the generation problem?" It turned out he was talking about the natural strange-

ness that sets in during adolescence or later between fathers and sons. I stumbled awhile and told him, though not quite in these words, that of course my parents' generation had kowtowed to a long tradition that started with Adam (Mr. Gladstone at the latest) but that my generation was something quite new and free and emancipated.

Twenty years later, I was spending a few days as a visiting professor at Yale and it was an unpleasant shock to discover that the current crop of undergraduates felt about me as I felt about my father. I protested again that my generation was something special, we had broken the bond with the Victorians. I had come to manhood in the late 1920's and surely everybody knew that the twenties were one of the watersheds—perhaps *the* watershed—of human history. The small class I was talking to stared me down, and one young man said, "The 1920's? You mean bootleg hooch and the Charleston and F. Scott Fitzgerald?" Not exactly, I said. Tell us, somebody else piped up, about the twenties.

Well, I admitted that there was much to be ashamed of in the hindsight of the Depression, when the factories closed down and paper-windowed shacks mushroomed down by the river, and there were suddenly millions and millions of slouching unemployed—granted, the 1920's were a dirty word. I suppose, I said, the symbol of the slaphappy twenties was a brassy Texas hoyden who ran a night club in New York and greeted every new arrival with "Hello, sucker!" after which she shoved them down at a table, ordered a bottle of champagne, and presented a bill for thirty dollars. But if a nice young man came in, or an old friend from some innocent locality, she'd countermand the order and bawl at the waiter: "Lay off this guy, thirty dollars a quart for champagne and you know it isn't champagne." She'd turn to the couple and snarl, "Tell your young lady to take gin and like it." The

name of this endearing fraud (*betrug*) was Texas Guinan,
and her favorite columnist, Heywood Broun, called the twenties "Tex and the Coolidge Gold Rush." In the days of her
glory, Broun wrote, "This was the land of easy riches for the
lucky. The vein was deep and wide and handsome. Whoopee
would never end." Well, it ended, from simple exhaustion of
the long orgy, and it wound up like a New Year's drunk,
collapsed at the entrance to the subway.

I quoted to the class Broun's epitaph on the twenties:
"The jazz age was wicked and monstrous and silly. Unfortunately, I had a good time." That seemed, through the strenuous thirties and the fighting forties, a reasonable judgment.
There was a rearguard protest from some of the critics, who
kept pointing out that the twenties saw the birth of many
considerable talents in American literature: Sinclair Lewis
and Eugene O'Neill and Hemingway and James T. Farrell
and Dreiser and Mencken. After the Second War, by which
time no comparable harvest of later talents had been brought
in, people were inclined to pause and say that perhaps after
all the twenties had something. There had always been, at the
gin-mill level, the aging young jazz hounds who said the
1920's were the golden age of American jazz. But whatever
virtue we tried to find in the twenties was always a resurrec-
tion job. We had always to dig it up and dust it off and say,
look, it's pretty good isn't it? Where else can you find a
brighter horn than that of Bix Beiderbecke? And who revolu-
tionized the written language? We didn't have to advertise
the name; Mr. Hemingway could speak for himself, and
usually did, in a defiant bark from somewhere down in Cuba.
But I don't think Hemingway ever praised the twenties as an
era. It was simply the climate in which he grew up.

Well, now, in the middle fifties, you know what's happened? The other day a bright-eyed girl in her middle twen-

ties came in to see me cradling in her arm a brown paper package. She handled it as if it were a foundling. It was a phonograph record. She wanted me to hear it with her and say what it was. And we opened it, like Canadian prospectors coming into the assayer's office with their first handful of suspected uranium. It was a record made by five undergraduates who were at that moment in Princeton. As I slid it onto the turntable, I noticed that all the titles were tunes written or improvised in the 1920's—"Ballin' the Jack" and "After You've Gone" and "I Don't Love Nobody" and so on. Once they started tooting away, the shock was that the band was right out of the middle and late twenties, not the early thirties but right in midstream, a banjo, and a ducking, sinuous, Trumbauer-type saxophone, and a jaunty muted trumpet, and the boy playing the piano was a gallant mixture of imitation Hines and the clonkety-bang style known as barrelhouse.

I never thought that anyone would revive the 1920's with the reverence, the determined purism of rich stamp collectors. Next thing, I said, they'll be bidding in auction rooms for an early Stutz Bearcat. "My boy friend," the girl said with breathless pride, "has one!" She belonged, she went on, to a crowd of young people up in Boston who had taken a pledge as binding as a nun's: they meant to live their lives as pedantically as possible in what they took to be the style of the 1920's. They made bathtub gin (she was grateful for the tip that distilled water is essential), they bound their breasts to conform to a boyish silhouette, they pinned up the cartoons of John Held, Jr., they danced only the Charleston (how about the veleta? I asked, and the girl made an eager note), they made up their mouths with a Cupid's bow, they were slaving to revive the dead and gone slang (just keep memorizing Sinclair Lewis, I told her, and any song written by De Sylva, Brown, and Henderson).

It is the first time I have ever watched the sentimental re-creation of a period I lived through, and though my nostalgia was stirred for the moment it also gave me the shudders. Why? Because their pretty picture left out the aimlessness, the pleasure mania, the bulging bellies of the German children. But then, so did we. As my own affectionate picture of the eighteenth century leaves out the reeking poverty of most people, the stink of the smartest streets, the disease-racked bodies beneath the ruffs and the rippling, lucid prose. Perhaps, as Henry Ford said, "History is the bunk." But in this case they will have to revel in their nostalgia without me. Because I was there, Charlie, I was there.

11

THE WELL-DRESSED
AMERICAN, MAN!

A few years ago, when my son had about a year and a half to go before he graduated from college, I was mildly astonished to hear myself saying to him what fathers of college boys have said for generations. "I have a proposition to make to you," I said. "You've worked pretty hard and well. Keep it up for the next eighteen months and come out with a halfway decent degree and I'll give you the fare for a trip to Europe." I was a little uncomfortable making this traditional speech, because I had not always been the father of a college boy. I am, in fact, in my fifties for the first time in my life. But I heard myself sounding like the fathers I knew in my time, all of them, I then believed, professional fathers born into middle age.

Of course, I expected my son would fall on his face in gratitude. Instead, he cocked his head and looked at me with that peculiar tenderness that twenty-years-olds reserve for the naïveté of their parents.

"Are you kidding?" he said. "I'll be off to Europe a month from now."

"Indeed," I said, icing up very fast, "and where do you expect to travel?" (I almost said, "And, pray, where do you expect to travel?")

"Oh, a little time in Rome and Florence, a month or so in Paris, I guess, maybe a stretch in Tangier."

I wondered how he expected to live on his frugal allowance. In staggered disbelief he explained to me, with great simplicity and patience, some facts of life that had been kept from me. The summer vacation before his last academic year was coming up, and the university laid on several charter flights to Europe, leave a certain date, back a certain date, at something less than half the commercial fare. My son is a cagey mathematician where rent, food, and expenses are concerned and he had done a calculation on which I could not fault him. Even allowing for the cost of the transatlantic fare, he could live noticeably cheaper for three months in Europe than he could by staying in his rooms in Cambridge, Massachusetts. Uncounted thousands of American college boys and girls have discovered the same thing. Many of them, even on the home ground, live much like cave dwellers. A room as we knew it is by no means the same thing as a pad. We were, I now realize, painfully fastidious in my day. Whatever the cut of our political or social jib, we required such things as beds actually raised above the floor, curtains on windows, chairs for sitting on. These things, I am told, are now looked on as Establishment fetishes. American and European college boys of today are throwbacks to the wandering minstrels of the Middle Ages. They live from hand to mouth, and friend to friend, and pad to pad. They have a universal uniform: one pair of trousers, one shirt, a guitar, a pack of Gauloises, a jacket (maybe), and a toothbrush (sometimes). The motto of my old school would serve them well. It is *Ubi Bene, Ibi Patria*, which being roughly translated means, "Wherever there's a handout, that's for me, man."

All the countries of Europe, and some of Africa, are now peopled by these identical types. They rustle around the continents like cockroaches, and you can never be sure, when you see them on the Spanish Steps, or in the Uffizi, or along the docks at Casablanca, or in the streets of East Berlin, whether they are American, English, Swedish, German, or even Russian. Every place they go they are at home with other wanderers from other lands. The language barrier does not exist, for I am told by a very earnest sociologist that this generation is passing beyond the need of speech into a *lingua franca* of gestures, grunts, and shrugs that establish—and I quote—"a subtle and vital form of identity-communication." No niceties of dress disturb them. On second thought, I'm not so sure of that. However, *our* niceties of dress are as alien and meaningless to them as the elaborate hierarchy of military orders among South American generals who have never seen a puff of cannon smoke.

Of course, today we all pretend to be unfussy and informal about clothes, and to have abandoned the social distinctions that they once used to signify. I doubt very much whether this can ever be so. I have lately been in London for a spell, and then in Devon, Dorset, and Surrey, then back to New York for three days, and am now in California. I am struck by the weirdly different uniforms that the inhabitants of any one place take for granted. A man lying on a beach at Brighton would not alarm anybody if he wore a cap, a tweed coat with an open shirt (the collar folded carefully outside the coat collar), a pair of dark-gray flannels, and boots. A woman coming to dinner in Surrey causes no alarm by appearing in the outfit in which a woman in Minnesota plays golf. Some of these distinctions are obviously imposed by the climate. And to prepare for the jaunt I have just enjoyed calls for some pretty thoughtful packing. Yet even here when people are in doubt they tend to disbelieve the travel-guide warnings and stay with their own prejudice. Every time we go to San

Francisco, I tell my wife that she should pack warm clothes for the evening and that a fur coat is a blessing for the fog-swept, chilly nights of July and August. This is so plainly ridiculous if you were born and brought up in the East that she dismisses my advice as raging hypochondria and later complains that she has not been warned.

But providing for the weather is comparatively easy. The really subtle challenges set in when you travel between the same social strata in different countries. My last three evenings in London were spent respectively at a tony dinner party, at a cozy supper with my stepdaughter, at a "happening" in a railroad yard in a dingy London suburb. No problem with my daughter: she is acquainted with my tastes and I with hers. I wore a suit she once admired and a tie with little tigers snarling on it, and which her friends might well mistake for a white hunter's special. At the socialite dinner party, whose hostess had casually mentioned "black tie," I had to fake it by wearing a black business suit and a black dress tie, which I always carry against such a sudden summons to the tables of the mighty. Nobody noticed the difference, except a modern young siren with eyelashes like quills who must have seen black wherever she went. She congratulated me on the cut and style of my dinner jacket, so much "cooler," she thought, than those old-fashioned silk facings. "Where did you get it?" she asked. I bunched up so as to hide the breast-pocket label that said, "New Haven, Conn." Spain, I said. She purred.

The "happening" was something else. I wore a suit—matching coat and trousers, that is—a necktie and a dark-blue topcoat. I looked, I was later told, like a fugitive from the Foreign Office. Everybody in sight was in jeans or stretch pants, in silver lamé, blue velvet, fuchsia corduroy, monk's cowls, dhotis; and many of them sported beards, leather jackets, and rhinestone necklaces or beads that jangled around their thighs. They were a tolerant lot. No one, I was assured, was outraged by me. The friendly attitude seemed to be: "If this cat wants to dress like an American ambassador, then okay, so long as he keeps his trap shut about Vietnam."

Dressing in America is trickier, for in a country of this size each region incorporates the prejudices of a separate country. I know exactly how New Yorkers of many social types dress for winter, spring, summer, and fall. I know, for instance, that it is necessary to warn a visiting Englishwoman that no New Yorker with the smallest pretension to style wears white shoes, in summer or any other time, in the city. But dressing in Hollywood so that you won't look stuffy, or flashy *in the wrong way*, is a separate trick that not one Easterner in a hundred ever masters. Because they have at the back of their minds a preconception of Hollywood—bikinis, fat cigars, picture ties, Klieg lights, two-tone shoes, Swiss silk suits, V-necks cut to the navel, summer prints of a psychedelic garishness. They know for sure that Beverly Hills is more informal than, say, London. Not so. Only in the movies. You arrive at a Hollywood dinner party in a smart blue blazer, light blue shirt, sleek slacks, a club tie, and black loafers, a costume that would be entirely acceptable at a summer drop-in dinner at the Garrick Club. But in Beverly Hills you find yourself surrounded by men entirely in dark suits, white shirts, and tiny patterned ties. The women, it is true, have a license to wear evening dresses or canary-yellow slack suits. Yet I suspect that this license too prescribes some nuances and forbids others.

Santa Barbara is only ninety miles from Hollywood but it is one band of the social stratosphere away. Although October is a hot month there, fashion obeys the calendar and dictates that it is the fall. The women put on warmer clothes, darker colors, paler shoes. At a Santa Barbara dinner the other evening there was a ravishing New Yorker present wearing a melon-pink suit of Thai silk. It became her greatly. We sat out on a terrace where it was around seventy-five degrees, and she stood out like a firefly in the night. She was thought by her hosts, I later discovered, to be attractive but odd.

That same evening I mentioned to my host a little detective work along these lines that I had done while driving in an airport limousine on the way from the beautiful coastline of the Carmel Bay to the Monterey airport. The only other people aboard were a handsome couple in, I should guess, their middle forties. The woman was pretty and effortlessly chic, and clearly a Californian, for though the day was blinding she wore an exquisitely fitting light-brown cashmere dress and alligator shoes. Her husband, though—lover, perhaps?— was a puzzle. He had on pencil-thin well-cut slacks of a tiny hound's-tooth pattern; a dark-blue jacket; a minihat—a rakish deer stalker, also of a tiny hound's-tooth pattern, and in the brim was tucked a little swirling black feather. If he had been an Easterner, I cannot think what sort of man he could have been. A very well-heeled advertising man, possibly, on holiday. But he sounded too relaxed, too professional; he looked with a steady, matter-of-fact gaze at the blue-brown headlands, the writhing Monterey cypresses, the foaming blue, blue ocean. A little wily conversation at the airport drew out from him that he was a distinguished gynecologist—but from Beverly Hills. He could not possibly, I told my Santa Barbara host, have been a gynecologist in the East. "Nor," he responded, "in Santa Barbara either."

To many people this may appear to be a very trivial theme in the great day of social upheaval and the equality of man. But, I am told at the United Nations, even in China the uniform of Mao Tse-tung has details that escape us which signify to the faithful that his worker's smock is not any worker's smock but the costume of the All-Highest. The Russians, once they were well over their revolution, got out a blue book for their crack regiments patterned after the blue book which once laid down for a British Guards officer the correct civilian uniform for every place and time. And my son now tells me that my own observation of Carnaby Street distinctions is naïve and unseeing.

It will be said that these are snobbish preoccupations. And so they are, and important to go into, since we are all snobs. All of us draw social inferences from the way people dress. In this, fishermen and farmers are just as snobbish as debutantes and hippies. And there is no one, however regal, however humble, who is not put off by some detail of dress he personally dislikes. I well remember the morning that one of President Kennedy's aides came in wearing a button-down shirt, an item that started in America in the very early thirties as an Ivy League fad. It remained so until a few years ago but was swiftly abandoned when it spread to bond salesmen and airline executives and then to Midwesterners, and then to cattle ranchers in convention, and finally to Englishmen. It is still retained by aging country-club types who have not noticed that they suddenly look old-fashioned. "For heaven's sake," said Kennedy to his bewildered aide, "take off that shirt. Nobody wears those things any more, except Chester Bowles and Adlai."

By remarking on these tiny things, John O'Hara for one cornered for himself a small but subtle and memorable view of life. For the rest of us, they can be invaluable signals and telling symptoms of what lies behind the appraising glance and the guarded handshake.

12

THE AMERICAN
NEUROSIS: INSTANT
HEALTH

There is a certain kind of novel, which has long gone out of fashion, that did not aim to take in the whole of life, or say deep things about even small relationships. It was written under the spur of an ingenious idea, which must have come to the author as suddenly as the punch line of a joke. The French do not seem to have a word for it, and failing their instruction we must improvise a genre: call it an Idea Novel. Arnold Bennett's *The Card* is one; and so, I suppose, is his *Buried Alive.* My favorite, though, is a forgotten story by the late (I presume) J. D. Beresford. It is called *The Hampden-shire Wonder,* and I have not had a copy of it for thirty years or more. It was about the small son of a famous county cricketer, a bowler, who for some reason I have forgotten—maybe just plain forgetfulness on his part—had never sent his child to school. This lapse came to the notice of the county school board, which got very worked up over the scandal of a celebrated cricketer having a cretin for a son. So they held an indignation meeting and hauled before it the father, who was something of a simpleton himself except in the matter of medium off-breaks. "Why," roared the chairman of the school board, the leader of the local gentry, "your son doesn't even know that two and two make four."

The son himself, a dropsical-eyed tot who had never uttered a word in the six or seven years of his retarded life, spoke up for the first time. "That," he said, "is by no means certain, for Pythagoras held . . ." The board nearly expired from the shock, as the reader does, and it turned out that the boy was a genius. Beresford artfully sidestepped the usual hurdle of this kind of disclosure—which is the need of the author to become a genius himself—by implying that the little monster's brain was bulging with so much wisdom and learning so far beyond our power to grasp that there was no point in having him communicate with anybody around, including the reader. The squire turned the boy loose in his library, and the last I remember of him was that day after day he climbed up on a throne of twenty-three volumes of the *Encyclopaedia Britannica* in order to read the twenty-fourth. He was left to his own learned devices, for if he had good reasons for knowing that if two and two don't necessarily make four, what hope was there for you and me?

It seems to me that even the most intelligent people in a democracy today are very much in the position of the county squire. We are confronted every day with new knowledge, in science and medicine, and new audacities in propaganda, that rob us of our lifelong assumption that there are some simple truths that can be taken for granted. A loud protest from the dairy farmers of Wisconsin and Minnesota was followed this week by a paper from a psychiatrist on what we don't know about airplane travel. The President of the United States announced that the guilt of Hiroshima had been purged by the discovery of a puzzling novelty called "a clean bomb"; and the Secretary General of the United Nations remarked that from now on it was probably going to be impossible for anyone to distinguish for certain between war and the absence of war.

What these bewildering items add up to is this: A. Milk is not good for you; B. It is not the foreign food that gets you down but your own character, you fool; C. A dirty bomb is a dirty deed but a clean bomb is a boon to mankind; and D. War is peace and peace is war and never shall the twain be kept apart.

Take milk, for example. *You* take milk, after what I'm going to tell you. Until very lately, no nation on earth, with the possible exception of the Swedes, has drunk so much milk as the Americans have done in the past forty-four years. I date this orgy of milk consumption, on the advice of a distinguished public-health expert, from the year 1913, because that was the year in which the United States government acted at last on the discovery that tuberculosis was caused by a transmissible germ and was not, as people had thought for centuries, a vague wasting disease picked up by poets and weedy people from city smoke or the night air. (Sufferers from respiratory diseases were always, and may still be, put on the top floor of the celebrated Johns Hopkins hospital so that they would avoid the miasmas that hovered at night over the surrounding countryside.) The government acted on the precise and historic discovery of Dr. Robert Koch that tuberculosis can be passed from a cow to human beings by its milk; and that the way to prevent this disaster was either to submit the herd to a tuberculin test or pasteurize the milk itself. The United States Public Health Service started a national campaign to make farmers do one or the other. The last risk had been taken out of milk. It was declared to be a "complete" food full of protein, fats, carbohydrates, minerals, and water. The American farmers responded wonderfully, so that by the late 1930's all but one of the three thousand-odd counties of the United States obeyed the law. (For some unexplained reason, Sonoma County, California, was—I believe—the last holdout.) I am sorry to say that Koch's good news, even though it had been first announced in London, was not so well received in Britain; down to the late 1920's and beyond, milk was not generally pasteurized in the United Kingdom. Pasteurizing, the farmers insisted, "took the good out of" the milk. It also took out the tubercle bacillus, a fact that became known to the country doctors of England in the Second War when London schoolchildren were evacuated in large numbers to the countryside, drank "fresh" milk for the first time in their lives, and promptly burst out in a rash of secondary tubercular infections.

But in America, so early as 1913, obstetricians started prescribing gallons of milk for expectant mothers. Within twenty years the height of the average American had increased by two inches, and the American female thigh had lengthened by three inches; not the same thigh, of course, but the thighs of the girls whose mothers were fed the magic liquid before the girls were born.

Some logic chopper is doubtless going to protest that because the long thigh came after the milk doesn't prove that one was due to the other. (A famous statistician, doubting the statistical method employed by the American Cancer Society in its studies of cigarette smoking, has lately shown that the decline in the sale of female corsets exactly parallels the rise in the number of baldheads who frequent burlesque shows.)

Well, America is a country almost heroically responsive to new knowledge, and the fame of Dr. Koch rattled through the country. Milk was not merely good for you. It was essential to a healthy body. So milk passed onto Ameri-

can menus as a routine alternative to coffee. And in my time
an American, male or female, who didn't choose a glass of it
with a meal at least once a day was about as odd as a resident
of Maine who swore off his state's fabulous lobsters.

Well, the milk fad—just as it is starting up in Britain
and France—is waning so fast in the United States that the
great dairy states feel as unsympathetic to doctors as the
tobacco industry. Some busybody, who I suppose is going to
become as immortal as Koch or Pasteur, has discovered
that what seems to clog the human arteries and cause clots
and heart attacks is a chemical snag known as cholesterol.
And milk is mother's milk to cholesterol. So are butter, cheese,
and all animal fats. The fear of heart disease is now as
rampant in the United States as the fear of the invading
British was to the simple Bostonians of the 1770's. And
cholesterol is the redcoat of heart disease. We are now being
urged, not by the dairy interests, you may be sure, to cut
down on meat and cheese and butter and most of all milk. Ice
cream, the routine glory of American cuisine, is so much of a
villain that we may expect the decline and fall of the institution known as a soda fountain. Skimmed milk is acceptable, if
only it were drinkable. If the cholesterol crusade catches on,
it is going to be a dim future for Wisconsin and Minnesota
and many other regions of the cow country. And by about
1984, Miss America will be a midget walking around on
stumps; but, of course, she will be sound in heart and limb,
and mighty unattractive.

Another of the two-plus-two-equals-five discoveries is
that just published by a ranking member of the know-it-all
club of psychiatrists. We have already bowed before their
contemptuous discovery that no generation in history has
known how to raise children without breeding neuroses in
them as big as carbuncles. And now we are told that when

you travel abroad and attribute those bilious days in bed to the water or the old fish, you are crazy, and what's worse naïve. The cause of what the French so magnificently call "bilial fermentation" is not anything you can touch and see. It is something called "cross-cultural shock." In their own language, "The act of transferring one psyche to an environment alien to the subject's own familiar mores produces a cultural trauma characterized usually by digestive disturbances." Being translated, what this means is that what gets you down is not the unfamiliar bugs but the natives. There may be something in this. Of course, a little food poisoning will help.

So now, they have you coming and going. Go abroad and suffer from cross-cultural shock or stay home and run the risk of a heart attack. Above all, stay off milk. And don't walk, jog! Sometimes, it hardly seems worth hanging on, does it?

13

L B J

One of the occupational burdens of a foreign correspondent is the request from the home office for a piece which the home office has already composed in its head. Many years ago, an English magazine asked me for an article and an accompanying photograph "doing something American, preferably sporting." I was briefly fascinated by the thought of what the editor imagined a sporting American to be (a rodeo rider? a Las Vegas gambler? a golfer in two-toned—or as they used to be called, "co-respondent's"—shoes?). For almost at once I came on a photograph taken by a friend on a hot summer's day on the south shore of Long Island. At that time I was mad about surf-casting, and here was a tanned and lithe fellow, young and black-haired, casting the long line with a masterful arc. I was in shorts and my knees were buried in the froth of the surf. It seemed just the ticket. I scribbled in a suggestion for a caption: "Cooke casting for striped bass on Long Island." Incidentally, I was in left profile facing the ocean, which was on the left of the picture.

When the magazine sent me a complimentary copy, I was in right profile and the ocean was on the right. This was not an error, though it involves a rather laborious photographic trick. I thought, Why print the negative? The editor wrote back, "If the ocean is on your left, it will look as if you were fishing in the Pacific—very confusing." But the printed caption alarmed me more. It said, "Cooke fishing in Florida." The editor had an answer for that one, too. "The English," he wrote on a crisp postcard, "know certain elementary things and we mustn't upset them. The Pacific is where Hollywood is; fishing would seem a waste of time. Cowboys come from the West. Fishing is in Florida—no use puzzling them by bringing up Long Island, which is where rich men keep their yachts."

It took me years to work up the nerve to write for a British audience about fishing. I still wanted to correct that caption, though I was undoubtedly the only living person who remembered it. I wanted to say that though they do surf-fish in Florida—and catch such inconsequential stuff as snook, permit, and various snappers—it is the loot of the deep seas, the white and blue marlin, and the inshore red and mutton snappers, the pompano and other lurid and tasty monsters, for which Florida should be respected; and that it is we in the North who have the thundering surf through which striped bass as weighty as thirty or forty pounds knife their headlong way till they are practically beached at your feet, and wheel around and beat it out to sea. It was all too late to explain. No use even mentioning to a transatlantic audience that striped bass is probably the most succulent of our eating fish. If it does not swim in Europe, it's probably tasteless.

This early episode provided my initiation into the war between correspondents and their editors. Lately, I have had another. Very soon after Lyndon Johnson took over the presidency I had a cable from an English editor saying, "WOULD APPRECIATE ARTICLE ON TEXAS AS BACKGROUNDER JOHNSON STOP COWBOYS COMMA OIL COMMA MILLIONAIRES

COMMA HUGE RANCHES COMMA GENERAL CRASSNESS BAD
MANNERS ETC." I promptly declined this assignment since
the whole piece would have had to show that the editor was
wrong at the start, and the end. If cowboys, oil, millionaires,
huge ranches, and general crassness were the true background of Lyndon Johnson, or even the elementary things
about Texas, clearly the editor could have written the piece
himself.

My first thought was: cowboys there are, west of the
Johnson country, which is central Texas, a landscape of pul-
verized granite planted with mesquite, very congenial to ar-
madillos and other armored divisions but the pasture otherwise so poor that the sheep eat the wild flowers and the goats
must nibble for the rest. Goats, they say, can live where all
other four-footed animals would starve. And this is goat country, and that is why Lyndon Johnson as a Congressman, or
some other Congressman from nearby, would be pretty certain to be on the House Armed Services Committee, because
goats produce mohair, and mohair produces army uniforms.

All right—oil. It used to be smart to say that Texas has
traded its open range for a sea of oil beneath. But it is very
likely that most of the people in and around Johnson City and
the Pedernales River have never seen an oil man. The great
oilfields lie to the east and the north, and to Johnson's family
and neighbors they are another world. In his early days, in
fact, Johnson had to fight the oil lobby on behalf of the poor
farmers around him, and you could say that the unceasing
struggle of the farmers against drought and floods, their need
for some elementary conservation and electricity—these were
the hard facts of life that first pushed Johnson into politics.

By now I hope I don't need to say that millionaires in
Johnson country are as scarce as they are in northern Scotland. Huge ranches? I must say that this magazine editor had

an uncanny knack for picking on the very attributes that aren't there. The celebrated King Ranch, from which this preconception springs, is in the extreme southeast of the state, right on the Gulf. It is the largest ranch there is, just under a million acres, and it is spectacularly atypical. The average Texas ranch is two hundred acres, and the ranches (meaning the farms) of the Johnson country are smaller still.

General crassness? Certainly, there are crass people in Texas, as there are in Maine and Berkshire and India and France. But when I read to the end of this sorry cablegram, what came perversely to mind was a remark of the late Lord Halifax when he was Ambassador to the United States. Whenever he could snatch a weekend or a few days away from Washington, he would go down to Texas and his Texas friends. It was his favorite state, and about its people he said, "They have the finest manners of any foreign people I have ever known."

Manners? Lyndon Johnson? In this, perhaps, he is an original, and only a week or two after he succeeded to the presidency, an old American statesman, an intellect and a wasp (in more senses than one), told me that "the problem the American people are going to have with him is to recognize that his 'country manners' do not preclude genuine compassion and a first-rate mind."

So if you are going to write a piece filling in the background of Lyndon Johnson there are some essential things that you have to picture. The granite soil, with actual high mounds of granite slabs; the heat and the barrenness of the country; the stern and tidy life of the nearby German town of Fredericksburg; the strong hold of the Methodists and Baptists on the Texas state legislature—hence no alcoholic mixed drinks are served in Texas from one end of its eight-hundred-mile stretch to another, and millionaires must tote their booze into a fancy restaurant in brown paper bags. The boyhood spent with people of Scotch-Irish descent, known there as Anglos, because the other neighbors are Germans and Mexicans. The Germans are a Republican pocket on the plain, and as a boy Johnson saw many old friends suffer cruelly in the First World War because of their ties of blood.

The most important mark of this part of Texas is its classlessness, of a special, highly regional kind. Thus, Johnson could be at one and the same time a small farmer, once a very poor one, and yet be well connected as to family (his father and grandfather could be high in state government and yet be close to bankruptcy). He is a country boy with Southern talk and Western habits. He knows the Old Testament as well as he knows the soils of Texas. And throughout his childhood, college was a distant thing to aim at but not to take for granted. The enduring ambition of his boyhood was that of his friends: the passionate desire of a poor farmboy to own his own farm and call it a ranch. The now famous LBJ ranch is a modest place, as such things go. And when Johnson first bought it and took old Speaker Rayburn down there to show it off, Mr. Sam said: "Lyndon, you told me you'd bought a ranch, why it's nothin' but an itty-bitty farm."

The pride of Johnson in these origins is something we shall all have to reckon with. What has already emerged from his presidency is the force of his remark, long buried, that he was "a Roosevelt man, lock, stock, and barrel." Roosevelt took to the young Johnson in the pit of the Depression and sent him to his own people to reclaim thousands of unemployed young men from the streets and the farm patches. It was, Johnson later said, "the most satisfying job I ever did have in my life." This remark attests, I think, to the genuineness of his so-called war on poverty, which the opposition said was a cynical election-year ploy. As a Roosevelt radical he

was well hated by the oil and insurance interests when he first
ran for Congress. And if we say that he was allied rather with
"the ranching interests" they include very conspicuously the
interest of the small farmers, the Mexicans especially, in
having sheep that stayed alive, electricity for their kitchens
and pumps, feed for their cattle, not to mention food for their
families.

There is another aspect of this regional pride that is
bound to affect Johnson's approach to negotiation both with
friends and foes. He delights to look on southwest Texas as a
training ground and a horoscope for the world outside. He
strongly believes that if a man can learn to harmonize the
conflicting interests and prejudices of Mexican bean farmers
and German bakers and Anglo retailers and Jews and real-
estate men from Austin, he can approach foreigners—men
from India and prime ministers from Westphalia—on the
same basis. He always provokes a stranger to talk about his
past and his origins, so as to gauge the real forces that commit
a man's heart before his head is involved. He startled a German delegation, on its first visit to the ranch, by saying that
the German demand for a milk subsidy, the Italians' concern
for protecting their rice and olive oil, the Netherlands' need for
a margarine tax, all composed not the dangerous battleground
of the European Common Market but the common ground on
which they would have to weave these necessities into a
system. "He talked to us," said one goggling German, "as if
we were his constituents."

It remains a great question whether this instinct for
what he calls "creative compromise" will provide the proper
magic for talking to the Russians and the British about Europe, or the South Vietnamese—and maybe one day the
Chinese—about Southeast Asia. There is another large question. It is whether a conservative country in a revolutionary

mood (I mean the United States) will be willing to let "a Roosevelt man, lock, stock, and barrel" finish the liberal revolution of Roosevelt's New Deal that was only halfway along when it was rudely arrested by the Second World War.

It is not simply to bolster your spirits on a dark anniversary [1] that I have attempted this little session on the couch, but to warn the intelligentsia, which mourns too inconsolably the bad day at Dallas, that it should watch and wait. Lincoln, too, was considered an oaf by the intelligentsia and actually dubbed "the Baboon" by the best-informed men in London, including the editorial writers of *The Times*. He fooled most of the people most of the time he was alive. But he didn't fool history. So it could be with Johnson.

[1] The assassination of John F. Kennedy.

14

WANTED: AN AMERICAN PROFILE

At a time when television, radio, the movies, and the jet excursion make everybody believe that he knows pretty well what a "typical" American is like, and Russian, and Japanese, and every other nationality, it is good news that the British Central Office of Information has drawn a profile of the average Briton. It is a crushing blow to any foreigner's preconception, and I wish it could be publicized all around the United States. For as the old haw-haw monocled Englishman has faded, a new stereotype has developed, and though it's quite different it's not much better than the old one.

When I first came to the United States, I was struck by a general assumption which Americans carried at the back of their minds. It was that the proportion of upper-class Englishmen to servants, Cockneys, and droll comic characters was about twenty to one; a contradiction in itself unless you think of the average Englishman as a medieval baron maintaining an army of serfs and private soldiers whose main business is to maintain *him*. The ordinary middle-class Briton barely existed in the American view. And since not one American in a thousand ever got beyond the South country—except on his way to York Minster and Scotland—the English city and the working population were left out too. Only two or three years ago I was asked by a lady in a lecture audience to say how you could best get a sharp, accurate picture of England and the English in three days. Two of those days, she warned me, were to be taken up with visits to Hampton Court and the Tower of London and an excursion to Oxford and Stratford-upon-Avon. I hinted that this itinerary itself would only reinforce the picture already in the visitor's mind. Did she really want to replace it with a picture of what most Britons were like, in the sort of place that most of them lived and played? She insisted that she did, she did. I urged her, then, to forget about Oxford, Stratford, and the Tower and spend a day and a night in the East End of London, another in Birmingham or Sheffield, and a third day at Blackpool.

Of course, this was very puritanical advice. You might as well tell a visitor to the United States to skip the Grand Canyon, Williamsburg, and San Francisco and settle for two days in Pittsburgh and a day in a village in Vermont. (At that, you'd learn more about most Americans in a short time than many a resident Englishman learns about them who spends his year in New York or Washington and dashes to Cape Cod or Long Island for his summer holiday.) But few tourists, after all, are "in" steel or rubber or molybdenum, and if they are, that's all the more reason why on a vacation they should stay out of Pittsburgh, Akron, and Climax, Colorado. They are out to enjoy themselves in delectable places. But holidays introduce us to highly atypical sights and sounds, which then pass over into our general impression of the people and the country we are holidaying in. Americans have been going to Europe in larger numbers and for a longer time than any other people have spent in visiting another. Yet the picture most of them cherish of the average British family is as woefully cockeyed as the Briton's picture of the average American family.

Today, I said, there has occurred a split, what intellectuals call a dichotomy, between the old preconception of Britain and the new. And this is disturbing to people, most of us that is, who like to shuffle the three and a half billion people of the earth into their recognizable compartments: Indians are poor and eat rice when they can get it; the Russians are soulful but paranoid at the same time; the Japanese are terribly ingenious and make marvelous cheap imitations of German cameras and English toys; the French would send for the cops if they were ever served a meal without a bottle of wine; and so on.

Unfortunately, this pat world is breaking up in a most uncomfortable way. The Russians are apparently developing social classes and are mad for the piano of Earl Hines (the best thing I've heard about them in a long time). The Japanese surpass the Germans, and everybody else, in optical and medical instruments and are about to snow us with their automobiles. Three Frenchmen in ten, it comes out from a survey by the French Institute of Public Opinion, never drink wine at all.

This brings us back to the new picture that is replacing the old. To this day, I suspect, most Americans would pick Terry-Thomas as the most typical Englishman now on view. But most young Americans, I'd guess, look on him as a precious relic to be treasured and fondled. They *know* he is a relic. I hasten to say that I hope Terry-Thomas himself, the man behind the gap tooth, will prosper and flourish for many years to come. I mean his type, the archetype of the sublime upper-class ass. The big jolt to this P. G. Wodehouse immortal was given most recently by an article in *Time* about

London, "the swinging town." It impressed probably as many Americans as it revolted. The question is not whether London is a miniskirt Babylon swinging down the reckless road to ruin but whether it is anything else. The picture was so artfully painted, the evidence so overwhelming of a general abandonment to free-wheeling morals, psychedelic clothes, rock-and-roll, and the philosophy of "I'm all right, Jack" that even if you suspected it was only part of the truth about a very small part of London, there was nothing else to put in its place. We were in the trapped position of the class whom the teacher told to "think of anything you like except elephants." I predict that by midsummer Carnaby Street will have more American visitors with more cameras than the Tower of London, Oxford, and Stratford-upon-Avon combined.

I'm reminded of an American magazine whose editors decided to do a big color spread on the Western Highlands of Scotland. You can guess at the trouble in store for the Scots by the editorial memo that described the project as "a fitting tribute to the hardy and colorful people of the Highlands." As the editors jetted over the Atlantic, their imaginations were agog with shepherds and their curious crooks and their voluminous kilts. The first town they stopped at could sell them many things—scones, clay pipes, Coca-Cola—but had no kilts in stock. But one of these editors was a far-seeing man. Himself a Southerner, and therefore the long-suffering victim of the Northerner's fantasy of goateed Southern colonels drowning in mint juleps, he had taken the precaution of bringing along a kilt. He bribed the pub owner, or innkeeper as they prefered to call him, to put it on. Which he did, backward. He was photographed in this object, for the first time in his life, outside his little hotel looking across Kyle of Lochalsh and brandishing a pewter mug which the transatlantic image-makers had bought in Edinburgh for just such an emergency. The preconception was fulfilled, the full-page tribute to Scotland was paid. Everybody was happy.

Well now, the spoil-sport Central Office of Information has gone out and questioned and surveyed the actual Britons. And what are they? Terry-Thomas? The butlers that used to appear at the rise of the curtain saying something like, "Excuse me, sir, there's a corpse on the dining-room table"? Comical Cockneys? Night owls rocking into the dawn with girls whose skirts do grow beneath their shoulders? Not at all. Seven out of eight Britons have never been in a night club or any other place in the evening except their homes. The busiest profession in Britain is that of housewife, for only one percent of the population has a live-in maid or other servant. Only five households in a hundred have any regular domestic help except, it says, "that donated generously by the husband." How's that again? That is not true to American observation at all, which faithfully reports that the English wife moves around the kitchen on a long leash while the English husband reads his paper, smokes his pipe, waits for his slippers, and fondles the dog or cat. It is something of a relief to know that there almost always *is* a dog or cat. The British Islands accommodate 4,200,000 cats and 4,100,000 dogs, not to mention 4,700,000 parakeets (a record world total), some of which, I suspect, land up on the menus of ambitious restaurants as snipe, partridge, and pheasant.

Need I ask what is the favorite vegetable of the British? No American would think so. But the deafening response of "brussels sprouts" is drowned out by the astounding fact. The true answer is one which, if John Kennedy had known it, might have provoked a warmer round of Anglo-American talks. For it was his favorite vegetable, as it is of most Bostonians (somebody will now do a survey and prove that most Bostonians are mad for hominy grits). Well, it's baked beans. And I am staggered to hear, as the Central Office of Information was, that Britons eat 230,000 tons of baked beans a year. All of them, that is.

And now, please, will Dr. Gallup do a profile of the average American and his habits and tastes? I don't dare to guess what they might be by now. From my shrewd English friends I gather that the average American rises at dawn, swallows a couple of Dexedrine tablets and a stack of pancakes, climbs in his monster car and hits the freeway, dashes to his Dictaphone for an hour or two, is sharply out at noon for two double martinis and a steak, dashes back to his car and the freeway, another brace of martinis, another steak, a game of poker, a stretch at the telly, a quick trip on LSD, a couple of Seconals, and a fitful sleep. I do remember that Dr. Gallup made a study about ten years ago, a study I've been trying and failing to ram down the throats of my friends here in the East who gag at the idea that they are themselves wildly unrepresentative Americans. Most of them assume, for instance, that at six thirty or seven in the evenings all work across this mighty land comes to a standstill, and that wherever two or three are gathered together the Scotch flows and the martinis. It is true that the cocktail was invented in America and received the blessing of none other than Charles Dickens, who was in most other respects a churlish admirer of American institutions. But the truth is that eight Americans in ten have never tasted a cocktail in their lives. Moreover the presumption of the upper-middle and professional classes that Americans eat dinner at seven thirty or eight in the evening is also a woeful legend. Ninety per cent of Americans have their big meal at six o'clock, without benefit of alcohol, unless you can count the gaseous compressed water that passes in these parts for beer. Only one American in ten has ever been in a night club, beating the British as homebodies by 10 per cent. In spite of the cherished folk tale that apple pie with ice cream is America's favorite dessert (or sweet), the amazing fact is that apple pie with ice cream is America's favorite sweet (or dessert). Beef, which I must say is of a fairly uniform lushness and fineness, except in California, *is* their favorite meat.

As for pets, there is no question that they are inordinately fond of dogs, most of which inhabit my apartment house. Cats? A French writer came here decades ago, stayed two weeks, and his subsequent book on (I think) *America, the Tragic Land* began, characteristically enough, "The central problem of American loneliness is that there are no cats." This is not strictly true. I have spotted at least a dozen in the last ten years.

Trust the French to touch the nerve of the national spirit, or, as they prefer to say about any country but their own, the problem. Surely this discovery offers a profound insight into the true character of Americans. At last we touch rock bottom. For Americans, as everybody knows, are loving people who want very much to be loved back. The trouble with cats is, they don't love anybody.

15

THE WORLD
GONE TO POT?

Anyone like me who was brought up in Britain had used
the slang phrase LSD ever since he could remember. It was
one of the last souvenirs of the Roman occupation and was the
normal phrase for pounds, shillings, and pence. It naturally
held a fascination for the smallest tot who ever stood on the
wrong side of the plate-glass window of a candy store. But
the initials never had the sinister fascination they now spell
out.

A letter from the federal government to two thousand
university and college officials reminded me at first of the
comparative innocence of my own boyhood, and then by free
association of two blind men, James Thurber and Aldous
Huxley. Most of all, it reminded me of a walk I took with
Huxley, around Christmastime 1959, along the road and
around the garden of his house high above the bowl of mountains which encloses Hollywood at its rim and Los Angeles in
its huge basin. Aldous Huxley was not a poet himself but a
man of fine insight into poetic experience. He was also a man
who held grimly onto some rather rum superstitions, and I
don't think it's unkind to say that southern California was at
least one congenial room in his spiritual home.

I mention both these characteristics, one of which is a kind of parody or excess of the other, because they both applied to something he said to me as we walked high up in the hills and he began to tell me about an experiment he was making with a certain drug. It excited him greatly. He called it lysergic acid, and I presume it was an early compound of the one that is now known as LSD-25. Huxley was, so far as any ordinary person could see or sense, a blind man. He could read through very thick lenses when he held the paper almost to his eyeballs. He could, he said, distinguish intensities of light. Sometimes his eyes were better and sometimes worse but not so that an acquaintance would notice. You had to guide him on a walk and you could believe he had any sight at all only when he went into his own house and moved easily around its familiar geography. It is necessary to go into the seeming limits of his sight because he was, during our walk, talking about the essential thing in a poet, his ability to see physical things more penetratingly than most of us, and to feel more deeply.

I remember we were treading carefully along the road, and I gathered that Huxley could not possibly see more than dim shadows and shapes farther than a few feet in front of him. He had just said that D. H. Lawrence had the most acute sensitivity of anyone he had known to the texture and tactile character of animals and birds and flowers. "Well," he said, in his gentle and intense way, "I have found out that with this drug one can be granted for a while a kind of exquisitely heightened sensibility, so that"—he said, as the gravel crunched under our feet—"every stone or piece of gravel on this roadway, for instance, comes to look like a separate and marvelous jewel."

In the past week or so, more than six years later, I have dared to wonder whether the drug quickened and improved the sense he had almost lost or whether it did, in fact, replace his loss with a vision. I put it this way because we have lately heard some sad and shocking testimony about the effect of LSD-25 on college students, who, in the present fashion, seem to take all sensation for their province, including the further reaches of consciousness, and unconsciousness, induced by drugs. LSD is absurdly cheap to make. It is one of the company of drugs now known as hallucinogens, and there is no doubt that in some people it produces exquisite visions. The big question is whether they are of the outer or inner world, whether in fact they heighten and deepen reality or fool the taker into believing that the kind of vision a madman sees is the real world that convention, habit, or sheer blunting of instinct hide from him. At any rate, the experience of a dose sometimes passes off with few bad effects that are noticeable. (We ought to say "noticeable at the time, and to the outsider.") There now appears also to be no doubt that LSD can, and often does, induce mental aberrations and psychotic states that may last several hours or days; that it may plant a chronic psychosis, or do temporary or permanent damage to the central nervous system. Sometimes, though apparently rarely, it drives the taker to suicide, murder, or death.

It was the director of the Food and Drug Administration who sent this letter to the presidents and deans, principals and science departments of the colleges and universities, warning them of the "extreme danger" of these "hallucinatory drugs," in particular of LSD-25, one tenth of an ounce of which can provide 100,000 tiny doses, each big enough, in the government's opinion, to be called "exceedingly dangerous."

This radical move was called for by the great prevalence of pep pills, barbiturates, and other drugs among college students. Lately, we have had scary news about the preva-

lence of LSD, in California especially. It is the kind of news
about which it is almost impossible to make a helpful comment. Older people deplore the pathological extremes which
this generation of college students seems to touch in its hun-
ger for experience. Doctors shake their heads, but the addicts
don't go to doctors unless they are thoroughly alarmed; with
LSD, the government suggests, the alarm may sound too late.
The hope about LSD is that it will be more often terrifying
than exalting, and it will be dropped, even by neurotics who
are tempted to go beyond the euphoria of pep pills and the
weed grown in back gardens known as marijuana. (Marijuana is always lumped with the other dangerous drugs, but
the day may come when we have to consider it as a special
case. The state laws are strict against its possession, on the
general assumption that it is a narcotic. But the scientists are
agreed that it is not, as—for instance—cigarettes are. It
spreads the time sense in some people, so that an oncoming
truck may seem to be a mile away instead of its actual few
hundred yards. In most people, I'm told, it produces much the
same sense of confident well-being and happy talk as a couple
of dry martinis, which are not so far, thank God, banned from
American life.)

Whenever the LSD topic comes up, we most of us—if
we have children of college age—are forced to ask ourselves
whether we are taking a merely reflex, stuffy view of the
failings of the young. We tend to lump drugs with the active
rebellion of the young against what they call the Establishment and we call society. I don't know the answer to this. But
there is one comment I should like to make. The generation
just ahead of me, which was young and dashing in the
1920's, was certainly indicted by *its* elders. It was told it had
violated the whole moral code and was fast destroying family
life. (If you were chic in the twenties, having children was

considered naïve or, since birth control was a prevailing fad,
clumsy.) In this country the brazen young defied the Noble
Experiment of prohibition with a flask of bathtub gin in the
hip pocket. There were, in every city, whole benches of
magistrates to bemoan that the young were leading the world
into decadence and damnation to the wailing of the newly
revived saxophone and the shameless gyrations of the
Charleston.

Well, I suppose that these people, who are now in their
mid-sixties or beyond, produced their quota of pleasure
hounds and even drug addicts. A remarkable number of them
wrote remarkable books, painted memorable pictures, composed so many charming and bouncy songs that without them
any band that plays for old-time dancing (what you might
now call "square" dancing) would have to fold long before
midnight. Other family-wreckers turned into statesmen, ar-
chitects, businessmen, conscientious plumbers and builders,
doctors, scientists, and the majority into law-abiding citizens
and devoted parents who, only a few years ago, provoked the
amazed admiration of their grandchildren by teaching them
how to do the Charleston.

The irresistible thing is to say that old people always
lament the morals and manners of the young and are always
wrong. The fact that is often overlooked is that sometimes the
old people have been right; and the trick is to know when you
are living in one of those times. An old Roman codger who
lamented in the fourth century A.D. that the empire was going
to rack and ruin was absolutely correct. A Greek doctor who,
let us say, in the first century A.D. feared that his trade of
medicine was seriously declining would no doubt have been
ridiculed as a fogey. But he could hardly have been enough of
a pessimist to guess that for the next twelve or thirteen
hundred years, medicine would flounder in a dark age of

quackery and superstition before it again enlisted the early
scientific method or the insights of Hippocrates, who knew
the difference between the fever of tuberculosis and the fever
of pneumonia, though he had never heard of a microorgan-
ism. Or consider an old English playgoer, in about 1630,
grumbling that the best tragedies had all been written and
staged in his youth. Another fogey, no doubt, but neither he
nor the young who scoffed at him could possibly have imagined that no decent tragedies at all would appear in English
for another two hundred and fifty years.

It's an old cliché, but annoyingly enough it's a true one,
to say that Americans are obsessed with the idea that progress is inevitable, that—as a faith healer of the 1920's used to
say—"every day and in every way we are getting better and
better."

The belief in progress is certainly a stimulant to achieve
it and is responsible for the tenacity of, say, American industrial research (applied research, to be precise) and for the
national delight in new things, as well as (I've been hinting)
for the complacency of seeing virtue only in what is new,
whether it's a plastic or a poem or a new way of talk. But it
does disguise from us the truth that civilizations have their
ups and downs and all of them, at last, snuff out. Because we
can "hang" glass buildings on a steel frame does not necessarily make us the superiors of John Nash or Palladio or
Louis Sullivan. The fact that we've seen in our time—in the
last thirty years only—the birth and glory of the great age of
bacteriology is no guarantee that it's going to go on. As a
political fact, simply, it has guaranteed the survival of more
people than can be decently fed and housed.

I put the question, and I do not stay for an answer. Just
in time, another medical item came off the ticker and may
help us to hang on with our fingernails through this barrage

of brimstone. A research scientist from the Neuropsychiatric Institute at Princeton, speaking before an impressive gathering of experimental biologists, has come up with the pronouncement that the only drug that some of us will ever take with a steady hand and a clear conscience is not only a pain killer but has very positive properties to relieve anxiety. The man has been measuring brain waves, of course, and he finds that this magic drug has a more reliable and harmless effect than the tranquilizers. It is called aspirin. When it is "buffered," he says, it will soothe you and strengthen you against "the real anxieties of the real world."

Fortified by two of these little white placebos, I look out my window and onto the park and, whether it is there or not, I can see that the forsythia at last is out, that the cherry is starting to blossom. I have a vision of the sap rising in the trees. I am humbly grateful for the faculty of sight. And I recall suddenly that James Thurber, in his brave crochety way, used to maintain that writers can actually be handicapped by sight. We were sitting out on the terrace of his house in Connecticut and I asked him what he meant. "Well," he said, "you are constantly distracted by the sight of the flowers and the buds bursting. I can sit here and I don't get distracted by flying birds or the sight of a pretty girl going by. Of course," he said after a thoughtful pause, "I can still *hear* a pretty girl go by."

III PEOPLE AND PLACES

16

GIVE CALIFORNIA BACK
TO THE ENGLISH

Several years ago I did a talk about San Francisco and right away I had a letter from an angry English lady. "You talk," she wrote, "as if California belonged to the Americans. You don't make it at all clear that California is a British possession. Drake," she concluded, "took it."

In that last sentence, which is just about as stark as the Indians Drake took it from, the lady spoke nothing but the truth. Drake took it, and I will tell you briefly how he did it.

In 1577, Sir Francis Drake sailed with five ships out of Plymouth. On this astounding voyage, which landed him again in Plymouth two years and ten months later, he reached Brazil, he put down a mutiny, he set two ships adrift, he lost another, he and his crew suffered for long stretches from scurvy and dysentery, and he ran into a storm "the like of which no traveler hath felt, neither hath there been such a tempest since Noah's flood." This one evidently outdid the flood, for it blew Drake helplessly for fifty-two days. When they all came to, they were already in the Pacific off the coast of Chile. This circumstance persuaded Drake to make a luxury of necessity and he set off on his famous orgy of looting the cities of that vast coastline, seizing a treasure ship here, lifting a load of silver there, terrifying the cities of Chile and Peru, ransacking the churches for their altar plate and golden crucifixes and hauling them back to the ship. In the end, he was glutted with loot, and since it was the wrong time of year to cross the Pacific for the Spice Islands, he sailed north to look for that three-thousand-mile all-American canal into the Atlantic which, I need hardly say, neither he nor anybody else ever discovered. But he came off the coast of California.

It can be very cold in central California, and the coastal towns of what is oddly called northern California are always being restocked with Americans who can no longer stand the infernal heat and mechanical sun of the mainland. It was very cold and foggy off the Pacific shore in that June of 1579, and the crew, even though they were Englishmen, began to sniffle and complain. Their noble ship, *The Golden Hind*, was corrugated with barnacles, and Drake looked for a place to put in and calk it. He found it "in a fair and goodly bay, into which it had pleased God to send him." Now this is only the first of several sore points that the scholars hasten to bring up. Some say it was a place long ago called "Drake's Bay" which, in fact, Drake never saw. Some say it was two other bays to the north. The most tedious and authoritative work of scholarship on this topic, put out in 1947, comes to the conclusion that there was no Drake's Bay. Sir Francis was suffering from one of those delusions or fantasies of Eldorado which later came to pervade the coast of southern California.

The bay that Sir Francis *thought* he saw lay a few miles north of San Francisco. An Indian paddled a canoe out to the ship and made a speech with gestures and threw a bundle of black feathers and a basket into the ship. Nobody knew why. But the Englishmen were provoked to go ashore and saw mobs of Indians dancing and waving in the hills. Drake, with all that swag aboard, was taking no chances. He built a stone fort and waited for them to come down. They came down at last in great numbers, the men naked, the women wearing short skirts of bulrushes. It wasn't enough for the Englishmen, who had the character to hand them shirts and bits of linen, which they had no idea what to do with. They acted, according to the ship's chaplain, "as men ravished in their minds." They ravished at a proper distance during the day and retired to the hills in the evening. In time, they adopted a regular routine. The men would toss presents to the sailors. The women stood off a way and "shrieked piteously, tore their cheeks with their fingernails until the blood flowed, tore off the covering from the upper parts of the body and . . . cast themselves on the ground with great violence." After a time they retired to the hills again and set up a dismal wailing and moaning. This went on for six days. American scholars have concluded from this performance, and from the presents they left behind, that the Indians thought the visitors were either dead men returned or supernatural creatures, a view of himself that Drake had come to share.

On the seventh day, a sort of leader or king was escorted down from the hills, and after another bout of singing and dancing and lacerating exercises by the females, he gestured to Drake to be seated. Then he made a formal speech, led a song with an attendant chorus, and hung a necklace of shell beads around the neck of the baffled Sir Francis. The women resumed their wailing and tearing themselves apart.

By this time, the Englishmen had put their heads together and come to a shrewd conclusion. This, they figured, was the ceremony that went with handing over your country to a conqueror. It may now seem to be quite an assumption, and it could hardly be a practiced ceremony since it's something you'd very likely do only once. But we should not forget that Drake's voyage was a kind of dry-run of empire building. The English were dimly reaching forward to the notion, which became a Christian conviction in the nineteenth century, that the first thing a native wants to do when he sees a fully clothed white man is to give up his country for his own good. Anyway, as the lady said, "Drake took it," whether or not he was intended to. Before he sailed away, the Reverend Mr. Fletcher, the chaplain, has recorded, "Our general caused to be set up a monument of our being there, as also of her Majestys rights and successors right and title to that kingdom; namely, a plate of brasse, fast nailed to a great and firme post . . . together with her highnesses picture and armes, in a piece of sixpence current English monie, showing itself by a hole made of purpose through the plate." *The Golden Hind* sailed off. California was took.

We now jump three hundred and fifty-seven years. A young department-store clerk was driving north from San Francisco on a sunny Sunday in 1936. He climbed a little hill, five hundred feet high, and looked out over the bay and breathed deep and felt that life was good. He started tossing rocks down the hill.

Under one big stone, he saw a piece of metal. It was black and battered, and he thought he'd take it home and shine it up a bit. He brushed it with soap and water and he read a few words cut into what looked like a brass surface. They made very little sense to him. But, as you would, he talked about it to his friends.

It took about six months to get the plate into the hands of a rather famous historian from the University of California at Berkeley, one Dr. Bolton. He had been looking for such a thing for years and jesting with his students about the immortality that would be theirs if they ever stumbled on a plate with a hole in it big enough to fit a dime. Dr. Bolton went to work on the plate with a microscope and made out all the words. Delirious with pride, he went off to the president of the California Historical Society and told him what he'd found. He needed money to acquire this moldy piece of brass for the university and the glory of California. They drummed up $3,500, which during the Depression was quite a packet, and the department-store clerk accepted it in, no doubt, a grateful daze. This is what the plate said:

> Bee it knowne unto all men by these presents
> June 17 1579
> By the grace of God and in the name of Herr
> Majesty Queen Elizabeth of England and Herr
> Successors forever I take possession of this
> Kingdome whose king and people freely resigne
> Their right and title in the whole land unto Herr
> Majesties keepeing now named by me and to bee
> Knowne unto all men as Nova Albion
> Francis Drake

Underneath and to the right was the hole for a sixpence —all right, then, a dime.

This was not the end but the beginning of a mystery. The Californians, including the department-store clerk, were convinced at once that it was indeed that "plate of brasse, fast nailed to a great and firme poste" that Drake's chaplain wrote about. English scholars, acting on that old Anglo-American team spirit which animates scholars just as much as boxers and golfers, were convinced in their bones that it must be a fake.

So the plate was sent to Dr. Colin Fink, head of the division of electrochemistry at Columbia University, and he called in a famous metallurgist and an equally famous spectographer from the Massachusetts Institute of Technology. They spent seven months on the plate. They got hold of an

Elizabethan sixpence, and it fitted. They examined the grooves cut by the letterings under a microscope at magnifications of two hundred diameters. They were corroded black all the way through, no suspicion of a fresh area. They found microscopic parallel lines near to the lettering that they were unable to reproduce with a chisel on modern brass. (The expert on armor at the Metropolitan Museum in New York pronounced that such lines can be found on old brass armor.) They tested and scrutinized and weighed in painstaking detail the metal structure, the patina, the soils of the place it had been found. They were convinced it could not have been rolled but hammered, since rolling came in a century later. The organic tissue of the plate was impregnated with minerals. It contained more magnesium than you can ever find in a modern brass. In the end they submitted their report: "It is our opinion that the brass plate examined by us is the genuine Drake plate referred to in the book, *The World Encompassed*, by Sir Francis Drake."

There was a commemoration dinner, and the universal cheer that went up from all true Californians (led by the English colony in Hollywood) was marred only by a faint growl from Captain Haselden, then the curator of the Huntington Library down in Pasadena. English Elizabethan scholars, who had been dashed for the time being, rose to cry "Hear! Hear!" to the doubts of Captain Haselden. A professor at Princeton complained that Dr. Fink had not explained why there was carbon on the patina; there is no record that carbon has been found on copper alloy, whereas a forger might fire it to make it oxidize more quickly. The literary gentlemen brought objections that didn't seem to have occurred to the electrochemist and the metallurgist. The plate is inscribed in Roman letters, which didn't come in until about the 1630's. Several letters—the *m*'s and *n*'s especially—cannot be matched in any known Elizabethan document. The date is put at the beginning, whereas, by invariable custom, it ought to be at the end. The opening words, "Bee it knowne," are smaller than the rest and crammed into a little space, suggesting that they were put in later. The spelling is whimsical, to say the least, though the scholars do admit that the Elizabethans weren't as fussy about spelling as we are and even spelled their own names several ways at different times, just like my daughter. "Her Majesty" is spelled "Herr," and it is never so spelled in any known document of the period. (They answered that one by getting from the Royal Geographic Society the prospectus of a London company formed at the time to exploit, or should we say to develop, the lands that Drake might discover. In it, "Her Majesty" is spelled "Herre.")

Well, the battle rages, in that smooth, ruthless way of scholarly battles. The literary gentlemen say it's a fraud but they begrudge it some skill; maybe it was done a long time ago, and certainly the brass is very old. The California Historical Society has it preserved and on exhibition. They are sure it's the real thing: "Just look at it," they say. I went and looked at it, in the university library, and I must say I think the scholars are splitting hairs. Drake took California, didn't he? My God, they have the brass plate to prove it. The logic of its authenticity is as solid as that of the old lady who was shown the brass plate inlaid in the deck of the *Victory* to mark the spot where Nelson fell. "I shouldn't wonder," she said. "I nearly slipped there myself."

17

H L M : R I P

The other night,[1] the most famous man who has ever come out of the city of Baltimore (pronounced by all natives Bawla-mer) showed to the door an old friend from the Peabody Conservatory of Music, came in to say good night to his brother, who had lived with him through the twenty years since his wife died, and went upstairs to bed. It was just after nine o'clock. And for a man over seventy-five who had had a stroke seven years ago, and a heart attack two years later, nine o'clock was the witching hour when the good things of day—and at that age, alas, of life itself—begin to droop and drowse.

A little man, a stocky man with a bull neck, eyes as blue as gas jets, white hair parted exactly down the middle in the fashion of the early years of the century, and tiny hands and feet that added four surprising grace notes to the solid theme of his body, which was that of an undersized German pork butcher. The Sage of Baltimore, they called him, after they had forgotten the furious years in which they had called him every scurrilous name they could coin for a rebel against respectability, gentility, and the social order he chose to call "the church, nobility, and commons": a chuckler at all bank-

[1] January 28, 1956.

ers, bishops, politicians, Methodists, feminists, city fathers, labor leaders, and "every other sort of faith-healer"—a life-long unbeliever. This little man was in the flesh a genial and even kindly skeptic, and he was very much at home in the society of which he pretended to be the scourge. He was, to those who knew him, Mickey Mouse playing Tamburlaine the Great.

He yawned and doused the stogie of his last cigar and he ambled slowly up the two stories to his bedroom. He turned on the radio to hear some music. There was a program that night of Beethoven, whom he had worshipped all his life and who combined, he wrote, "the glory that was Greece, the grandeur that was Rome"; and Bach, whom he summed up in the single metaphor "Genesis I: 1"; and Mozart. Since the two-hundredth anniversary of Mozart had let loose on the night air a silver flood of his music, let us hope that it was mainly Mozart. If so, no more angelic sounds could have been arranged for the end of an old man who seven years before had roused himself in an oxygen tent long enough to say, "Bring on the angels."

Around eleven o'clock, his brother passed along the corridor and heard him snoring, with the music still on. Next morning, a colored houseman, one Rancho Brown, having prepared the coffee and laid the breakfast table, went upstairs and knocked on the old man's door. "Eight o'clock," he said. "Eight o'clock, Mr. Mencken, sir." But Henry Louis Mencken did not answer and never would again. He had departed what he called "the cosmos we all infest" sometime in the night and embraced without any struggle the end he had groaned for these many years. When all your life is bounded by books and ideas, and you yourself have a magic way with them, it is a bitter judgment on a man to find for his last seven years that he can neither read nor write and is reduced—by an affliction they call a semantic aphasia—to a vegetable, contemplating other vegetables in his small back garden, laying a brick or two, shambling off in the evenings to the one entertainment he had always despised: the movies. The fact was, or came to be, that they provided the most animated and passionate contact he had with human beings (about twenty years after everybody else he fell violently in love with Myrna Loy), but he could not bear to renounce the anathema of a lifetime, and he explained his fondness for the old movies they showed around the corner on the muttered grounds that "their imbecilities amuse me." In the fall of 1948 he had come down with a cerebral thrombosis, which left him paralyzed and babbling for a time, but, to everyone's surprise, the paralysis left him and one morning he woke up and demanded a boiled egg and a stein of beer.

His old enemies lamented that he might have been stricken but he was not yet cowed. He went home to the row house on the edge of Baltimore where he had lived since he was three, where his brother, August, a retired engineer, nursed and did for him. And H. L. Mencken, the American Bernard Shaw, the cheerful juvenile delinquent of genteel American culture, the three-volume-classic authority on the American language, the man who could read at a glance a page of anything—theology, criticism, medicine, law, the news—the man to whom the English language was green pasture to romp in, a three-ring circus to perform in to the delight and terror of the onlooking "boobs": this man got home and extended his index finger and, at the prompting of a patient nurse, learned to identify it like a three-year-old. He learned all over again the simple physical nouns and the things they stood for. "Fin-ger, finger," he repeated, and "plate," "spoon," "elbow," "chair," "floor," and worst of all, "book." For it turned out that the damage had settled in the part of the brain that synchronizes sight and meaning, the ability to see and the ability to make sense of what you see. This disability never left him. He could focus the written page but what he saw was an orderly array of meaningless symbols. So he never read again. He could see and he could talk, pretty much as he had always talked, with sass and pungency and scornful humor. The last time I saw him he made little of the then general fear of the Russians. He had been out on the streets looking at the billboards and store signs. "Why do they fuss about the Russians? It appears to me," he said, "that the Chinese have already taken over." But sitting in his library with several thousand books buried on the walls, he was like a crippled castaway surrounded by the mocking ocean, the one element he had loved and mastered.

Henry Louis Mencken was the grandson of a German who had deserted the troubles of 1848, settled in Baltimore, and left to his son a prosperous cigar business. Young Henry was meant to take it over but he was temperamentally unfitted to following in anybody's footsteps. As a boy in the 1880's he lay on his back on the kitchen table and shot lemon rind from a catapult at the flies which, in the days before fine-mesh door and window screens, camped on the ceiling. "The hired girl," he wrote, "when she was in an amiable mood prepared us enough of these missiles for an hour's brisk shooting, and in the morning she had the Red Cross job of sweeping the dead flies off the ceiling." Having tasted what he called "the red mammalian blood that leaked from the biggest horseflies," he looked around in adolescence for fatter fry. For a time he masked these bloodthirsty instincts in a bookish stoop, which alarmed his father so much that he sent his son off to a gymnasium hoping—said Mencken—"to make a kind of grenadier of me. If so, he was in error, for I remain more or less Bible-backed to this day and am often mistaken for a Talmudist."

When he was nine, young Mencken read *Huckleberry Finn* and it opened up to him astonishing vistas of life in the world outside. He decided a little later on that to be a newspaperman would offer the priceless opportunity, as he put it later, "to lay in all the worldly wisdom of a police lieutenant, a bartender, a shyster lawyer and a midwife." At nineteen he descended on journalism with a whoop. He was extremely spry and industrious and he very soon went from a reporter to a city editor and rollicked in the absurdities, the pomp, the small scandals and big bores with which any self-respecting big city abounds. "The days chased one another," he wrote, "like kittens chasing their tails."

Now, he looked around for the horseflies. He found them in public life and in the late-Victorian beliefs which, before the First World War, gave life its earnest meaning and society its complacency. He had developed a stinging prose style and an essentially humorous view of human idealism. Like Voltaire in one country and Shaw in another, he let fly at his own. And for about ten years, through the prime of his forties, he skinned every respected institution in the land which he thought had grown fat and uncritical. He regretted the arid theology of the puritan fathers and debunked the heroes of the Revolution. George Washington himself he thought would be today "ineligible for any office of profit or honor" in the republic, and he begged the American fiction of the 1920's to cure itself of its "marshmallow gentility." The new young realists swarmed to Mencken like Polish underground refugees to London during the blitz, and he started a magazine and printed their first, and then considered pretty revolutionary, work. O'Neill, James Farrell, Dreiser, Sherwood Anderson, Ring Lardner, and more. They were the rude natives he defended at the gates of the Governor's garden party. Through the 1920's and until the Depression gave people simpler and more urgent troubles to think about, Mencken was the rebel god of American letters. Soon after that his influence wilted, for he was suddenly a gadfly in a charnel house, and he turned to his work on *The American Language* and to the writing of his enchanting memoirs. Every four years he would enjoy a ribald excursion into his old never-never land by way of reporting the presidential nominating conventions.

This outrageous, cocky, gallant, cynical, sentimental, greatly gifted man went out suddenly last Sunday without even a coughing fit, snoozing in his bed as the dawn came in over the city he had loved and terrorized. If he could have seen the way he went, you may be sure he would have fired off a final impenitent chuckle. For it contradicted something he had noticed long ago: "The human tendency to make death dramatic and heroic has little excuse in the facts. . . . A man does not die quickly and brilliantly like a lightning stroke; he passes out by inches, hesitatingly and, one may almost add, gingerly . . . the abominable acidosis sneaks upon us, gradually paralyzing the adrenals, flabbergasting the thyroid, crippling the poor old liver, and throwing its fog upon the brain. We pass into the blank unconsciousness of infancy and then into the blank unconsciousness of the prenatal state and finally into the condition of undifferentiated protoplasm . . . the dying man doesn't struggle much and he isn't afraid. As his alkalis give out he succumbs to a blest stupidity. His mind fogs. His will power vanishes. He submits decently. He scarcely gives a damn."

Living or dying, it was Mencken's special glory that he didn't give a damn. He was all of a piece, from the boy on the kitchen table firing slingshots at horseflies to the old man whose last political comment to me was that the old soldier, General MacArthur, "is a dreadful old fraud but he appears to be fading satisfactorily." "All of a piece" is a phrase we seldom hear any more; we prefer the solemn word "integrity." It may be the word I am looking for, though it is taken as a Christian concession to allow the word these days to men who are wholly dull or wholly predictable because they give no rein to the warring impulses in all of us, to men who would better be called conventional, or prudent, or obstinate, or plodding, or enslaved by the codes they never made. Mencken was an original with the courage to live by his sometimes outrageous convictions. Like all writers of surpassing talent he was offered huge sums to do some other man's bidding. But he early on turned down the big money and never wrote a piece he didn't want to write. In a persuasive plutocracy, he was impervious to the seductions of the rich because he liked his life and was devoid of envy. "In the face of another man's good fortune," he once wrote, "I am as inert as a curb broker before Johann Sebastian Bach."

Of the advice he gave me as a starting newspaperman in the late 1930's, I have always been grateful for one rule, or rather three, which a reasonably honest man might get to respect but only after a long convalescence from painful bruises: "Never accept a free ticket from a theater manager, a free ride from the chamber of commerce, or a favor from a politician." He lived absolutely by this rule. He wanted to have his say, and he knew that a very gifted man who isn't interested in money is very hard to tame.

With his father's admiring help he became an agnostic as a boy and stayed one for the rest of the seventy-five years, four months, and eight days of his life. There was no weakening at the end, no yielding at last to lifelong temptations to throw in his lot with this sect or that, religious or secular, no sloppy concession that there are no atheists in foxholes. As old age came on he was noticeably more tolerant, even of types he abominated, like evangelists, city politicians, and golfers. He was challenged toward the end by an old opponent to confess what he would do if he discovered there was an afterlife by the simple fact of finding himself in one. He replied that if he did indeed "fetch up beside the Twelve Apostles, I should simply say to them: Gentlemen, I was wrong."

He prepared for his end with singular sprightliness and care, appealing in his will for no parsonic "whooping and heaving" at the grave, a little poetry perhaps but nothing that would offend his irreligious scruples. In an astonishingly well-ordered life, his secretary was asked to appear at the same split second every morning. He answered every letter by return of mail. He took a daily nap at the self-same hour. He locked away his files at six precisely, and they were as elaborately card-indexed as the personnel records of the Pentagon. As the sun faded from the front parlor he mixed the martinis, for he was ready to observe the second half of another lifelong rule: "Never accept a drink by day or refuse one by night."

In such a life it would have been an odd oversight if he had not prescribed the proper sentiment to go on his tombstone. Since he ordered that there should be no fuss or ceremony at the end, he was cremated, and the only service was a reminiscent get-together of a few friends. But he had not overlooked his epitaph. He wrote it over forty years ago. It is chiseled on a brass plaque that greets you today in the lobby of the Baltimore Sunpapers building. This is it: "If, after I depart this vale, you ever remember me and have thought to please my ghost, forgive some sinner, and wink your eye at some homely girl."

18

THE ROAD TO CHURCHILL DOWNS

I was recently invited to go down to Kentucky as a house guest for a few days and wind up with a front seat at the Derby. In the early days of May this is about as sure a guarantee of heaven as a city dweller, or even a countryman, could ask for on this earth.

Kentucky is technically a border state, lying poised between the North and the South, but it deserves far more than its neighbor, Ohio, the description "a Northern state with a Southern exposure." Being not quite in the South it has striven to be very much *of* it. There are no Southerners quite so Southern as the professional Southerners of Kentucky, and by practice as well as by blood they have taken on the legendary pace of Southern life, its customs and cookery, the slow twist of vowels into diphthongs, and that attractive Southern irony which is prepared to believe the best of human beings and expect the worst.

It was a little warmer than usual the day I tumbled down into Kentucky, but the Ulstermen, or as they say here the Scots-Irish, who settled here a century and a half ago soon accustomed themselves to a semitropical drowse that would have choked their cousins in Aberdeen. It was at Aberdeen, by the way, that I crossed the Ohio River, and along its banks the Judas trees were in full flame. The town is terraced high on the steep slopes of the hills as they crowd down to the river, as if rushing to make a last stand before they give way to the rolling meadows of the Bluegrass country.

I tossed in the word "Bluegrass" there in a casual way, but have no fear that it is going to go unexplained. This whole talk, if it takes the turn I hope, is going to be about the Bluegrass region, which for a hundred and seventy years has bred the fastest, proudest, most gleaming of America's race horses. On top of the Fayette County courthouse is a weather-vane in the shape of a golden stallion. It is no more possible to go through the Bluegrass country and ignore the horses than it would be to go through Nevada and ignore the slot machines. From Maysville, the first town across the Kentucky line, down to Lexington, the capital of the Bluegrass, is sixty-three miles, and there are some interesting oddities. There are handsome houses overlooking the river that were built in the spacious times when the steamboat minted fortunes as fast as the railroads that superseded them. But this was, and is, trapper country. The first white men who really roamed this hinterland were the French, the fur trappers and traders who made the most of a huge continental landscape where, unlike Europe, the mountain ranges ran from north to south, and the rivers also. There is hardly a river in the main river systems of the American mainland that has not left the relics of the French fur trappers, for they extended Napoleon's empire up the Mississippi and the Missouri and the Ohio to places far in the north. Even Chicago, it may strike you, is pronounced "Shick-ago" and not "Chick-ago" because the first people to come on it were French rivermen. Chicago is an Indian name, but the French had trouble with the "chi" sound, as they still do (they can't even say "Good night, chairee"), and they had to say it "Shick-ago." The incoming Yankees picked up the pronunciation and it has stayed that way ever since, except, of course, out of the mouths of Englishmen, who live eighteen miles from the French but have had little truck with them.

But in this first valley that I went through, the French had been quietly obliterated by the Scots-Irish, who have a habit of taking over any place they settle in; and if they don't absorb it, they preserve the gift of not being absorbed either. Until I arrived on the edge of the Bluegrass all the names were such as Cochran, McConnell, Marshall, and Keith and Duncan. In a charming small town called Washington one of the houses that is a required stop for tourists is a two-storied Georgian brick house. It was built at the turn of the eighteenth century by a man who had loaded a large family on a flatboat, sailed down the Ohio, and made a home here. The point of visiting the place today is that in the grounds many of the Marshall family are buried. And there stands still the modest tombstone of a certain Mary Keith, who turned out to be the mother of John Marshall, an early and great Chief Justice of the United States Supreme Court. The epitaphs on Scottish tombstones are not, as I recall, very flowery, not even when they were written in the eighteenth century, which both in old England and in New England consigned its beloved to the care of Providence with grand flourishes of the language. But some of these Kentucky leavetakings are as chilly as the Highlands. That of the mother of Chief Justice Marshall is no exception. It reads, "Mary Randolph Keith, born 1737, she was good, not brilliant, useful not ornamental, and the mother of fifteen children." The mind reels at the size of her progeny if she had been ornamental.

Well, by the middle of the afternoon I had come to the end of the winding river-bottom roads and was on a long undulating upland and the true Bluegrass country. You will want to know, as everybody who has never seen it does, if the grass is really blue. It is not. Even the natives admit that it is merely green in summer. But no matter how much the Kentucky guide insists that "only in May do the blue anthers of its blossoms give the grass a distinctly steel-blue tint," a stranger needs to wear special tinted glasses to make it appear so. The way not to disappoint your friends is to photograph it in color in the very late afternoon, when the slanting light of the entire Western hemisphere spreads a film of milky blue on anything, even the complexion of your favorite girl. It is only fair to say that you do notice the greenness of the grass, but it would not startle an Englishman or an Irishman and it would not be much of a surprise to a native of Oregon. However, let's not be hoity-toity about this local product. It is as indigenous to this region as the Monterey cypress is to that small coastal stretch of central California. It is not matched as turf, and as pastureland is surpassed, I should guess, only by the two famous sections of eastern Pennsylvania and southwestern Belgium, which a League of Nations survey chose as the finest in the world.

The Bluegrass is a small central plain, less than eight thousand square miles, which lies on a bed of limestone and is richly veined with underground water. And this is the perfect —they say essential—recipe for the two glories of Kentucky: fine horses and bourbon whiskey. It is the limestone which endows the waters that pass through it with phosphorus and calcium. Which, as every stable boy knows (and I just learned), are two ingredients of bone and rippling muscle. This is why the Kentucky thoroughbreds are strong and fast and beautiful to look upon. This is why, as you drop south from the eroded hills of southern Ohio and up onto the downs of the Bluegrass country, the road signs change from adver-

tisements for familiar gasolines and cigarettes to elegant
signs by elegant stud farms that say: "Brood mares, boarding
and training"; "Track entrance, 100 feet"; and "Blue Grass
Seed."

In deference to people who were brought up in my own
self-denying faith, I will quickly explain the essential ingredients of Kentucky's second famous product and then pass
on. It may be regrettable but it is also true that the water that
courses through the limestone has a distinctive flavor. There
are simple, strong people who slake their thirst with the
natural product alone and go on, I'm told, to live blameless
lives. But there are others, the first of whom was one Jacob
Spears, as long ago as 1790, who looked on the Kentucky
water as the merest raw material for a confection that has
done the state some service. The United States abounds, as
you may have heard, in maize, so much so that like the
English with their wheat, the Scots with their barley, and the
Australians with their oats they have adopted for it the usual
counter-word for the staple crop: corn. Mr. Spears earned the
gratitude of uncounted generations by having the wit to take
the maize and grind it and mash it and add the magic limestone water, and then distill the compound and age it. And
that's how bourbon was born, so called after the name of the
county that gave birth to this splendid firewater. Not surprisingly, Mr. Spears's first distillery was in Paris. And the heart
of the Bluegrass country is between Paris and Versailles.

These towns were so named, as were many others
nearby, in grateful remembrance of a stripling boy, a nineteen-year-old Frenchman, the Marquis de Lafayette, who offered himself in the service of the American Revolution to
General Washington and beat you know who, and has ever
after symbolized the special one-upmanship that the French
enjoy in America. This is nothing to dwell on, but you surely

can't expect me to toss off the remark that I have just driven from Paris to Versailles without explaining that we are still in Kentucky.

It has a wide undulating green horizon, strikingly devoid of evergreens but spotted here and there with those jetting, fanlike American elms, which, alas, have been blighted by the Dutch bug all the way from Ohio to the New England coast. The Bluegrass is rich country in more senses than one, for it must cost a modest fortune to maintain even the five-barred white wooden fences that ring the paddocks and enclose the fields and swing like switchbacks between you and the horizon. Inside these pastures is practiced that strange and compelling ritual of breeding race horses which so obsesses the insider and leaves the outsider feeling that he has been mistaken all his life about what a horse is. In sickness and in health, in affluence and depression, no babies anywhere in Kentucky are so jealously and delicately cared for. After the weaning comes the precisely regulated diet—a mixture of oats and corn, bran and flax seed and vitamin extracts—then the trimming of the feet, the breaking to the halter, the gentling into the paddock routine, then the exploratory trotting and cantering, and then the speed trials; all this going on for two years or more before the magic truth is revealed or exploded: whether or not the blood of the horse's ancestors and the skill of his training will merge to produce a true race horse, perhaps a great one.

In the late winter and early spring, you could have seen on the doors of some stalls record charts—for temperature, diet, and other clinical peculiarities of the tender patient inside—which are as anxiously consulted as those in a surgical ward; because no discipline is too fussy, no care too excessive to the men who match their knowledge of blood lines and skill in training methods in the gaudy hope that one day the people may flock to see their ward run on the first Saturday of May in the Derby at Churchill Downs. And there can be few Kentucky owners and breeders who do not nurse a faint hope that later on the people may troop to a second shrine comparable with Kentucky's first.

And what is that? It is Faraway Farm, outside Lexington, and to some knowing people it is as much of a pilgrimage as Lenin's Tomb to an obedient Russian. Up against the sky and standing on a small hillock is a handsome statue of the greatest race horse of his time, who won nineteen times in twenty-one starts, collected a quarter of a million dollars in only two seasons, sired two hundred and thirty-six horses, one hundred and seventy-six of whom were winners: the fastest, the most beautiful, the proudest son of Kentucky—Man o' War. You amble up to the statue with your hands in your pockets and a few other visitors come up, and the men take their hats off. You are surprised to find that you have done the same.

All this, you will have assumed, is an easy buildup to the climax of a holiday in Kentucky: the breathtaking spectacle itself, the Derby. Well, to be quite honest, I can think offhand of a dozen other spectacles that catch my breath quicker. A hooked bluefish, for instance, a glass of lager, the dimple in the chin of Ava Gardner. For I was shaken to discover that if, while the race is on, you lose your program or have a coughing fit you can miss it altogether. If anybody had asked me, I should have guessed that the Kentucky Derby was something like the bicycle race around France, and that we were going to sit through the last day of it. It turned out it takes two minutes, and for this the whole population of Louisville, and several hundred train and plane loads of gamblers from the East and West, and breeders from Ireland and Argentina, and "kinfolk" from the South, make plans for a year, finagle for tickets, pay regal prices for a bed, and line up for food— for a hundred and twenty seconds on the first Saturday in May. Other people's enthusiasms are always a riddle, but I shouldn't take kindly to a sneer at mine. So I will say that the reason for my being in this strange place was a promise I had given, in a wild moment a year before, to my ten-year-old daughter. By the peculiar grace of God, she has not yet become aware of one half the human race—I mean boys. That being so, what else is there on earth to rave about but horses? Her weekends are spent bouncing round the park, the only dress catalogues she handles feverishly are ones for riding gear, her room is plastered with more ribbons and horse prints than a presidential convention with campaign buttons. She flew in on a flawless day over the velvety pastures and the rolling farms and the gleam of horseflesh, and she said at once, "Why can't we live in Kentucky?" I said, "I'll tell you why. Because a little later on you'll discover that they breed boys in other places than the Bluegrass."

The object of this trip, then, was up at dawn and out with Ned, a slim young man in blue jeans and a high-buttoned shirt, with tendons as bowed as the horse he couldn't sell. There was a choice of colts, fillies, ponies, for this was a working farm, and a working farm for other less favored beasts. Cows sloshed their tails around in the heat of the day, and at night sheep complained to the moon and the air was dense with birds that trilled, barked, whistled, shrieked, and glucked. The sun came up like a yellow rose and fell like a sweating orange. It was ninety-four degrees the first day, ninety-two the second, ninety-six on the great day itself. But the tempo was easy and nobody was going anyplace but Churchill Downs. We lay on the grass and had lunch of Kentucky chicken hash and potato pancakes and the best succotash (corn and lima beans) I'd ever eaten. We had a box overlooking the finishing post, and for the first time since 1880 there was a challenge from the losing jockey, and a very tense pause before the stewards decided that in the stretch Tommy Lee and Sword Dancer were bumping each other in a rhythmical and entirely legal way.

Some people, I don't doubt, will be sensing with suspicion or disfavor the sort of society I seem to be sketching: a horsy, arrogant, vowel-chopping—or vowel-smearing—upper crust. Not your cup of tea perhaps? Not mine either, I assure you. While I feel like a vaudeville clown in the presence of dignitaries of the church and state, I am practically T. S. Eliot in the presence of horsy people. I know less about a horse than—certainly—a horsefly. An Argentinian, in a mad attack of mistaken identity, asked me if I'd brought any promising fillies along. I said I had brought a ten-year-old filly with me. My daughter hopped to my side and growled in a whisper, "You can't be a filly if you're older than four." How about colts, I asked. "Same thing," she said, and blushed for her city-slicker father. The Argentinian thought he was in the wrong town and wandered off.

But the great surprise, and the delight, of this interlude in the Bluegrass was to mix with a lot of people who were expert and hospitable and easygoing with their knowledge, and impossible to grade socially. You never knew whether the young tow-haired man in the corner was a Yale sophomore or a groom. For three great days, Jefferson's original image of America was restored—that of a pastoral republic where the rich, the poor, and the in-between mingle, eat, drink, joke together, have the same manners, the same idioms, and an overriding gentleness and naturalness. A small, uncorrupted society united in a lovely landscape by a genuine love of the same thing—a horse. (I discovered, much too late in life, that the same sense of an innocent community can be guaranteed by the pursuit of a ball with a liquid center.)

On the plane coming home, my daughter rattled on in ecstasy till she had to catch her breath. I jumped in with the damping reminder that it was wonderful but it was not at all like life. "What d'you mean?" she said. "Well," I said, as we looked down on the approaching industrial landscape of the Jersey flats, "we might have had bad seats, or stayed in a crummy motel, or keeled over from the heat, or been bedded down in Louisville, or there might have been no horses to ride. Everything was perfect," I said, "but it isn't always so."

"I don't get it," she said, and fell asleep.

19

THE COLONEL OF
THE PLAINS

When Colonel Robert McCormick, the publisher of the Chicago *Tribune*, died in Chicago even his enemies among the Midwestern papers couldn't suppress a sigh over the passing of their feudal baron. Right or wrong, he was their man, the son and champion of that part of the country that is variously known as the Midwest, the Heartland, the Farm Belt, the Isolationist Belt, and the Cow Country. Local pride in America is a complicated emotion, which permits—at different times—the separation and the overlapping of different loyalties: to the town, the county, the state, and the allegiance that embraces and swallows them all—regional pride. For, if I may say so, this is a big country; more, it is a continent and its natural regions span four time zones and a range of terrain from true desert in the Southwest and semitropical swamps in the Southeast, up through semidesert and high plateau country to wheatlands and lush pasture country and, in the West, to the forest primeval, until the whole northern verge of the country shears away to Canada and on to tundra. A man from the state of Maine, who lives on the rocky edge of a glacial coastline, can be as much of a stranger to a man from southern California as a Laplander is to a Hawaiian Islander.

Nowhere is regional pride so jealously upheld as in the midcontinent, whose capital is Chicago. Colonel McCormick was born there and he liked to think of himself as the chosen monarch of all he surveyed. He was, in fact, not chosen at all. He was the self-appointed defender of the Midwest against its perpetual legendary rival and persecutor, the financial East. He saw himself fondly as the original pioneer, the valiant son of New England who had the get-up-and-go to desert the effete comforts of New York and Philadelphia and hack through the forest and emerge at last to build a plain, brave, wholesome life on the vast Central Plain. So he thundered through a long life against the New York bankers who supposedly held the Midwestern farmer in thrall. He half-believed that industry was born in the Midwest. He was quite sure that self-reliance and honest-to-God Americanism were. Till the day he died he never ceased to lament that New York and Washington and Boston were little better than British outposts drugged by the decadence of Europe and periodically perverted by a loyalty to Britain which he considered little short of treason.

I have deliberately painted no picture of Colonel McCormick himself but rather let off a volley of his favorite gunfire in the hope that through the clearing smoke you could picture for yourselves the honest, granity outline of him: a rugged, downright rough diamond, unaffected, unlettered, but unbowed, the very archetype of the Irish and Germans and Poles and Swedes and Czechs who built the railroads and ran the factories and sowed the prairie soil and intermarried to produce a new man in the world whom we know as the Midwesterner. Well, let me now give you a closer look and unveil the details of this splendid statue of a man. It is true that his grandfather was the same McCormick who developed the McCormick reaper, which reaped the grain and raked the cuttings off the platform and bound the sheaves in a mechanical operation. This great invention guaranteed a historic development of wheat farming on the endless high plains, where the climate had always been ideal but where there were never enough human beings to harvest it by hand. It also guaranteed that the next generation of McCormicks would be very nicely taken care of.

So the first thing is that young Robert Rutherford McCormick was born in the lap of luxury that he came to despise. His father was a diplomat who was sent, when the boy was only nine years old, to serve in the American Embassy in the hated colonial capital of London, England. Consequently, the boy had a rather lonely childhood, and his humiliation as a native Midwesterner began very early in life. For he was first sent to school, and to a fashionable prep school, in England. From there he went to Groton, in Massachusetts, which in those days was considered, and still might claim to be, the American Eton. There, by the way, he met another little boy, not at all a solitary type, a genial, sunny, slighty dudeish Easterner. This boy was to become his lifetime enemy, a symbol of everything he disliked about the Eastern United States: the effortless assumption of breeding, the rather prim, la-de-dah manners, the mawkish concern for old Europe and the tendency to run to her aid in time of trouble. This other boy's name was Franklin Delano Roosevelt. At Groton, McCormick was one form ahead of Roosevelt, so by the stern code of schoolboys he was able to regard young Roosevelt as a junior and a whippersnapper. In later years, it was something to be grateful for.

From school, McCormick passed on to Yale, which was then hardly a plebeian retreat. By this time, his family was in what used to be called Petrograd and is known to us as Leningrad. The boy had the best reasons to feel neglected and put-upon. His family lived abroad and the apple of its eye was his eldest brother, who was being trained to succeed his grandfather as the publisher of the Chicago *Tribune*.

Suddenly, in 1910, the brother died and Robert Rutherford inherited the paper. In the next ten years, he transformed it into a technically brilliant production. He bought up huge forests in Canada. He always regretted having to secure his pulp from the country which, he calculated, would be the jumping-off ground, or staging area, of the next British invasion of the United States. But, on the Salvation Army principle that the devil's money is as good as any, he imported the forests and downed his pride. He took the incoming immigrants under his wing, much as William Randolph Hearst did in New York; and it must be said that he shared a forgotten virtue of Hearst in his early days: which was that he understood profoundly the social plight of the shoals of newcomers, from central Europe especially, who poured into a new land with a new language and strange habits, different in different places, and who were already too old to go to school and learn the language or the elementary facts of American history and American customs. Hearst deliberately set out to teach them and to make his newspapers family newspapers in the novel sense that they helped to make the immigrant feel like a member of the American family. Of course, this entailed a good deal of flag-waving and bombast; but Hearst, and McCormick after him, took to heart the remark of the other Roosevelt (the "manly one," as he was sometimes known in the family to distinguish him from Franklin the dude). America, said Theodore Roosevelt, was too far-flung already to be able to afford millions of what he called "hyphenated Americans." If all these strangers were to be melted into the pot of a single powerful brew, the sooner the better for people to stop identifying German-Americans, Polish-

Americans, Italian-Americans, and so on. What Hearst tried to do for the workers of the cities of the East, Colonel McCormick did for the new Chicagoans and the Midwest. They rewarded him by buying his paper. And the Colonel—he earned the title in the First World War and never afterward dropped it—quadrupled the circulation of the *Tribune* and chose, about twenty-five years ago, to call it flatly "the world's greatest newspaper." In case there was any doubt about it, he printed the slogan as a subtitle at the top of the front page.

The Colonel lived in what was called "quiet luxury" in a thirty-five-room house. He had a bony long rectangle of a face, a guardee's mustache, the quizzical gaze and the slightly bloodshot eyeballs of a retired Indian officer or a master of foxhounds. He wore two wristwatches, one on each hand, for he was always afraid of anyone's getting the jump on him; and in his crusade of saving America for the Americans and setting it free from all foreign entanglements, it was always later than you think. He took tea at precisely four thirty in the afternoon, a custom indulged in in this country only by the most rabid Anglophiles. His voice could hardly boast a single Midwestern vowel, uvular *r*, or cadence. In horrid fact, he had more than a trace of a British accent. So that if you went to Chicago looking for that archetypal Midwesterner you would never have found him. He looked indeed like a Tory clubman, a Bond Street polo player, of the vintage of 1912. Freud, thou shouldst be living at this hour!

How is one to explain this remarkable contradiction between the spirit and the flesh? Well, I have talked about him because, although he was rare enough to be that rare thing, an American eccentric, he yet embodied a conflict in the Midwestern character which usually throws up no signals on the surface. It lies in the sort of dislike that involves a strain of envy. Colonel McCormick, I think it fair to guess, was secretly angry with cultivated Easterners and Europeans of his own type because they were so obviously and irritatingly more self-assured than the Midwestern natives and immigrants with whom he had thrown in his lot. But make no mistake, his feeling for the Midwest and its destiny was very genuine. I got the impression from him that he wished American history might jump a hundred years so he could demonstrate that the Midwest had just as many good clubs and representative museums and fine universities and civilized people as the detested East. His criteria of civilization were the same as the Easterners', in spite of his prodigal's embrace of the farm and the factory and the honest uproar of the streets. If he had only known it, he was Colonel Don Quixote tilting at windmills that had collapsed long before he died. For the first thing a foreigner has to learn when he arrives in this country is that it has no unchallenged capital city. Washington is the capital of government, New York of publishing and show business and fashion. But the vast, and vastly separated, regions, like the old Greek states, have their own capitals. And in the hundred years of its growth, Chicago need hardly bow to any other American city for the quality of its medical schools, its art collections, its social amenities. It is actually a national leader in advanced engineering, agriculture and Oriental languages. It was the cradle of modern American architecture. It was to Chicago that Sir William Craigie came to edit, on the model of the great Oxford dictionary, the dictionary of American English. Chicagoans know all this but they still fear that they are best known for Al Capone and the railroads and the endless troop of livestock that come into Chicago as cattle and go out as steaks or tennis racquets.

As you push west from the Eastern seaboard, it is impossible not to notice the Midwestern chip on the shoulder, which

Colonel McCormick elevated to the dignity of an epaulette. Old Tocqueville, over a century and a quarter ago, spotted and pinned it in two marvelous sentences. Writing about the bleak New England coast where this nation was born, he says, "This tongue of arid land was the cradle of those English colonies which were destined one day to become the United States of America. The centre of power still remains here; whilst in the far backwoods the true elements of the great people to whom the future control of the continent belongs are gathering almost in secrecy together." Secrecy is the word. In Midwesterners of whom Colonel McCormick was an ideological caricature, there is always the secret fear that perhaps the Midwest has not in fact achieved "the control of the continent" or the grandeur it imagined for itself in its youth.

20

ALCATRAZ

In the middle of San Francisco Bay there rises an island built like a battleship. In one direction it looks across a mile and a tenth of thrashing water to the docks and the white city rising on the hills. In the other, it looks toward the Pacific through the break between two tawny hills, which are spanned nowadays by the red arch of the Golden Gate Bridge.

Summer is the coldest time in San Francisco, and on dank summer nights when the Pacific fog comes whirling in the vertical struts of the bridge actually twang and wail like a harp played by the witches in *Macbeth*. Looking down to the few damp lights on that island it is not hard to imagine that Duncan is lying there on his last night. If this is a morbid image, it is of the sort that springs to the minds of San Franciscans all through the year and causes some of them to wish that the place would sink or be sold by the government and turned into something less intimidating—a rocket pad, a hydrogen bomb lab, say.[1] For the island looks like a fortress, and when it has not been armed as such, first by the Spaniards and then by the United States Army, it has been a prison of one kind or another. First it was a so-called discipli-

---

[1] It was too expensive to maintain, and in 1963 the federal government abandoned it.

nary barracks for renegade Indian scouts. Then for captured
Filipinos. And always for army traitors. The Spanish lieutenant who discovered it in 1775 might well have called it the
Alcazar if he had not been struck by clouds of pelicans that
floated around it. So he called it after the bird itself—Alcatraz.

This genial christening has long been forgotten; and
since 1934, when it became a federal prison, Alcatraz—the
mere name of the place—has sent a shiver through the tourists who come to peer at it from the shore. For the mile or
more of intervening water separates them from the most
atrocious murderers, the stoniest rapists, the subtlest jail-
breakers now extant in the United States. It is not, as the
popular gossip has it, a prison for lifers. It is, the warden
insists, a "corrective" prison for men who know how to
organize sit-down strikes in state prisons; for incorrigibles;
for the bred-in-the-bone mischief makers of the Republic; for
the men who employ a life sentence as a lifelong challenge to
discover how, with a twisted hairpin or a stolen razor blade,
to break away from any prison they are put in.

A removal to Alcatraz is thus considered in the under-
world as a kind of general's baton, the reward of distinguished field service that cannot be overlooked. And the
guides on the steamers that ply through the riptides close to
the island never fail to call off the roster of the incurable
desperadoes who have battled the state prisons and landed
here: "Limpy" Cleaver, Machine-Gun Kelly, Gene Colson,
and Al Capone. If a man goes through Alcatraz with an
impeccable record he may shorten his stretch there; but invariably, on the day of his release, two guards appear from the
state prison that could not hold him. A warrant is sworn for
his instant arrest, and he goes off in handcuffs back to the
state that claims him, for another twenty years, or whatever,
or perhaps for life.

I myself seem to have a mystical relation with Alcatraz. On the first day of my honeymoon, in the spring of 1946, I was driving my wife across the four-and-a-half-mile span of the Oakland-Bay Bridge, ticketing the wonders of the bay, and like all newcomers she wanted to see and shudder at Alcatraz. I looked over my steering arm toward the island and saw little puffs of smoke peppering the blue sky. And I said, offhand, "Down there where the whiffs of grapeshot are coming from." Well, by the time we got back to the city from a trip to the Berkeley hills, the newspapers were inky with fresh black headlines. The puffs of smoke had not come from a trap-shooting exercise. They announced the now celebrated Battle of Alcatraz. The inmates had seized the arsenal and tied up two guards, whom they subsequently killed. For two days the men shot it out with the guards, and it took the arrival of the Marines to break them.

Again, in 1958, I flew into San Francisco on the last Monday in September and had barely had time to unpack before the wailing of klaxons started, and two men had vanished from Alcatraz.

Now the trick of escaping from Alcatraz by the water route (and unless you have a friend with a silent helicopter there is no other) is worth a little thought, surprisingly more than the men who have tried it have cared to give it. The distance to freedom is, as I said, no more than a mile and a tenth. But it is a ferocious stream that empties into the Pacific with an ebb tide swollen and quickened by the waters of the Sacramento River. Close by the island, even on the most placid days, the water is slashed by riptides and gurgling with whirlpools. You might conceivably plow through these hazards if it were not for the implacable enemy: the extreme, unvarying cold of the water. A guard I met had jumped in one hot afternoon to rescue a mother and child, from one of the staff families, who had been playing by the water's edge and stumbled in. He fished them out in five minutes and was confined to a hospital for two days with chill and shock. The doctors calculate that an average healthy man with a reasonable layer of blubber on his bones could stay alive in these waters for not more than twenty-two minutes. But it takes about forty minutes for a log of wood to achieve the ambition of the inmates, namely to catch the full ebb tide, drift down to the Golden Gate, and be deposited on one of the nearby beaches. In the last twenty-four years, nineteen men have tried it. Five never got beyond the range of the catwalk guns and were shot to death. Twelve were captured in the water, or —feeling the ice around their spleen—chose to slosh back to the comparative comfort of a longer lifetime on the island. Two vanished and are presumed long dead.

Mind you, it can be done, but not on the ebb tide on a foggy night, and not by you or me, or Al Capone. Johnny Weismuller, when he was the world's champion swimmer, looked the prospect over and thought better of it. In 1936 Babe Scott, the nineteen-year-old daughter of a police sergeant, made it on the flood tide at high noon, on a brilliant hot day with an accompanying launch, nips of brandy, a well-greased body, a cheering press boat, and several other amenities which the warden and his men do not provide for intending escapists.

In the first week of October 1958, soon after the latest attempt, a San Francisco gym instructor hit the water in the same place, at the same time, in the same weather, as the two men who escaped. He was an extraordinary animal and the attending doctors and guards were amazed that he lasted for over half an hour, when he was taken out half-frozen. "No doubt about it," said the warden, "Burgett's body is at the bottom of the bay." Of the two men who had plunged in in

September, one was a criminal of the first chop, Clyde Johnson, a forty-year-old bank robber who during a short, busy
period had been listed as Public Enemy No. 1. The other was
comparative small fry, Aaron Walter Burgett, a twenty-
eight-year-old gunman, lately from St. Louis. Johnson, the
tough guy, was caught when the water was no higher than
his hips. But Burgett had gone, it seemed, for good.

And so I telephoned the warden and asked if I could go
over. And on a shining day, with the water as silver and green
as a bluefish, I took the launch from the army pier and went
to Alcatraz. I sat beside a priest who was one of the prison
padres. I could get very little out of him except the line:
"There are some marvelous men over there, they just happened to get caught too young."

I quoted this thought to a prison guard, a personable,
and seemingly a kindly, man. "All parsons," he said, "think
that all men are basically good. 'Tain't so. Shall we go?"

Although the island looks formidable from the city, it is
an agreeable, even a romantic, place close up. It has tumbling
hills and is banked with ice-plant in the spring. It has protected playgrounds and little lawns for the children of the
sixty-five staff families who live there. It also has natural
caves, which have often been blasted with tear gas, but last
time only the vapor came back, not Burgett.

From the terrace of the warden's house, the view is
magnificent in all directions and the deep water slaps close
by. "If I lived here," I said brightly, "I'd have no time for the
prisoners, I'd sit on this terrace and fish all weekend."

"What do you think?" the warden said, almost with a
touch of hurt. "We get beautiful bass."

The central building is huge, and its three main units—
cell blocks, mess hall, kitchen and yard—are very compact. In
an outer office, with a big switchboard and panel that made it

look like the control room of a submarine, a guard pressed a button; an iron door swung open and we were in the main cell block. The floors glistened. Most of the men were at the workshops making leather or tools or binding books. A few were in their cells, which are small and house one table, one washbasin, one toilet, a short bookshelf. One man had two volumes of Gibbon's *Decline and Fall of the Roman Empire*, and he was stretched out on his bed halfway through the third. In some cells there were paint brushes stuck in bowls. It seems that a third of the men take to painting, if only to copy in a crude fashion the pneumatic beauties of the pinup magazines. Most of them bend with painful diligence to copying some of the fifty personal snapshots they are each allowed.

We moved on into the mess hall. At the entrance to it, there was a high wallboard, like the ones they have in American cafeterias, a black plastic board with white block letters slotted in to proclaim the dinner menu. The day I was there it was clam chowder, grilled rockfish, wax beans, carrot sticks, mixed salad, corn bread, ginger cake, coffee. Sometimes, I thought, it hardly seems worthwhile slaving away piously on the outside. We moved into a great kitchen, gleaming with stainless-steel surfaces and refrigerators. A staff cook was slicing carrots. The chef, a chronic bank robber, was tasting the soup with a lacy gesture.

Through and beyond the kitchen you come out of a door and onto the catwalk, where the guards roam cradling their machine guns and overlooking the men down in the yard. The big yard, which looked about half the size of a football field, appeared from the catwalk to be the floor of an empty swimming pool. It was fifteen feet below, enclosed by walls packed and meshed with barbed wire. The yard had a baseball diamond, and half of the men were playing there and the rest

were lounging around. They all wore a light-blue denim
uniform. It was the general poise and ranginess of them that
provided the big shock. Back on the mainland you imagine
gorillas baying behind bars; and there they are, as coltish and
easygoing as an air-force crew. Average age, by the way,
thirty-four. It makes you feel suddenly very old, and very
lucky. I looked down on them with a fascinated kind of awe
and then across to the splendid vista of the mountains and the
city, and the freedom that is so near. The men see it only for a
few taunting seconds every day. When they leave the mess
hall they have to go along a ramp near the catwalk before
they troop down the steps to the yard. For that brief moment
they glimpse a mile of green water and beyond, sharp as a
graveyard of white tombstones in the spring sun, the city of
liberty. It is a sight tantalizing enough to breed great patience
in the vilest of men—Aaron Burgett, for one. He had gone ten
years with a faultless record, so blameless that he and Johnson had been assigned to the elite crew. They were the only
two inmates to make up the garbage detail, and they could
therefore roam the island picking up the daily refuse of the
shops and garages and homes of the sixty-five families. After
ten years, they saw their chance with a new guard.

On the afternoon of the 29th of September they whipped
on him with a knife, tied him to a tree down by the water, and
rescued some plastic laundry bags from the garbage cans.
Burgett fashioned his, after long practice, into a pair of water
wings and took off.

Pretty soon the klaxons sounded, and the San Franciscans shivered with the familiar guilty thrill. For, what the
warden cannot say, from considerations of public morale, is
what the public knows very well. The citizens may shudder at
the klaxons but that is only a respectable cover for the unholy
hope they cherish. It is that one day one man might make it

by water, that Warden Madigan might receive, sometime around Christmas, a postcard from Miami or Blackpool. "Having loverly time," it says, "wish you were here. Signed —Aaron Burgett."

These uncivic thoughts were frozen in their tracks on the 16th of October. Many logs and much debris, and even rafts, float by the island. One such object on that day had an almost human look, almost but not quite. It was the rather frightful remains of the corpse of Aaron Burgett.

21

MARSHALL

It has been a habit of these letters to honor, as W. H. Auden put it, "the vertical man," the Americans in all their variety who are up and doing. But Americans themselves are great celebrators of their eminent dead. And when the calendar reminds us of a great one who was born or died fifty or a hundred years ago, he is obediently honored in the tomb by people who would have feared or hated him in the flesh. For Americans, an impetuous but ceremonial people, are soon ready to pay tribute to a man once the wind is out of him.

Lately we observed as a holiday the date kept aside as Columbus Day, which celebrates the discovery of this country by a man who neither discovered it nor ever saw it. And a few days later we nodded respectfully in the direction of Harpers Ferry, West Virginia, where—a hundred years ago—John Brown, a near-lunatic with a hot eye and a single purpose, started on his wild and brief campaign to set up a free state in the Appalachians as a sanctuary for escaped Negro slaves. Next day, a man died who had been born just across the Pennsylvania border from Harpers Ferry who had an equally single purpose but who was so prosaic, so deeply disdainful of drama and public exposure that not one American in a million would have recognized him on the streets, and not even his close friends knew a pungent or delightful story about him. He was almost impossible for a newspaperman to know, for he winced at the word "newspaper" and he therefore acquired no public personality, not even a couple of identifying adjectives in *Time*. In the last few years of his life he used to drive downtown most days from his small house in Pinehurst, North Carolina, buy his groceries in the supermarket, tote them to his car to the accompaniment of a nod from the townspeople, a bit of gossip with the drugstore clerk, and then get into his car again, receive the flourish of a salute from the traffic cop, and drive home again. Yet on a bright day, wherever in the world the American flag flies, it was lowered and flown for him.

I hope I won't be misunderstood if I say that he was a most un-American figure because he was so remarkably self-effacing. The United States has as many people as anybody afflicted with self-effacement, but it usually springs from social discomfort, or genuine shyness, or that other form of shyness which, as somebody wisely said, is a sure sign of conceit. This man was not shy, but the subordination of self to teamwork was almost an instinct with him, and I suppose few men who take to soldiering took to it for a better reason. Most Americans were willing to credit the reports of his eminence but it was something they had to take on trust; for General George Catlett Marshall, of all the great figures of our time, was the least "colorful," the least impressive in a casual meeting and the least rewarding to the collector of anecdotes. He was a man whose inner strength and secret humor only slowly dripped through the surfaces of life, as a stalactite hangs stiff and granity for centuries before one sees beneath it a pool of still water of marvelous purity.

He was always uncomfortable when anyone mentioned

the great Plan that bears his name, the plan to repair the fabric of European life after the devastation of the Second War. He took no credit for it, and he was nearly right. For it was first conceived by underlings in the State Department and seized on by Undersecretary Dean Acheson when he realized that all the largesse of UNRRA and Breton Woods, and the loan to Britain, and other loans to Greece and Turkey, were far from enough. It was time to jettison Europe or to throw out a lifeline. Acheson developed the Plan, and it was worked on in the White House, and he floated it as a trial balloon in a speech at Cleveland, Mississippi. No one in the country took particular notice of it. Marshall had been in Europe and when he came back, Acheson told him about it, not without misgiving, for Americans had not marveled at his trial balloon, and a sudden Communist stab at Hungary might puncture it once and for all. Marshall, it must be said, now saw the necessity of speed and a public forum and contrived within two days to speak at the Harvard commencement. He was no orator, and the dramatic novelty of the Plan went unnoticed by everybody except a trio of British correspondents and the British Foreign Secretary, Ernest Bevin, who sat by his bedside in England and heard a transatlantic broadcast and responded to it at once as "a lifeline to sinking men . . . the generosity of it was beyond our belief . . . we grabbed it with both hands." So it is not for the Marshall Plan that we honor the General.

Imagine now a sturdy, well-knit man, stiff-necked it would be fair to say, certainly in the physical sense, with sandy hair and mild blue eyes and a homely, underslung mouth from which issued unspectacular remarks in a throaty voice. A student of war, from the books and the maps but also from the arms contracts and the quartermaster records, and from a personal knowledge of the battlefields picked up on

private walks when the bones of the dead were long over-
grown.

It is possible—we shall never know—that in his private
imagination he was another Robert E. Lee who dreamed
dreams of high deeds in the cannon's mouth. But for almost
fifty years he was fated by his superiors and, in the crisis of
his career, by his own conscience to return as always to the
drawing board, to revise the training methods of a tank corps,
to compute the comparative tactical efficiency of a 55mm.
machine gun in close combat and in desert warfare, to gauge
the competing need for anti-aircraft of the slums of Chung-
king or the docks and ports of Iceland. A high subordinate
who worked with him assures me that in the history of
warfare Marshall could not have had his equal as a master of
supply: the first master, as this West Point colonel put it, of
global warfare. I suppose we must defer to this expert judgment. It was enthusiastically seconded by the three or four
senior British generals during the Second War. But to most
of us, unifying the command of an army outpost or totting up
the number of landing barges that could be spared from
Malaya for the Normandy landings is hardly so flashing as
Montgomery's long dash through the desert, or MacArthur's
vigil on Bataan, or even the single syllable by which General
McAuliffe earned his immortality: "Nuts!"

A layman is not going to break out a flag for a man who
looks like a stolid golf-club secretary, a desk general who
refused an aide-de-camp or a chauffeur and worked out of an
office with six telephones. Even though 1984 comes closer
every day, this is not yet an acceptable recipe for a hero.
Though no doubt when Hollywood comes to embalm him on
celluloid, he will grow a British basso, which is practically a
compulsory grafting process for American historical characters in the movies. He will open letters with a toy replica of

the sword of Stonewall Jackson (who was, to be truthful, a lifetime's idol).

But in life no such color brightened the gray picture of a man devoted to the daily study of warfare on several continents with all the ardor of a certified public accountant. In a word, he was a soldier's soldier. Nor, I fear, is there any point in looking for some deep and guilty secret to explain his reputation for justice and chivalry. There is, however, one voice that has been silent. No syllable of praise or criticism has come from a soldier who can coin resounding epitaphs when he so chooses. General MacArthur has said nothing, and I dare to wonder about his silence only because it reflects a conflict of character and temperament that was conducted on both sides with shattering dignity. It will by now be no surprise to learn that on Marshall's side it was a most undramatic quality: the gift of making at fateful times sensible decisions that elevate another man and swing the spotlight away from you.

We have to go back to February 1956 for the last public word about Marshall written by General MacArthur. "General Marshall's enmity towards me," he wrote, "was an old one." Discounting the word "enmity," let us say that the original row—the sort of thing that elephants and politicians never forget—goes back to the First World War, when Marshall, a colonel on the Operations Planning Section of the American Expeditionary Force, was planning the recapture of Sedan, the historic town which three German armies in the last century have broken through to lay waste the lands of France. Marshall's plans did not allow for the impetuous ambition of a young brigadier general to summon his own division and take Sedan at a bound. The brigadier general was, need I say, MacArthur. He leaped through a loophole in the Marshall plan and took Sedan in his dashing stride. From then on he vaulted ahead of Marshall in everything but prudence. By 1930, when he became chief of staff, you would have had to scan the army lists with binoculars to see what happened to Marshall.

After the First War, you might have thought that his appearance at the side of General Pershing as a personal aide would have assured a flashier or more enterprising type some quick preferment, but it was downhill again for another fifteen years. As late as 1933, for instance, he was appointed senior instructor to the Illinois National Guard, an appointment that would have thrilled a scoutmaster. But for an able soldier, fifty-two years of age, it was the pit of his career. Once MacArthur retired, in 1935—and it may be no more than coincidence—Marshall had his feet on the ladder again. Two days before the Germans swept into Poland he was made chief of staff.

I said that in the supreme crisis of his career it was his own conscience that sent him back to the commanding obscurity that was his habitat. Nobody has told this incident better than the late Henry Stimson, Roosevelt's Secretary of War. In a letter to the President in August 1943, Stimson wrote, "I believe the time has come when we must put our most commanding soldier in charge of this critical operation [that was to be the invasion of Europe]. You are far more fortunate than was Mr. Lincoln or Mr. Wilson in the ease with which that selection can be made. . . . General Marshall already has a towering eminence of reputation as a tried soldier and as a broad-minded and skillful administrator." The British had, in fact, suggested him. Churchill assumed he was already picked and Stalin had vouchsafed a wily nod of approval. There came a day in Cairo when President Roosevelt and Marshall lunched alone. It seems to be accepted among Marshall's close friends that he had all his life yearned for a combat command. The most majestic command in history was his for the asking. Roosevelt had already made up his mind but, as usual, allowed himself room to maneuver (and lament) if things didn't turn out his way. He asked Marshall whether he would prefer to stay in Washington as chief of staff or take the supreme command. Stimson kept some notes, made from Roosevelt's account of the lunch, and in them he says that Marshall declined the gambit. It was, he said, entirely for the President to decide. He warned the President that if he was chosen to go to Europe, there was only one man he could think of to replace him in Washington. It was the new general Dwight D. Eisenhower, who had commanded the North African landings. The President decided that Eisenhower had neither Marshall's grasp of worldwide strategy nor his familiarity with Congress. So he picked Eisenhower, and Marshall congratulated him, and the lunch was over. At the end of it, Roosevelt said, "I couldn't sleep nights, George, if you were out of Washington." (Roosevelt is the only known man who ever called General Marshall "George.") When Stimson heard of this he was, he said, "staggered." He gave to his diary the note that "at the bottom of his heart it was Marshall's secret desire above all things to command the invasion of Europe." But Marshall himself had advanced the deciding argument. Who else would oversee the war of supply, who would review the war in both oceans, from the necessary desk in Washington? He never by any sign showed that the President's decision was not the perfect one. The British too were staggered and apprehensive, and it was a British official who put down in *his* journal: "In Marshall's presence ambition folds its tent." Stimson put down an older sentence he had once quoted about Marshall: "He that ruleth his spirit is better than he that taketh a city."

When the dust and the glory came blowing up over the

battlefields, Marshall was the father confessor and guru to
Eisenhower. To MacArthur he was still a sullen office figure,
smarting at long range over the humiliation at Sedan, but it
was Marshall who urged on Congress the award to MacArthur of the Medal of Honor. Twelve years later, when Eisenhower was campaigning for the presidency in Wisconsin, he
deleted—at the personal urging of Governor Kohler, of Senator McCarthy's Wisconsin—a passage in praise of Marshall
from a speech that he was about to give. Not a word ever
passed the lips of Marshall about this dismal episode, and
when McCarthy called him a traitor for the failure of his
postwar mission to China, all Marshall said to a personal
friend was: "The hardest thing I ever did was to keep my
temper at that time."

There is a final story about him which I happen to have
from the only other man of three present. I think it will serve
as a proper epitaph. In the early fifties, a distinguished, a very
lordly, American magazine publisher badgered Marshall to
see him on what he described as a serious professional mission. He was invited to the General's summer home in Virginia. After a polite lunch, the General, the publisher, and the
third man retired to the study. The publisher had come to ask
the General to write his war memoirs. They would be serial-
ized in the magazine and a national newspaper, and the settlement for the book publication would be handsome indeed.
The General instantly refused on the grounds that his own
true opinion of several wartime decisions had differed from
the President's. To advertise the difference now would leave
Roosevelt's defense unspoken and would imply that many
lives might have been saved. Moreover, any honest account
might offend the living men involved and hurt the widow and
family of the late President. The publisher pleaded for two
hours. "We have had," he said, "the personal testaments of

Eisenhower, Bradley, Churchill, Stimson, James Byrnes. Montgomery is coming up, and Alanbrooke, and yet there is one yawning gap." The General was adamant. At last, the publisher said, "General, I will put it on the line. I will tell you how essential we feel it is to have you fill that gap, whether with two hundred thousand words or ten thousand. I am prepared to offer you one million dollars after taxes for that manuscript." General Marshall was faintly embarrassed, but quite composed. "But, sir," he said, "you don't seem to understand. I am not interested in one million dollars."

22

THE SUBMARINERS

It was just after midnight on a Wednesday in April, and my telephone rang. A friend of mine wondered if he might come over for a nightcap. I was delighted. I am what they used to call a night owl and now call more mysteriously one of the night people; but my friend turns into a turtle about nine in the evening and I welcomed him as a convert to the small hours and the life of Riley. "You heard what happened?" he said. I had not heard. The U.S.S. *Thresher*, a submarine, was long overdue on a well-plotted mission. My friend was an old navy man, with the sentimentality but also the compassion of the service, and he came in shaking his head and murmuring about "those poor bastards." Possibly, we reflected, we knew some of the men aboard. For we had gone off together a couple of summers before to spend a few days at Groton, Connecticut, at the mouth of the Thames River that flows into Long Island Sound. We had gone to look over the Submarine Training School, where indeed the crew of the *Thresher* and many more like them had been converted from sailors into submariners, as they call themselves. Offhand, I can't think of an assignment since the war that sounded so ghoulish at the start and ended in such fascination on my part for a new subject, a new profession, you might go so far as to say a new type of twentieth-century male.

When I arrived at the Groton base, I was as excited as an urchin and as apprehensive as an undertaker at the sight of two submarines at the docks and the thought that I would soon be on one, and in one, and down in one. They look at first like some joker's attempt to build a whale. The navy engineers are, in fact, engrossed in just this kind of task. They are still trying to decide what is the essential function of a submarine so that they will be led to design the perfect and appropriate shape.

So I started with a submarine designer and hastened to tell him that I was an ignoramus. He looked at me and said, "What do you suppose a submarine is basically supposed to do?" I was about to tell him, but he quickly added, "That's not a leading question. It's a question. I honestly have no idea." (We were both relieved.) "We're beginning to learn," he went on, "that a submarine is not a ship, and it's not an airplane, but it's more like an airplane than a ship. And maybe more like a fish than either."

I shuffled as you do when you are seeking some practical information from a butcher or an insurance man, worse yet a pharmacist, and find yourself in the presence of an amateur philosopher. You want to tap his special knowledge and he wants to show you he's a deep, wise man. It took only an hour or two to appreciate that this naval designer was, on the contrary, a troubled wise man. We began at the beginning.

The first submarine was invented there at Groton, or to be precise a few miles away at Saybrook. It was designed in the shape of a Boy Scout's water bottle. It had a frame and a treadle, and its one-man crew bicycled, so to speak, out into the Atlantic by dead of night, detached himself and the frame, which became a bicycle raft, and attached the big bottle to the hull of a British ship. He then peddled his way back to land and waited. His hope was that the bottle would soon become a bomb and blow up His Majesty's ship. You must have guessed that all this was going on in the 1770's. The intrepid bicyclist was the inventor, and this escapade marked the first journey of a submarine. His name was David Bushnell, and his target was H.M.S. *Eagle*. His bottle contained one hundred and fifty pounds of dynamite. Somehow, the thing never went off. Bushnell survived, but so did H.M.S. *Eagle*.

Anyway, it was a beginning, and Mr. Bushnell's intentions were honorable. So he is honored in the submarine museum at Groton with a life-size model of his ingenious but unsuccessful invention. After that, submarines were designed in the shapes of yachts, pipe organs, kazoos; and the ones from the First World War now look like castle towers on skis. Later they got to look like swordfish.

The engineers and designers and naval strategists and psychologists have been putting their heads together all these years while we were going about our business assuming that they certainly knew theirs. While all the while they were going around asking themselves, "What *is* a submarine?" like Joxer Daly in Sean O'Casey's play going into his trance and asking himself, "What *is* the stars?"

"The big breakthrough," the designer told me, "came with the *Skipjack*." It is a nuclear submarine and it very strikingly resembles a shark. It resembles a shark on purpose, for it took the best brains in the navy to rediscover the profound truth that fish tend to swim and birds tend to fly because they are designed for that purpose. They found that the more a submarine resembles a deep-sea fish, the better it works. It stabilizes better when it has both dorsal and caudal fins.

But since submarines have been learning to dive deeper, they have passed out of the element of the sea into a band of water so light and airy and so motionless (they retreat to it in hurricanes) that it approximates to an atmosphere and is called by the submariners "the clear element." The big discovery about this peculiar layer of water is that it radically transforms the motion, the speed, and the whole behavior of a submarine. They now realized that what they needed was a machine that could sail like a ship, dive like an old submarine, but, in the clear element (which behaves much like the air a few miles up), fly like an airplane. So they developed retractable ailerons, like airplanes, or—as I facetiously suggested—like pigeons. "That's it," cried my designer. "The more we study what a submarine can do at different depths, and what the nature of war is going to ask us to do, the more we look at birds and fish all over again. The ideal submarine," he was now ready to pronounce, "would be a cross between a seagull and a dolphin."

For all I know, this may be deeply secret information. At any rate, I was allowed to gather that the day when a submarine went as deep as possible to lie below surface craft, at which it was meant to fire torpedoes, seems to be about as dead as trench warfare. The whole training of a submariner, which is about as long as a psychiatrist's, though more rigorous (the man has to come up with verifiable results), is to inspire him to go to sea, after seven years of study and practice, and to submerge and slink off nine thousand miles to the Baltic shelf or wherever, to stay down for a month, six months, a year, until the White House presses a button, which lights up in the *Skipjack* or the *Nautilus*, which then presses its own button and fires a Polaris or its less primitive successor into the lap of the chairman of the particular republic which by that time has graduated as the supreme enemy of the United States. This is the ultimate fate of the seadogs of Sir Francis Drake and Admiral Nimitz. No wonder the submariners are a special, long-suffering, and meticulously chosen type. (A navy psychiatrist goes off on first missions, and special missions, to check on the "health" of the men's adjustment: the adjustment, that is, to months of waterbound claustrophobia.)

The submariners are recruited from the cream of Annapolis, the United States Naval Academy. They go to sea for a year or so on what has come to be called "routine surface craft," what once were proudly known as ships: they serve on a destroyer, a cruiser, or other pleasing anachronism. This part of their training is, I can only think, a tender tribute to the traditions of the navy and no doubt will soon be abandoned. Then they go to Groton and learn how to handle an ordinary, pre-atomic, submarine. They go to sea in one, and six months later they move over to nuclear submarines. Most of their specialized nuclear training is not done at sea but indoors in what looks like a mammoth movie set. It is a life-size model of a submarine bridge and is controlled from a huge electronic console (the movie-theater organ) at which sits a devilish coordinator—a man, no less, who feeds into an electronic brain in the basement every possible kind of problem of weather, of fire, of dynamics, of handling and mishandling, of natural and unnatural shock. The brain reflects and refines the signals the coordinator throws him and throws them back in a perilous form at the poor trainee on the bridge. He is, of course, required to react instantaneously— and correctly. Watching these men, I saw one or two first-class disasters. "Fine, Jackson," the instructor would tartly comment, "you're now at ten thousand feet, angle forty-five degrees vertical, and going through the ocean bottom." The point of this monstrous Link trainer is, of course, to save the training submariner from fatally enacting at sea the mistakes he makes in the theater.

The human aim—if you can call it that—is to produce men whose reliability, of intelligence, reaction, and temperament, can be trusted 99.9 per cent of the time, 100 per cent in an emergency. Consequently, the school at Groton is turning out crews markedly beyond the normal skill and steadiness of the old valiant men of the ironsides. You may well wonder, as I did, what sort of human being undertakes to become this kind of automaton. He is permitted the doubtful boon of eating anything he wants at any time of the day or night. But otherwise he has to be psychiatrically tested and then psychologically trained to withstand months underwater, in very confined quarters (the cloisters, so to speak, are reserved for the weapons), with the same limited company, to eat on a table the size of a chessboard, to sleep on his back under air-conditioning pipes that allow no lateral movement.

I assumed when I first heard about the conditions of their trade that the only fit type must be a neurotic brooder, a compulsive eater, and an agoraphobe with an I.Q. of 200. It was a surprise, and an eerie one, to find them professionally superb, and socially, at least, as amiable and humorous and level-headed as you or I. I saw enough in a week or more to grant that, from the captain of the base to the lowest rating, they are distinguished for exceptional intelligence, good nature, and absolute dependability in a crisis. They are, to be brief, superior craftsmen and superior men. We could use them anytime on land. Of such were the one hundred and twenty-nine who went down to the sea in a ship to see what it could do, and never came up again.

23

THE PALM BEACH STORY

The scene is a small airport, no more pretentious than a country railroad station, on the Florida mainland across from Palm Beach, a long sliver of an Atlantic island about twenty miles long and never more than a mile wide. The time is early on a Friday afternoon in the first week of January. The cast contains, in the order of their appearance, no stars as yet but what Hollywood used to call "general atmosphere"—that is to say, people.

They are mostly in sports shirts and slacks, for we are at the latitude of the Moroccan desert but are saved from the sweat and languor of the tropics by the wind from the Caribbean and what you might call the liquid air conditioner of the Gulf Stream, which swings closer to land at Palm Beach than anywhere else on its long meandering course up and out into the North Atlantic. So it is eighty-three degrees and balmy, and the little cumulus clouds puff by like balls of cotton, and the wind flaps at the shirts and ruffles the summer skirts of the women. There are about a hundred people sifting around the small low building and a big jet is making its high whistling noises outside on the tarmac. This is the airport for the most exclusive and luxurious winter resort on this side of the ocean. I am aware that "luxurious" and "exclusive" are two words plucked from advertising copy suggesting snobbery allied to great wealth. Well, that is a handy definition of Palm Beach. When the noon jet arrives from New York, there is a small army of men in blue uniforms waiting by the baggage-claim area: more chauffeurs per head of the population than any other place, I should guess, in the Western world.

So far as we know, the first white men who saw this slim island lying in a turquoise sea were a few draft dodgers from the American Civil War. At any rate, the first house was built there by such a fugitive, and he felt fairly sure that justice would not pursue him, for the island was nothing more than an offshore sand bank. Not until 1876 did other people apply to the state to purchase little lots, and they bought them for a dollar an acre. Today, there is very little available land between the spacious acres that surround and enclose the stone and stucco mansions and the well-combed golf courses that cater to their owners. But if you should happen to have eighty thousand dollars lying around, there is an acre or two I could get for you. All you would have to do then would be to clear the tropical underbrush and build a house.

The transformation of this island from a sand strip to a millionaire's winter garden was anticipated, by history but nobody else, when in 1878 a Spanish ship came too close to the shore and was wrecked. As I just remarked, the Gulf Stream is only a couple of miles offshore and because it runs at a brisk seven knots northward, cargo ships and even liners have to slice across it and then turn smartly and hug the shoreline on their journey south. This Spanish ship, plowing across a boiling sea on a moonless night, ran aground. It was carrying a cargo of coconuts and they were washed ashore, and the shells broke and the nuts were scattered along the sands. The few settlers there went out and picked up the nuts and planted them and the others took root where they drifted. Very soon the island began to resemble a backdrop for a Hope-Crosby *Road* picture. And for a time, the draft dodgers and their brood, and the few people from the mainland who had built there, had the Dorothy Lamour retreat to themselves.

But not for long. In the 1880's, fashionable people from the frigid Northern cities, from Philadelphia in particular, got the habit of retreating to the warm South for long winter holidays. The Palm Beach natives were surprised by the appearance of a large yacht or two in the lake that separates the island from the mainland. It was the period when ingenious wealth took to railroads as now it takes to the takeover bid, or what in this country is called conglomerates. (I can think of a shrewd contemporary who has set up an unlikely empire combining lead-mining with sugar with motorcar bumpers with a motion-picture company. Eighty years ago, he would undoubtedly have been a formidable rival of Harriman, Jay Cooke, or Henry M. Flagler.)

Flagler is the man, a Philadelphian, who did a little reconnaissance work on Palm Beach before coming to a lordly decision. He owned the main railroad line that ran down the Florida peninsula. He decided that Palm Beach was just what the doctor ordered. He extended his line down the mainland, threw a bridge across the lake, installed a private track, and simply carried his friends over into Palm Beach. To accommodate them he obligingly built a hotel. Tents and shacks sprouted like bars and lunch counters around an army camp. But not for long. The Flaglers and Stotesburys and Wanamakers and C. Volney Kents were not accustomed to such unmentionables, not, at least, as neighbors. This problem was solved in the most forthright democratic way: him that hath can command. Flagler commanded Addison Mizner, an odd and gifted architect, boxer, and tycoon, to set an architectural style for the place. He was the first man to abandon the Saratoga style of resort hotel, with the high-pitched Northern roof and the white clapboarding and the long porch and the shipboard rows of wicker rocking chairs. He built instead a Spanish villa, in the agreeable indoor-outdoor manner of Latin terraces and courtyards, with a martello tower and red-tiled roof. It set the general style for the next forty or fifty years. Even through the Second War, Palm Beach happily weathered the so-called international style, for the simple reason that Palm Beach was fashioned by wealthy Wasps who were unmoved by the thought of retirement to boxes of cement and steel and later of steel and glass. Today, amid their palms and poincianas and luxuriating gardens and the towering feathery Australian pines, they sit and dine and nap and gossip in this oasis of service for the very few amid the surrounding American desert of conveniences for the very many. There are no visible telegraph poles, no billboards or garish signs, no banging and hammering of builders in the afternoon, the sacred hour of the siesta. (It is a depressing thought, by the way, that in a great democracy such an example of civic good sense is secured not by an act of the state legislature or a popular referendum but by the fastidiousness of the very rich.)

For the next forty years or so new wealth moved in, and its possessors were only required to conform to the strict and unpublished mores of the Anglo-Saxon Caesars who ran the place. In the 1920's there appeared even the son of an Irish saloonkeeper and ward heeler, moreover a Catholic. He had acquired a fortune, but he did not strain to hob-nob with the established nobility. He had a vein of Irish pride and a stock-pile of self-reliance. His family was his joy, and he gathered them around him, and as the big family grew, it grew closer.

On this Friday afternoon in January then—if you can lean back so far—some of these confident types could be seen mingling with the well-tanned old folks and the prancing children from West Palm Beach, the pleb enclave on the mainland. They were all strolling around the airport waiting for this plane or that, picking up handsome daughters and grizzled old aunts, all under a flashing sun and the puffing clouds.

Just before three o'clock there darted in a half-dozen medium-sized men in dark suits wearing tiny white buttons on the left lapel. They split up and walked in and around the people. They nodded to the airline counter clerks. They sought out the manager and nodded some more. They accosted an incoming pilot and walked out onto the field. They shaded their eyes and looked across to a private runway far away to the east. They came in again and checked with the flight tower. The instructions had been received and would be acted on. The airport would be closed to all incoming and outgoing traffic twenty minutes before and after the takeoff of a great red and silver-gray jet that was warming up on the private runway. The blue suits drove off there in a car, and they walked around the great plane at a slacker pace. An army pilot appeared and chatted with them, and then a copilot and a bevy of stewardesses. The big plane roared and whistled awhile and then a fuel truck snuggled under its belly and for fifteen minutes or so there was a chugging sound. The plane was examined for spots on its spotless body. I have never seen a cleaner plane. Certainly there has never been a plane with cleaner fuel, for overnight and again that morning a gallon or two of it had been siphoned off and tested for foreign bodies. All was well.

Now a station wagon appeared and one or two rented cars. The men in the blue suits separated and stood with one hand in an inside pocket, and peered to recognize the new arrivals. The crew of one car was dressed for a West Side rumble: swarthy men in glaring sports shirts and sneakers and slacks of many colors. They were all known to the blue suits. They were press photographers. A second car disgorged a blond girl, a soldier, and a white-haired man. The soldier was a slim, quick-moving man, a general, who looked —if such a thing is possible—like a handsome Phil Silvers. General Bilko, perhaps. The blonde was no Mata Hari but simply a reporter. And so was the white-haired Apollo, in spite of his striking resemblance to a Riviera admiral in an old Jerome Kern musical. Other cars disgorged an assortment of men dressed like insurance salesmen on a golfing holiday. All peered at and passed for security. They, too, were the press.

At a private signal, they were all waved back against the fence, and the general and the blue suits moved toward the plane. In through a private entrance to the private field swished a large black private limousine. Here, at last, was the star of this outdoor matinee, the most acceptable, the absolutely top social resident of Palm Beach. For him the Stotesburys must down their private planes. For him the Wanamakers must stay behind the ropes on the airport terrace. For him the C. Volney Kents must keep their respectful distance.

He had his own covey of jumpingjacks in blue suits and

white buttons. They went aboard. The general saluted. The star, a tall thin man with ropy, light-brown hair and shoulders hunched, was convoyed across the field by a flying wedge of blue suits. They all went aboard. The blue suits on the field looked at their watches. It was exactly one minute after four, as the orders had specified. The plane door was slammed, the engines roared, the plane taxied and turned and roared again and hurtled screaming down the runway. Multimillionaires a mile away narrowed their eyes toward the sun and mused on the many aspects of fame and fortune. The grandson of the Irish saloonkeeper and ward heeler, John Fitzgerald Kennedy, thirty-fifth President of the United States, was airborne for Washington, the next Congress, and the facts of life. His Palm Beach interlude was over. "Okay, people," shouted an airport official, "you can relax."

24

GLENN IN ORBIT

In the dear, dead days of American vaudeville there was a comedian, a beguiling dude whose whole character was nothing but pretense. He always appeared in a flowing Ascot and a blue blazer as tight as a belly band, and he tossed his head as if he had just won the singles at Wimbledon, when everybody knew that he wouldn't know a tennis racquet from a harp. He sang after a fashion, and again the audience knew well that he had only one song in his repertoire. He would breeze in, lean against a grand piano, insist with an imperial wave that his accompanist take a bow, and then he would say, "What would you like me to sing tonight, did someone say 'Tea For Two'?"

Well, did someone say Colonel Glenn? There is no other possible topic. I should guess that, the other morning, only the unemployed and families depressed by a grave illness had their minds on anything but the ordeal, and the triumph, of John Glenn. For twenty minutes after the launching of the *Friendship Seven* from its pad at Cape Canaveral, the New York police department reported that not a single call had come in to any police station. Even crime stood still.

At Grand Central Station in New York, the concourse was entirely filled by an audience that stood, like an Easter crowd in St. Peter's Square, all facing one way, looking up to a giant television screen. For long stretches they stood in a cowed, inhuman silence that we never see in life but always see in movies showing the people outside Ford's Theater on the night of Lincoln's assassination or the citizens of Melbourne waiting for the drift of the atomic cloud and the end of the world. Many more millions feigned pneumonia, or feigned nothing at all, and stayed home and did no more work than the dutiful millions who got to the office and locked themselves in with a television set. The Columbia network had a model globe in its studio and a capsule to scale synchronizing its visible orbit with the progress of the actual flight. We always knew where he was and when. They had also a mockup of the inside of the capsule with the astronaut's head and helmet in the left foreground looking at the panels that John Glenn was looking at and controlling. And at the base of the panel was a slot for the hours, minutes, and seconds he'd been aloft. The numbers ticked over for the whole four hours, fifty-six minutes and induced a hypnosis much more irresistible than anything I've felt during a space movie. Whenever a tape was played of a conversation between Glenn and a tracking station, and whenever a lump of jargon came up that might be mystifying, the television studio switched to someplace that could unravel the puzzle. Several times we were winged out to a lab in St. Louis which had constructed the core of the capsule. And when the fright about the heat shield seized us (and none of us, including John Glenn, was told at the time what a hellish hazard that might be) we were taken to another city to talk to the man who designed the shield. An immense part of the American population sat or stood in a trance following every overheard phrase, burst of static, accident, and stage of the first global orbit of an American astronaut.

I think I'd expected something very glossy and slick, something so impossibly technical that we should have to keep telling ourselves there was a man out there. But thanks to the sensible decision of Mercury Control to play back all of its ragged exchanges with him—and thanks also to the trouble that developed at the end of the first orbit—the dialogue was continuous. It took, perhaps, that first orbit to make the immobile millions sense that a very alert and vivacious man was in trouble somewhere between the stars. But after that there were tales of mighty shushings in railroad stations and airports, and cabdrivers shutting off their meters and halting at a curb to see it through. So that through all the catechism of cabin and oxygen pressure, and respiration, and the temperature of the suit and the capsule and the rest, a recognizable human being kept darting through. His "Boy, oh, boy!" delight at the beauty of the unidentified particles that swam past his window like fireflies. His thanks to the people of Perth, who had turned on every light in the city by night and spread sheets and blankets on rooftops as reflectors. The waggish request to the Marine commandant to file a flight chit for him, since he had just finished the four hours a month flying time that would entitle him to a bonus of $245.

All the experts admit that there is little the Russians could learn from this flight. There is one thing, though: a lesson in imagination, the feeling of buoyancy you can transmit to a whole nation when all the doors are unlocked on a great event and every secret episode and mishap recorded and broadcast. We have a very shadowy memory of Gagarin's feat, only the official confirmation that he did it, and the vivid little vignette of Khrushchev kissing him on both cheeks outside the Kremlin. But John Glenn, by merciless exposure, became Christopher Columbus and Lindbergh and Rock Hudson rolled into one.

It was the failures, and the hints of failure, that kept intact the thread of suspense without which there is no good drama, or good broadcasting. At the end of the first orbit he casually mentioned that he was having a little trouble with the automatic control of the capsule's keel, or kilter. This system fires two sets of jets of hydrogen peroxide, small ones of no more than a one-pound thrust, if the capsule should start to drift. If it drifts a lot, more powerful jets are fired to bring it rocking back on keel, but these use up a lot of gas.

The first time he was over Mexico he touched on this anxiety. A warning light had gone on to signify that he was using his gases too fast. So he switched off the automatic control and handled it by firing the gases electrically and steering the ship by hand controls. It worked fine. But at the back of his mind, surely, and at the front of the minds of the men in Mercury Control, there was an extreme possibility that nagged at us then through the rest of the flight. Suppose the manual system didn't work. Suppose the capsule lurched and rocked and he couldn't keep it on keel. Suppose it turned around so that the nose was up and the forward, blunt end down. Then—how would you bring him down? Suppose the rockets fired the wrong way and he'd go higher and higher and be gone forever from the earth. He would live only as long as his oxygen. As he was coming over the California coast on the second orbit a decision had to be made, and made in two minutes, whether they'd let him go for a third. Mercury Control judged that he was in complete command. And he judged so too. So off he went.

But there was something as bad, or worse, that was kept from the Colonel, and the universe of his well-wishers, until twenty-three minutes before the end. During the first orbit

Mercury Control saw a warning light go on that signaled the loosening or unlatching of the heat shield. This is a six-foot-in-diameter plastic dish that is fastened to the front end of the mushroom-shaped capsule. That was the end his head was lying against, and it faces the direction of flight, while he faces the rear of the plane, so to speak. Immediately below the shield is a linen bag that expands like a concertina to cushion the shock when the capsule lands on the water. Below the bag again are three packages containing the rockets that brake his speed and fire him out of orbit and back into the earth's atmosphere. Binding this triple package, the so-called retro-pack, are three metal bands. When the rockets are fired, the bands fall, or burn, away. The package can be retained there but it is usually discarded. In that case, the plastic shield is the astronaut's barrier against a fiery death indeed, for the shield is constructed to withstand the three-thousand-degree heat that flares up when the capsule rips back into our atmosphere at a speed of over seventeen thousand miles an hour.

For two and a half orbits Mercury Control thought the heat shield had come loose. They pored over models of the wiring systems and blueprints of the rocket. They chose not to tell him. But the time would come when they would have to; for the time would come when they would have to order him to fire the rockets. It came on the third lap, over California. They gave him a strange order. They told him to retain the package that held the rockets. They thought it might provide a second line of defense to the vanished, or about to vanish, heat shield. I think the two most poignant lines in this remarkable play were spoken a few minutes before he was to fire and start his descent:

Glenn: "Can you tell me the reason for this?"

Mercury Control: "They'll tell you over the Cape."

Then they ordered the fire. Glenn was sure the heat

shield was secure, it was just that the switch was on the blink. But if it *had* gone, and the rocket package didn't hold, then he would in the instant burn to a cinder. There was a crackle of static and the swish of a carrier wave. And no word. This nightmare pause was inevitable, for as soon as the capsule enters the ionosphere there is so much ionization that no radio frequencies can get through at the best of times. So we waited, and we thought of the family waiting, and the Mercury Control experts at Cape Canaveral frozen in their sweat. For two and a half minutes there was nothing. Then they called him. And two words came squawking in, loud and clear and blithe: *"Friendship Seven."* Never did the word "friendship" have a more blessed sound.

When he got back on the ground and was sitting with the press, he added a little shiver to the record of this ordeal. After the firing, and while the capsule was tearing on its downward path, he saw chunks of flaming material going by the window. They might have been—like the firefly particles —some unexpected natural phenomena. It was, in fact, the rocket package burning up and vaporizing. But he didn't know that at first glance. He thought it was the heat shield itself breaking up. And he became, he said, suddenly "super-sensitive along my backside" because that would be the first place the heat would burn through. He had worked the controls on the heat shield a thousand times in practice, and there had never been a hitch. But now all he could guess was that the heat shield had been damaged somehow by leaving the retropack on, and chunks of the shield were flying by. "If that had been the case," he said, "it would have been a short trip from there on." It had given him, he mused, "a moment of some concern."

25

OUR FATHER WHICH ART IN HEAVEN

A few days ago a headline appeared in a Philadelphia paper that must have struck thousands who saw it with more terror, heralded the approach of Doomsday with more certainty, than if they had heard a rumble on the horizon and looked up and seen the slow-motion growth of a mushroom cloud. The headline said, "God Is Dead!"

This spasm of terror could not have lasted long. Because plainly there are millions of people still going around unafraid. More to the point, there are thousands, how many hundreds of thousands we cannot know, to whom this man was the only true God, a five-foot-two dapper Negro who appeared on this earth, according to his own testimony, "about the time of Abraham," and who died in the master bedroom of a manor house on a seventy-three-acre estate hard by the well-tended grounds of Philadelphia's Main Line socialites. He died with rings on his fingers, a watch on each wrist, and, in a nearby cupboard, a stack of five-hundred-dollar silk suits. He had fulfilled more gloriously than anyone of his race the yearning of the original folk hero who pondered on mortality, as he looked down on his love "laid out on a long white table" in the St. James Infirmary:

When I die I want you to bury me
In strait-laced shoes, box-back coat, and a Stet-
    son hat,
Put a twenty-dollar gold piece on my watch chain
So the boys'll know I died standin' pat.

Nobody knows for sure, perhaps not even he knew, his
true name or where or when he was born. The likeliest story
is that he was born on a rice plantation in Georgia. Some say
in 1865, which would have made him just a hundred when he
died. The unbelievers say in 1882. He became a half-time
gardener and half-time preacher in the early 1900's, and his
name was George Baker. He disdained always to discuss such
trivial things as names and dates. "My enemies," he said,
"call me George Baker."

His disciples called him Father Divine. They gave him
all their worldly goods and set him up in this mansion with its
gold plate and its manicured grounds. Everything—a large
donation from a prosperous real-estate agent, a contribution
from a grocer, from white or black, young or old, and also the
widow's mite—was handed over to the estate, known as
Heaven, in the Pennsylvania countryside. Here Father Divine
was surrounded by eighteen secretaries, a forty-year-old Canadian wife (white), the trappings of wealth, the devotion of
those Angels, so called, who formed his court and the Angels
who were passing by and chose to stay for a night or a week
or a month. No Angel was too poor or miserable to have bed
and board in Heaven. They paid according to their means,
whether it was twenty dollars a night or one dollar. The
meals cost fifty cents at most, in the depth of the Depression
five cents, one nickel, tuppence.

From all this Father Divine took not a penny. He had no
income and he paid no taxes. This privilege naturally excited

the curiosity of mere citizens, and from time to time nosy outsiders would call on him—tax agents, process servers, and the like—and, coming slap up against the high marble wall of his serenity, they would try to find out why he thought himself to be God. He was, for an unlettered man, as subtle as a medieval schoolman and as grandiose as the Old Testament. With great dignity he spoke his piece: "I do not have to say I am God. And I don't have to say I am not God. I said there are thousands of people *call* me God. And there are millions of them call me the Devil. I do not say I am God, and I do not say I am the Devil. But I produce God and shake the earth with it."

I suppose his most godlike moment occurred when the news came in of the dropping of the atomic bomb on Hiroshima. His followers were very likely more petrified than the rest of us, because it must be hard to live with God and see the mighty horror of some of His works. Father Divine said simply: "I am the author and the finisher of atomic energy. I have harnessed it."

But these proclamations did not satisfy some of his questioners. The police, for instance. In 1931, after an outdoor feast, an occasion of great—and rather noisy—joy in Heaven (which was then located in Sayville, Long Island), Father Divine was arrested as a public nuisance. He was unperturbed. It had happened, he hinted, to his son. If you are God, they said in effect, give us some sign, define God. They should not have done it. Little did they anticipate the Father's stunning reply. "God," he pronounced, "is not only personified and materialized. He is repersonified and rematerialized. He rematerializes and He rematerialates. He rematerialates and He is rematerializatable. He repersonificates and He repersonifitizes."

The police fell back in deep thought. But to the Father's

disciples it was as clear and satisfying as the Twenty-third Psalm. They cried, "Thank you, Father, thank you" and "Amen! Amen!"

He was sentenced to six months in prison. It was a low point in his life but not the lowest. He had, as a young man, preached in many dingy places in the South and in the tenderloin district of Baltimore, and back in Georgia he was once given the terrible choice of being committed to an asylum or getting out of the state. That is when he came North and landed in New York, and a few loyal exiles set him up in a slummy West Side house, where by day he found jobs for impoverished Negroes and by night set himself up as the Lord and Master of us all.

The big feast at Sayville, Long Island, and the subsequent court action naturally made the New York newspapers. It was played up as what they then used to call a "zany" story. It was the first time that most people had heard of Father Divine, and for a day or two the papers ran facetious feature stories about the colored man who thought he was God. In those days a colored man with delusions of grandeur was always good for a feature piece. Those were the days when the nation chuckled every evening at its radio sets over the drollery of Amos and Andy, two impersonators of Negro clowns. It was also the time when the most successful Negro actor was Stepin Fetchit, a melancholy nitwit who moved through a life of misfortune with the speed and comprehension of a giant turtle. Those were the days, I am saying, that will not—dare not—come again.

Well, that arrest and conviction was the best thing that ever happened to Father Divine. The presiding judge fined him five hundred dollars and sentenced him to six months in jail. During the sentencing, the presiding judge appeared to be in the best of health. But by now you will surely have

guessed what happened to him. Four days after the sentencing he dropped dead. The Father's followers, who had been
made to feel like delinquents, now felt like the Chosen People.
They ran through the small towns and the big city and stood
on street corners and cried, "Peace, brothers," and "The
Lord done struck down the judge!" Father Divine was challenged for an explanation. It was brief and regretful: "I
hated," he said, "to do it."

If there was a turning point, when a half-baked religious
cult grew into a movement with a national, even international,
following, this was it. He moved to a great estate up the
Hudson, close by Franklin Roosevelt's riverside home, and he
declared that his was a movement that anyone could join and
through it "feel God within him. It does not belong to me
alone as a Person, any more than the light of civilization
belongs to an individual . . . the individual comes to be the
expression of that which was impersonal, and he is the per-
sonification of God Almighty!" There have been grave and
reverend theologians who have made less sense.

Looking back on this movement now, most Americans
would, I think, say that it could only have happened here and
that it could not happen again in our time. It appealed to
simple people, and gullible people, and the innocent and the
good, and also to legions of the half-crazed, as all cults do that
promise short cuts to the understanding of God or man. But it
was not, by its own lights, a fraud. The regal amenities of
Father Divine's Heaven are, of course, hard to overlook.
Beggar on horseback is a perennial theme. No cartoon of
Peter Arno's will outlive the institution of monarchy more
surely than the one showing the king in a long white ermine
robe and saying, "All I have under this is my underwear."
But the personal code that Father Divine imposed on his
followers was strict and well observed. Most Angels dis-

carded their personal identities and with them their worldly habits. They called themselves Peace or Faithful or some such holy abstraction. I remember we had several part-time maids in succession—one named Faithful Honor, another Goodness Abounding, and they were the most decent, able, and trustworthy servants you could employ. They were not allowed to smoke or drink or swear, and personal cleanliness was almost ahead of godliness. There were many subsidiary Heavens as well as the one where the Lord Himself lived, and in all of them men and women, whether married or not, were kept apart. Father Divine took a poor view of "the undue mingling of the sexes." And in an age in which sex is not only a social and artistic obsession, and—I might add—is made out to be depressingly complicated, Father Divine's attitude was refreshingly direct. He was against it.

It is easy today to feel half-amused, half-tender toward this diminutive Georgia gardener who mesmerized so many, in what the papers are condescendingly calling a simpler time. I don't think the 1930's were simple at all. But the social revolution of that time did not include the Negro as a special case. His 1930's came in the 1950's. So it is tempting to sum up Father Divine and his cult as a typical bit of early-twentieth-century revivalism cagily tempered to the lean days of the Depression by adding, as an annex to Heaven, a soup kitchen, a clean bed, and the prospect of a job. We like to think that we have come a long way since the breast-beating paternalism of the old colored preachers. It is true that we now take a more majestic view of political equality, we put out manifestos about the coming Great Society, we employ the brave little handkerchief of the anti-poverty program to swab up the filth and flood of the Negro ghettos. But in none of these is there any adjuration to faith, no set of civic rules that any mayor dare suggest, no appeal to the good life except through the oldest of the Christian churches. Father Divine may have been simple, or crafty, or deluded or preposterous. But unlike our police departments and sociologists and most progressive teachers and politicians, he never told his flock that they could enjoy the blessings of God and the world, the flesh and the devil, all at the same time. He is already a comic legend, but he did preach "peace, communal life, celibacy, personal honesty, the equality of all colors of men." In the late years he was a bemused old man, but he was never bemused enough to think you could have all these things for nothing.

26

A LONELY MAN

On a Saturday afternoon at the end of May, in 1967, a single-engine plane, looking very like something out of the early comic strips, wobbled and ducked over Roosevelt Field, one of the earliest airports around New York, and buzzed the tower. A small crowd of people on the ground looked up and waved and clapped, and then somebody unveiled a marker. And they all retired to an old hotel in one of the oldest country suburbs on Long Island and joined other crowds who had jammed the bars and the assembly rooms all day long to celebrate the same event.

It had been forty years to the day since a skinny, flat-chested, blond, twenty-five-year-old Midwesterner had left Long Island on a most peculiar journey. He had stayed the night of the 19th of May, 1927, in the same hotel where all the carousing and celebrating were now going on. He had ambled out on a miserable day, through rain and heavy ground mist, to an airplane he had built himself, at a total cost of six thousand dollars. There were no great crowds that time. There was a wet and restless pack of newspapermen who kept sloshing in the drizzle between three planes, which were sitting there in a film of mud waiting for favorable weather to take off and have a shot at a twenty-five-thousand-dollar prize that had been put up by a New York hotel owner. There was no question which of the three competitors would make the most impressive copy. He was Lieutenant Commander Byrd, who had been to the North Pole and was already a national figure. But the lonely one, the skinny young man from the Midwest, was more challenging if only because he was so preoccupied with his plane, tinkering with it, frowning, wading back for a monkey wrench or a screw, smiling little, talking less. The reporters had all heard of him, of course. He had been a flying cadet in the Air Service Reserve, as it was then called. He had been a mail pilot. He had made small items in the papers as a parachute jumper. Only a week before he had flown this crate from San Diego, California, to St. Louis to Long Island in the breathtaking time of twenty-one hours and twenty minutes, which was a new record for a coast-to-coast flight. They had heard about his wild ambition to make the coming flight alone. He was known as what they called a stunt merchant, a flying fool. He was about to live up to his nickname, for he decided on the wretched gray morning of the 20th of May that the time was now. The weather reports, such as they were in those days, said that there would be fair skies over most of the Atlantic. He decided to risk it. He arranged his long limbs in the tiny cockpit, pulled his goggles down, and splashed off through the rain puddles on the runway. He wobbled into the air and bounced back on the ground again; up again and then down. At the end of the runway, to everyone's relief, he was airborne. None too soon, for he just managed to clear the telephone lines at the end of the field.

I suppose, at eight o'clock on that May morning, not one American in a thousand was preoccupied with his name, and in most other countries not one person in a hundred thousand had ever heard it. The wire services noted that he had taken off alone, in a homemade plane, with the mad ambition of being the first man to cross the Atlantic alone. I can't recall ever having read about anyone who swooped so suddenly into world fame. It is strange to look back to the morning papers of the 20th of May and hunt for the first stories about him; and then to turn to the evening papers and get the impression that Alexander the Great had reappeared on the earth and was headed straight for you. It was not necessary to know anything about flying. The farmers rang through to the nearest newspaper office, and the telephone switchboards were clogged on three continents. Stockbrokers and parsons and racing touts and new brides and politicians and intellectuals and steelworkers had been galvanized in a few hours. By what? There had been transatlantic flights before. There had been the dramatic close call of Alcock and Brown. As long ago as 1919 a British dirigible had flown thirty-one men from Scotland to Long Island and turned around and flown back again. Only three years before, two American army planes had crossed by way of Iceland, Greenland, and Newfoundland.

There were two new things that combined to stir the imagination of people everywhere. He was not going to hop islands or countries. No Newfoundland to Ireland for him. He was going for the whole stretch: New York to Paris. And he was going alone.

He had not publicized these dramatic facts, though they were known to the sponsors of the prize. But what catapulted the populations of America and Europe into a two-day delirium was the shock of the news, not that he was going to take off but that he had already gone. That night, there was a championship bout in Yankee Stadium (Sharkey was fighting Maloney). Before the fight started, the announcer stood in the ring and bawled at an audience of forty thousand fans and asked them to rise and pray for the flyer. Like some vast chorus in an open-air performance of *Guys and Dolls*, they stood and bared their heads. By then, nobody knew where or how he was.

Today, we should hear about him every mile of the way. But he had no radio, no radar, no sextant, only an instrument panel slightly less impressive than the dashboard of a modern car. You remember when John Glenn fired his retrorockets, and we heard a scramble of talk about heat coming up from somewhere? And the long crackle of radio waves and he'd gone? You remember we'd been told that the fearful heat of reentry could bore through the nose of his capsule—and for five minutes there was the chance that he'd been burned to ash? Five minutes! This boy was lost to us for nearly thirty hours. It was the agony of Glenn diluted but stretched over a day and a night. Then the headlines boomed that he'd been seen over Ireland, then that he was crossing over England. Then he was over the Channel. Then the night fell. From his own account, he experienced the most enraging episode of the flight. He knew he was over France but he did not know the way to Paris. He sputtered along in a daze of exhaustion and at last he recognized Paris. Now he had to find Le Bourget. After half an hour more, which he later said felt like another night, he was struck by a curious broad shaft of fog, a sort of pathway of diffused light. Of the hundred thousand Parisians who were thrashing around down there, a hundred or more had cars, and they'd been told to turn their lights on. This was his rudimentary glide path. And he came on it and bumped in and trundled to the edge of the field. And then an ocean of humanity broke around him. "I," he said, "am Charles Lindbergh."

There was never any need, anywhere in the world after

that, for the next forty years, to introduce himself. I was at a party in Nairobi two years ago, a diplomatic affair, and the main room of an ambassador's house and the terrace outside were flashing with all degrees of political grandees. But they were as excited, in a subdued way, as a gaggle of teen-agers in the lobby of a hotel housing the Beatles. I sensed this restless curiosity but I didn't know the reason for it. Pretty soon a dark, fragile, handsome woman came in and at her side was a very tall, very clean, very tanned, white-haired man with the same boyish face, now matured and fully modeled. It was, of course, Lindbergh. Diplomats don't normally rush at a great man for his autograph, because it's impolite and because they are always rather hoping that somebody will rush at them. There was no fuss, no vulgar staring. The Lindberghs fell in with a little group, but at their coming there was a kind of rustle of pleasure, a palpable feeling among these eminent men that they were really hobnobbing with the famous.

By now the gruesome and the distressing periods of Lindbergh's life have been forgotten—the kidnapping of his child, the obscene trial, the exile in England, and the later incarnation as the hero of isolationists, the cat's-paw of an American nationalist party. This weekend, it was nothing but the unique flight of May 20 and 21, forty years ago.

You mention it today to people who were alive at the time and, as with the death of President Kennedy, they will tell you at once where they were when it happened. I was in school in England, and the morning after the great night scene in Paris, our science master skipped the lesson and recalled his own heroics in the Battle of the Marne. The geography master took on a special glow of pride and demonstrated over and over again that he was the living expert on the geography of the North Atlantic. Everybody paid Lind-

bergh the most naïve and sincere form of tribute: they
wanted to be in on the act.

So, on this Saturday morning, the crowds milled around
the Garden City hotel on Long Island, and till long past
midnight they toasted Charles Lindbergh. He was not there.
He had turned down the invitation. He is an acutely shy man
with an acute loathing of crowds. Perhaps the first huge night
at Le Bourget was a trauma. He was thoroughly secluded,
across Long Island Sound, in Connecticut. At sixty-five he
has three absorbing interests. He is the technical adviser to a
famous airline. He has long been interested in the construction of an artificial heart. And all the rest of the time he
spends between here and East Africa. His great concern is to
preserve, in the jet age, the lonely leopards and the wilde-
beeste and the gazelles of the Serengete Plain.

27

A RUINED WOMAN

The new Madison Square roof garden had been conceived as the last, or latest, thing in midnight entertainment. It was designed by the most famous contemporary American architect, the man responsible for the great arch in Washington Square, the Century Club on Fifth Avenue, Mrs. Vanderbilt's vast marble cottage in Newport. He was a virtuoso who could enlarge on Jefferson's idea of a university and turn his hand from a railway station to a tombstone or a stained-glass window.

The new theater garden had a stage built like a Chinese temple, and the outline of its pagoda was traced with electric lights. New York had not seen in a long time such an elegant audience as attended the opening, which staged a gay piece called *Mademoiselle Champagne*. Close by the stage at a privileged table was the heir to several railroads, a black-haired, black-eyed young man, and his exquisite young wife, who—like so many beautiful American showgirls before and since—had parlayed her fame into somebody else's fortune.

The architect himself, Stanford White, came down from his penthouse to be present for the closing number of the new musical. He strolled in and nodded in a benevolent way to his friends and admirers. He was a handsome man in his fifties, well set up in the Edwardian manner, and it is hard to say at this distance of time whether he would have been known as a cad or a bounder. If there were distinguishing escutcheons, I imagine the cad would be couchant and the bounder rampant. In his sleek way, then, White was a bounder, for he was a rampant ladies' man. While the last scene was being performed, and the chorus was dissolving in a foam of petticoats, the young railroad man, one Harry K. Thaw, got up from his table and threaded his way between the other tables and stopped at Stanford White's. He put his hand in the breast pocket of his dinner jacket, took out a pistol, and fired steadily, three times, at White's head. The architect fell against the table and sent it crashing to the ground. Harry Thaw stood for a moment like some Florentine avenger, his right arm high above his head and holding the pistol with its barrel down, to show that justice had been done and everybody else was safe.

This breathtaking scandal took place, I forgot to say, on the night of June 25, 1906. But when the murderer's wife died (in January 1967) even *The New York Times*, which takes an almost episcopal view of scandal, retold the story in four columns. Harry Thaw's trial attracted the most eminent lawyers of the day and great crowds. He was, to put it mildly, a spoiled brat and a wildly neurotic boy; and the introduction of evidence of insanity in his family was enough to acquit him but it sent him to a state hospital for the criminal insane. He fumed there for nearly seven years, escaped to Canada, was extradited and set free two years later. Not long afterwards he was up on charges that included whipping a high-school boy. Again he was confined, for seven more years. He came out in 1924, very little was heard of him again, and he died abroad in the late 1940's.

Long before that his wife pursued in cabarets and increasingly dingy theaters the vanishing fame which had been hers for simply being very beautiful, being married to Harry Thaw, and being the tragic cause of a murder. Evelyn Nesbit, as she was born and known on the stage, and recognized in Charles Dana Gibson drawings, made the most for a time of the morbid publicity. Or rather, Willie Hammerstein did. Willie Hammerstein was one of those dedicated impresarios to whom all of life offers simply the raw material for a specialty act. When two young showgirls shot a society swain in the leg, Hammerstein went bail for them, conceived a new act, and billed them outside his Victoria theater as "The Shooting Stars." The pathos of Evelyn Nesbit Thaw, widow, provided Hammerstein with a script and a gold mine. He was puzzled to find that the public was too numbed to look on Evelyn just yet as a performer. So Hammerstein sent her off to Europe for a time. She returned seven years later and, by a bizarre coincidence, the week that Thaw escaped from his asylum. Hammerstein, denied for so long of the revenue from a "property" he was subsidizing, saw the hand of God in this. He put her on as "Mrs. Thaw" and published gaudy stories to the effect that she went in fear of her life. He bullied the city into providing her with a uniformed detail of police guards, and at the end of two months he pocketed an eighty-thousand-dollar profit. It was some sort of peak in the career of Evelyn Nesbit.

The fascinating point of this affair seen down the perspective of sixty years is Thaw's courtroom defense. He had murdered Stanford White, he said, "to protect the purity of the wives and the homes of America." Nobody guffawed. He claimed the protection of the "unwritten law," the right of a husband to vindicate his wife's honor. For Evelyn Nesbit had told Thaw, before she married him (and she told him truly), that White had seduced her. For a year or two after this confession Thaw went on begging her to marry him. But although she was certainly no prude and went off to live with him on a long stay in Europe, she felt—according to the compelling taboo of the day—that she couldn't marry him. At last she gave in to Thaw's beseechings, and I suppose in the usual movie ending they would have gone out hand in hand prepared to grow together in wisdom and penitence. But now Thaw began to writhe with jealousy. He could never accept the fact that his wife was not a virgin when he met her. In Italy and other Latin countries this is still, I believe, a formidable defense against a murder charge. I doubt it would be any at all in Chicago or Manchester today. I go further. I doubt that among a majority of Britons and Americans it would any longer be a cause to thrash and brood, or nag away at a fiancée, or put off a marriage. But there seems to be no question that Evelyn Nesbit felt, as the mores of the time intended you to feel, an accursed being; as she put it, "a ruined woman."

I don't have the figures at hand, and I wouldn't anyway want to toss them around before a family audience, but I seem to have heard that scores, hundreds, perhaps thousands, possibly millions of girls today come to the wedding ceremony as, so to speak, ruined women. Yet as late as twenty years ago, birth-control pioneers in Massachusetts and Connecticut were being brought to trial for dispensing contraceptive information even through the most respectable medical channels. Only ten years ago, it would not have seemed possible that the United States government would give out such information, as it does today, not to married people alone but to anyone who asks for it.

The first sexual revolution of the century, in the 1920's, aimed at destroying the so-called double standard: the idea

that boys will be boys but a girl's purity should go on forever. The second sexual revolution, that of our own decade, is
out to destroy something quite different: the idea of sin itself.
A glossy London magazine has a layout this month of glossy
young London couples who are living together without benefit
of clergy. The woman principal of one of the most distinguished of American women's colleges says that the students'
sex life is their own business. In the Metropolitan section of
the Los Angeles *Times* it is reported that a famous American
movie actor and his Italian mistress, "who have two sons,
Frank, 2½, and Daniel, 1½, yesterday took out a marriage
license at Santa Monica Courthouse."

I honestly don't know much about the character of Evelyn Nesbit, and there is no call to take her at her lawyer's
priceless valuation in court. But I'm pretty sure that her
subsequent sad life was due less to her personal quirks, or
even to a neurosis that complemented or massaged Harry
Thaw's own, than to the vengeful moral code of her day. She
must have suffered agonizing episodes, very difficult to conceive today, when she kept making ritual confessions to Thaw
about her pitiful ruined state.

They made a movie about her some dozen years ago,
and Evelyn Nesbit herself was brought in on it and employed,
by a masterly understatement, as "technical adviser." It was
called *The Girl on the Red Velvet Swing*, the point of the title
being that Stanford White, whose architectural whimsies included a series of hideaways or love nests around town, used
to take her to one such retreat which was furnished with a red
velvet swing, on which she used to fly through the air with
the greatest of ease. It was, indeed, in this nookery that she
testified that White had got her drunk. She swung to and fro,
and then he broke out the champagne. She knew no more
until she knew she was ruined.

Now surely, the experience was nothing new, even in 1906. Let us consult the late Dr. Alfred Kinsey. Not, I must say, with much enthusiasm. For his studies of human sexual behavior are on the whole about as stimulating as a compilation of graphs by the Bureau of Labor Statistics, with their mathematical insistence on "frequency of outlet" and no mention of the incidental frequency of passion, humor, charm, or tenderness. But the old mole did dig up some interesting findings. One of them is his overriding conclusion that human beings in the 1950's were not unlike human beings in the 1890's or the early 1900's. After interminable interviews with several generations, he doubted that anything new about sex has been discovered in our time, or the time before that. The striking difference was not in the way people behaved but the way society thought they behaved. What doomed Evelyn Nesbit was not her sin but the social doctrine, which I guess she embraced as eagerly as anybody, that her sin was not to be expiated. Once a ruined woman always a ruined woman.

This belief was strong enough, even in the 1920's, to have provoked a memorable passage in H. L. Mencken's report of another murder, the notorious Gray-Snyder case. Judd Gray was what would have been called a normal decent man, a modest corset salesman, good citizen, churchgoer, leading a virtuous drab life. One day he met a Mrs. Ruth Snyder. He was taken with her, and he fell. He went with her to the electric chair in 1928 for helping her to butcher her husband in an act of incredible ferocity. In prison he wrote a sort of confession in which he is always saying, with unquestionable sincerity, how helpless he had become since the day he met Mrs. Snyder. When Ruth said "Do this," it was performed. Mencken analyzed his plight with, I think, acute insight: "His initial peccadillo shocked him so vastly that he could think of himself thereafter only as a sinner unspeakable and incorrigible. In his eyes, the step from adultery to murder was as natural and inevitable as the step from the cocktail-shaker to the gutter in the eyes of a Methodist bishop. . . . Once the conviction of sin had seized him he was ready to go the whole hog. . . . Its moral is plain. Sin is a dangerous toy in the hands of the virtuous. It should be left to the congenitally sinful, who know when to play with it and when to let it alone. Run a boy through a Presbyterian Sunday school and you must police him carefully all the rest of his life, for once he slips he is ready for anything."

I think this must have been as true in Babylon in 538 B.C. as in Queens Village, Long Island, in 1928 A.D. We have been making a big fuss for some time now—in fact, for something like sixty years—about how we have relaxed once for all the cramping prudery of the Victorians. But the way things are going, I expect they'll be back any day now. Close the theaters for a generation, and the next generation is ready for the filth of the Restoration. The mothers of the early Victorians, who put petticoats on piano legs, were ladies whose ball gowns were scooped out just below the nipple. I do not myself believe much in the idea of progress. I prefer the pendulum theory of history: we swing to this extreme and then the other, and most of us are uneasy as soon as we leave the ground and fly off into space. But I believe that for the time being, anyway, we have swung away from the notion that a boy or a girl who makes a slip or two is predestined to damnation.

Except, possibly, in Texas. I mentioned earlier the unwritten law, the right to kill your wife's seducer, as a strange and remote statute, a primitive relic honored now only in the Latin countries. I ought to have added that it lingers on, like some other discomforts of Spanish law (the community-property law of California, for instance), in the states of this country that were founded by the Spaniards. Texas is such a state, but a learned judge in West Texas tells me that it is no longer possible there to shoot down a prowling Mexican with impunity, and even the unwritten law is not automatically sanctioned, as the following story will show.

A few years ago an army officer who lived in a small Texas town was stationed for a brief spell in Colorado. When he came home he heard the rumor that his wife had been having an affair with a local bartender. She had certainly been seen with him. This suspicion preyed on him as the certainty of it preyed on Harry Thaw. One night, the officer went down to the saloon of the suspect and drank a few beers and bided his time. At last, the bartender walked off to the men's room and the officer followed him, shot him dead, and immediately called the police. His wife's adultery, by the way, was never proven.

When the jury came back to render its verdict, and also in Texas to announce the sentence, the judge asked if they were all agreed. They were. The verdict was guilty of murder in the first degree. The judge was mildly amazed at the change that had come over his fellow Texans, at their seeming indifference to the unwritten law. He was even more amazed when the foreman gave the sentence: "Life imprisonment in the state penitentiary." According to custom, the judge asked," Have you anything more to say?"

"Yes, your honor." The foreman paused. "Sentence," he said, "suspended."

28

ROBERT FROST

It was a splendid day in Vermont when they buried Robert Frost, the sky without a cloud, the light from the white landscape making every elm and barn as sharp as a blade, and the people crunching quietly through the deep snow and squinting in the enormous sun.

It is a harmless sentimental custom to bury men who have been supreme in some craft with a visible symbol of their mastery: one thinks of composers whose tombstone is inscribed with a lyre, and cricketers who were laid to rest with a floral wreath of a bat and a ball. Few men must have gone to their graves amid such an exhibition of the tools of their trade as Robert Frost did the other day. From the smallest object on the horizon, a clump of evergreens or a mountaintop, to the most domestic scenery that was close at hand—a maple tree, a country store, a spade—everything the mourners saw or passed among had been the subjects of his poems and the objects of his lifelong meditation. He was once called "an original ordinary man," but whether we ordinary men are ready or able to understand an original among us is another question. And I wonder how many Americans could have honestly agreed with President Kennedy that Frost had "bequeathed this nation a body of imperishable verse from which Americans will forever gain joy and understanding." Because if his poetry was as plain as its surface, it was very ordinary indeed. And if it was as deep and difficult as his best admirers said, the understanding audience for it must have been as small as it always is for great poetry.

However, President Kennedy had taken him up, and in the last year or two he became a sort of unofficial Poet Laureate more honored, I suspect, for his connection with the White House than for any spontaneous response of the American people to the body of his work. At any rate, when he died, either eighty-seven or eighty-eight years of age (no one is quite sure), his last days were full of honor, love, obedience, troops of friends, as his early days had been full of menial farm chores, odd jobs that never paid off, and easygoing obscurity.

He was born in San Francisco of a New Hampshire journalist and a Scottish mother. His father died when he was ten, and his mother took him back East to settle in Lawrence, Massachusetts, and he became and remained a New Englander. From his nineteenth year to his thirty-eighth he managed to get only fourteen poems into print. In the meantime, he had tried and failed to be a student at Dartmouth College, but he did later stick out two years at Harvard. In the five years between these two grim efforts to be formally educated he was a bobbin boy in the mills, a cobbler, a smalltown editor, a schoolteacher, and at last a farmer. But the soil of New England, as he came to reflect later, is a glacial relic, for most of the year the victim of alternating fire and ice. For this reason, or possibly because he was too obsessed with the natural objects of the countryside to be a good farmer, he had to eke out a living; which he did by going from his chores to teach English at one country school and to try teaching "psy-

chology" (a new fetish discovered by William James) at
another.

So in his thirty-seventh year he was neither a prosperous
farmer nor an accepted poet. From his long meditations on
the country life and landscape of New England he had shored
up two small books of poems: *A Boy's Will* and *North of
Boston*. Neither of them found a publisher until he moved to
England in 1912 with the set intention "to write and be poor
without further scandal in the family." There he lived and
walked in the West Country and was befriended and admired
by Wilfrid Gibson and Edward Thomas, two early Georgians
with whom he seemed at the time to have a lot in common. He
had left America with a family reputation as a dilettante, but
when he came back he was greeted, by a small audience, as a
pro. He had no more trouble making a modest living, and for
nearly thirty years, on and off, he lived on another farm, was
the so-called poet in residence at Amherst, and did other
agreeable stretches as a teacher at the University of Michigan, at Harvard, but mostly at Middlebury College in Vermont, and then again at Dartmouth. He put out his books of
poetry at about five-year intervals until the 1940's saw him at
the peak of his productivity and his authority, bustling
around "collecting sticks"—as he used to put it—for what he
would ignite as annual "poetic bonfires."

From 1924 on he took the Pulitzer Prize for poetry at
regular—about six-year—intervals. This habit, because it set
him up as a solid Establishment poet, made his more intellectual admirers begin to think that there must be less in his
work than met the eye. Indeed, Frost suffered for a long time
from the incapacity of the critics to overcome certain stock
responses to the various schools of poetry that were then in
fashion. Because he had been a friend of the English Georgians, he was for too long taken by some people to be an

over-simple rebel against the developing technology of modern life, an expatriate cricket-and-ale rustic. And because, when he got back to America, he met the high tide of the "new" poetry of the Chicago school, he had to be looked on as a New England Sandburg. And because, in the 1930's, he maintained his lifelong lack of interest in politics, the socially conscious writers of the New Deal dismissed him as a cranky escapist. We never seem to learn—though the evidence is stacked high in any library—that contemporary prejudices about a writer very rarely seem relevant in the long view. Frost was, in fact, as absorbed, and in some ways as difficult, a poet as Emily Dickinson, whose entire meditations on life were conducted inside the house in Amherst, Massachusetts, from which she barred all visitors and rarely stirred in more than twenty years. Frost was, let us say, an outdoor Emily Dickinson, which is a curiosity almost too bizarre to bear thinking about. Even when he was writing what later was admitted to be his finest poetry, his admirers were again of the wrong sort to satisfy the literary lawmakers. The people who called him "our classic New England poet" also tended to see Will Rogers as the Mark Twain of the 1920's, and Pearl Buck as the traveling George Eliot of the 1930's. This is a kind of reverse sentimentality and a usual reflex of highbrows, who are often more concerned to validate a man's reputation than to enjoy him. It never troubled Frost much, and it would be a mistake to think of him at any time as a martyr. But for many years it made good men back away from him.

Other people, who were willing to be impressed, were put off for more honest reasons. They turned with pleasurable anticipation to his work, and what did they find? They found verses as flat and bare, and frequently as limp with bathos, as the verses on a country calendar. But if you persisted with him, you found that he had persisted ahead of you. Sometimes he reads like a man with no poetical gift whatsoever who is determined to slog his way through some simple fact of nature and discover, at all costs, some universal truth. But what ought to give pause to the unwary is that there *is* always a mind at work, a wriggling, probing, and in the end a tragic mind. The very titles of his poems are deceptively ordinary. "The Cow in Apple Time," about a cow drooling cider, sounds like a humdrum cheerful thing. But it is not. Listen.

> . . . Having tasted fruit,
> She scorns a pasture withering to the root.
> She runs from tree to tree where lie and sweeten
> The windfalls spiked with stubble and worm-
>   eaten.
> She leaves them bitten when she has to fly.
> She bellows on a knoll against the sky.
> Her udder shrivels and the milk goes dry.

It was not until after the Second War, when the flame of the Harriet Monroe revolution had died down, and left so many of its fiery figures mere cinders along the way, that another generation of critics noticed Frost still there, still writing his knotty monosyllables. They began to be excited by the suspicion that here possibly was an American Donne, or a Yankee Theocritus, or—a harder thing to grapple with —Robert Frost, an original. The idea that a huckleberry or a birch tree, or the games a boy played with that birch tree who was "too far from town to learn baseball"; the idea that these things could bear the most unsentimental and profound con- templation was at first frightening, until the reader inched his way through the roughness of the underbrush and, like "A Soldier"—in Frost's poem—discovered that

. . . the obstacle that checked
And tripped the body, shot the spirit on
Further than target ever showed or shone.

By the time that he was being accepted as a pure and gritty-minded pastoral poet, about as far removed from the Georgians as Thomas Hardy from Brer Rabbit, he himself was rejecting the physical world as a treacherous harbinger of winter and sickness. You could say more simply that he was a genuine poet and the oncoming of old age stirred him:

Petals I may have once pursued
Leaves are all my darker mood.

At the age of seventy he was ready to upbraid God for the fate of Job and for His general cruelty to the human race. This challenge, in "The Masque of Reason," was too much for him, but by now the critics were ready to grant that unlike any poet before or since, Frost had used the ordinary vernacular of a New England farmer to probe a few fundamental doubts. In poetry that is subtler in structure even than most vernacular, he transmuted rocks and flowers, wind and berries and hired men, and striking mill workers, and boys swinging on trees, into the purest symbols of what is most hardy but most perishable in the human condition.

To the great mass of Americans, I suppose, he was simply a noble old man, said to be a great poet, who had come to be a colorful human adjunct to the refurbishing of the White House, rather like one of those plain hooked rugs, woven by a grandmother, with which wealthy New Englanders or Virginians living in exquisite Colonial houses will sometimes pay a small tribute to their origins. He must have

learned to live with the knowledge that to most of his countrymen he was known only by a couple of lines from one poem,
"Stopping by Woods on a Snowy Evening," just as John
Donne must groan in his grave at all the twentieth-century
people who know him only by the thought that "No man is an
island." In our time, which is the age of mass marketing, we
have to package our great men as quickly and simply as
possible to make them acceptable to the family trade.

At the end, though, there was a lucky occasion on which
his true readers and his uncomprehending large public could
see him alike for what he was. In the icicle brilliance of
Kennedy's inauguration he stood in twelve degrees of frost
and tried to read aloud a poem specially written for the great
occasion. The sun stabbed at his failing eyes, the wind
slapped at him, the white light from the snow was too much
for him, and he finally gave up and spoke out, stumblingly,
what he knew, his fingers kneading his palms in a secret fury
and his white hair blowing in sloppy waves against his fore-
head. It was an embarrassing moment for the President and
the officials who had brought him, and for the huge crowd.
But it was as good an end as any he might have imagined: an
old farmer stripped down at last to a blinded oak of a man,
tangled in his own branches, made foolish by the sun and the
cold and the wind, by the simple elements he had once re-
joiced in but which now he had come to mistrust as the
mockers of humankind from Eden to Washington, D.C.

29

THE NON-ASSASSINATION
OF JOHN F. KENNEDY

After ten months of investigation, Chief Justice Warren and his presidential commission have turned in their report, in twelve thousand pages of testimony, on five hundred and fifty main witnesses and twenty-five thousand others and they have come to the conclusion that Oswald alone killed President Kennedy and was not the agent of a conspiracy.

Like most other critics and onlookers, I have not myself questioned five hundred witnesses or studied the railroad pass or examined the ballistics tests. But in a country where the Congressional inquiry is the great and effective instrument of public curiosity, it is not likely that everyone will bow to the commission and say amen. And I have no doubt there will be a bellow of scorn in Europe at the commission's rejection of the various conspiracy theories: the automatic line of the Russian press that Oswald was a tool of the far right (his original target, by the way, was an idol of the far right, General Walker); the notion that Ruby executed an assignment to silence Oswald's tongue; that Oswald was a cunning Trotskyite; that, according to the bland conclusion of the Egyptian press, Ruby was, on the contrary, the tool of a Zionist plot.

These theories aside, there was in the minds of many intelligent Europeans a doubt, expressed on the day the commission was appointed, that it would ever get to the bottom of the assassination. It was useless at the time to say that it would have been hard to find seven men more diligent in public service, more distinguished, less apt to have an ax to grind. The intelligentsia of most countries has one human frailty in common: it instinctively resists a simple explanation. And once you remember that a world power always arouses unconscious resentment of its power, it is not hard to guess that there are many intellectuals, in Europe especially, who will resist *on principle* the idea that an American presidential commission could be thorough and dispassionate. To anyone who has honest doubts and natural fears, I would say that it is worth first looking honestly at yourself and asking if you aren't trying to give vent to the underlying pressures of anti-Americanism. Once you admit this bit of self-knowledge, I think you then leave your intelligence free to agree or doubt, to accept the loner theory or find compelling reasons, from the evidence itself, that perhaps there is another murderer still at large.

The night the report came in I thought with sudden vividness of another time and place. And if you can bear it, I want to go back to it, for I doubt you have ever heard of it. Yet it bears on the main question of belief in the Warren Report.

The place was Palm Beach. The time was the 11th of December, 1960, a shining, clear, hot Sunday. At ten minutes to ten that morning a car that was being driven along one of the oceanfront boulevards slowed down and was parked across from the mansion of Joseph P. Kennedy. Inside the house were other members of the Kennedy family, among them the new President-elect of the United States, his wife

Jacqueline, and their two children. It was on a patio of this house two and a half weeks later that an informal but televised press conference with the incoming President would be famously interrupted by the four-year-old Caroline, clomping in in her mother's high-heeled shoes and guaranteeing her father about a couple of million new votes in the next election.

There was nothing against any citizen's parking his car on that street and walking across the road to look at the high hedge of trees and to gaze up the long driveway. Even so, you would not have gazed or loitered for long, because at the entrance to the driveway stood two men whose white buttons in their lapels, one hand in a pocket and the habit of rolling on the balls of their feet instantly gave them away as members of the Secret Service, assigned to the President and his family by law the moment his election seemed sure, in the early morning hours of the previous 9th of November. Across the road there was a highway patrolman banking his motorcycle with one leg braced against the sidewalk. He was there simply to prevent too many sightseers crowding around, impeding traffic and so on. Not until Mr. Kennedy became President did the Secret Service keep the roadway in front of the President's temporary White House permanently clear for a block or two. For reasons we shall see.

We go back now a couple of days to the Friday morning, December the 9th, to Washington and to an office that is known as the Protective Research Section of the United States Secret Service. It contains in its files about fifty thousand records of people, some known, some not, who have written threatening or obscene letters to the incumbent President of the United States. The White House mailroom adds to these files something like fifteen hundred more letters of the kind every month. Every new such screed—it might be nothing more substantial than a dribble of block capitals on

the back of an envelope, and it has been a letter forty feet long
—is sorted out and passed on to the Secret Service, because
most of these letter writers are what is known as repeaters.
With the help of handwriting experts, psychologists, and
spectro-chemists working on the ink and the paper, the Service can usually find out who wrote the first letter no matter
how laboriously its authorship has been disguised. If a man
writes two letters, the Service claims a batting average of
98 per cent in tracking him down. But once the agents
have worked on a letter and its follow-up, and traced the
writer, they have to make a delicate decision: whether he
is a victim of what used to be called "dementia praecox" and
is now called "schizophrenia with paranoid delusions"; or
whether he is sane enough to be held responsible for his
actions. At any rate, they must decide whether to charge him
with threatening the life of the President, or to keep secret
their knowledge of him and his whereabouts. The point is
that such people are most dangerous as their illness deepens,
and it is difficult in medicine or in law to get a confirming
diagnosis on such slender evidence as a couple of letters.
However, some writers are so flagrantly assertive, so proud of
their identity as a potential assassin of the great, that they
must be taken and proceeded against. It is invariably done
quietly in their own town, and many of them are at this
moment away in mental institutions. If the Secret Service in
this country, or its counterparts in Britain and France, were
to publicize the threats to their rulers that come in every
week, the citizenry would get the idea that every president
and every prince was in imminent peril.

Now—on Friday the 9th of December, 1960—there
came into the Protective Research Section, from the White
House, a letter. It was from a post-office inspector in Belmont,
a small town in New Hampshire. It warned the Secret Service

that a local character, Richard Pavlick, had uttered threats
against the life of President-elect Kennedy. The Secret Service went through its files, made careful checks of the place
and the name, though they had nothing on paper to go on.
But here's another thing. The Secret Service has noticed over
the years that a man is never in greater danger than when he
has just been elected and is still President-elect. The tentative
theory is that when a new leader is crowned and his inauguration is inevitable, the fact of the man's new and now irrevoca-
ble eminence is itself a mockery of the maniac's urge to have
the people reject him. The vote, the cheers, the country's
acknowledgment, all taunt the impotence of the killer's crusade to prove that the man is a fraud or a dictator. It is often
put more subtly than that. And often the potential or actual
killer explains that the new man was not his first intended
victim. This man Pavlick, for example, harboring his delusions up in New Hampshire, wrote a letter for publication
after his crime. It said he was sorry for what he had done but
"it is hoped that by my actions a better country and a more
attentive citizenry has resulted, then it will not have been in
vain . . . It was unfortunate for the Kennedys that John was
elected President because it was Jimmy Hoffa [the convicted
president of the Teamsters Union] who was to have been my
target of destruction, because of his 'go to hell with the
United States' attitude and because of the gutless cowards
called the Congress of the United States who are afraid to clip
his wings."

None of this was known to the Secret Service when it
got the warning from the postal inspector in New Hampshire.
But it did begin a routine check of airplane flights out of New
Hampshire and Boston, and it put a special watch on incoming passengers at Palm Beach airport. Through manifests
and reservation clerks and airline agents and the rest, this is

not hard to do without alarming or even disturbing the troop of daily passengers. The Secret Service was not unduly worried. There was no evidence that weekend that Pavlick was anywhere but his home town in New Hampshire.

However, the nub of the story is that on the morning of Sunday the 11th of December, the car that drove along the Palm Beach boulevard and parked opposite the President's house had Pavlick at the wheel. And he it was who parked it there. It contained seven sticks of dynamite so rigged as to be set off by the pull of his hand on a switch. Pavlick's intention was an act of immolation on the pyre that would rid the country of the President-elect. He knew that Kennedy would be going, shortly before ten o'clock, to Sunday mass. His timing was correct. On the opposite side of the road, right in front of the Kennedy house, was the Kennedy car surrounded now with the Secret Service detail. Pavlick and his car were twenty yards, say, to the rear and across the road. Once Kennedy was in his car, Pavlick would press the ignition, start his car, roar into the President's car, and pull the switch. The report of the then chief of the U.S. Secret Service is laconic: "There was enough dynamite to blow up a small mountain and, unquestionably, it would have wiped out Senator Kennedy, Pavlick and all the Secret Service agents, as well as anybody else nearby."

Well, the President-elect appeared on the verandah of the house and, by great good luck, Mrs. Kennedy and the two children came out with him. They embraced and laughed. And in that moment the name of Pavlick, which would surely have reverberated around the world as Oswald's has done, quietly expired in oblivion. Pavlick was suddenly stopped by a passing impulse, of fascination, remorse, tenderness even. He did not, he later said, "wish to harm her or the children. I decided to get him at the church or some place later." The

President-elect waved to the few passersby as happily as he was to do at the Dallas airport. He climbed in his car and was on his way. Pavlick drove off and was on *his* way. Having postponed the great deed, he decided to take a day or two more revising and perfecting his mental blueprint of the Catholic church that the Kennedys attended.

Not till three days later did the word come from Protective Research to the head of the White House detail in Palm Beach that the suspect Pavlick had left New Hampshire and was headed quite possibly for Palm Beach. Within twenty-four hours they tracked him down and took him in. He had a file of photographs of the ocean-front house, of the church and the layout of the streets around it. Once, at least, he had been inside the church when the President-elect was attending service.

Pavlick is put away for good, and I have heard no appeals on his behalf and no suggestions, by intellectuals or scandal sheets on either side of the Atlantic, that he was sponsored by any political conspiracy domestic or foreign. No one on the outside seems to have gone into the circumstances of his life and his well-rigged plot. Of course, the great difference is that he failed. So we shall have to take the word of the Secret Service and the medical authorities who committed him that he was a loner and an intelligent maniac.

IV POLITICS

30

THE BUSINESS OF
AMERICA?

Nothing dies harder among the intelligentsia, among writers especially, than the notion that they have a natural and superior understanding of the art of politics. This presumption is as widespread in the United States as the Latin belief (which is now being embraced everywhere) that when things go wrong with the government, the people who know best how to set it right are the university students. On the verge of any political crisis—the choice of a presidential candidate, the invasion of South Korea, the Russian threat to Berlin—American newspapers print full pages of indignant manifestos, in print as fine as a company prospectus, from novelists, professors of economics, dramatists, clergymen, and assorted Ph.D.'s. They state a case, usually on the assumption that the President and the Congress are too doltish to have weighed it for themselves. The other evening a fairly celebrated novelist, looking from his high and privileged ground at the menace of Berlin, shook his head and remarked, "I'm afraid that politics don't seem to attract any really first-rate intelligences." It is a well-worn complaint but I think it is deluded.

In the first place, the writer, the artist, even the professor and the clergyman have an advantage over their raw material that in politics belongs only to the dictator. They begin by being in command of the situation. The novelist begins with his imagination and a blank piece of paper. The industrial designer, once he is hired, is asked by his docile backers to say what money and materials he needs. The clergyman is presumed to own the road map to heaven and is there to instruct his flock on the proper steps to take.

The politician cannot begin at the beginning. He starts with the human mess, with a situation already in transition. Not unnaturally, he tends to give weight to the kind of intelligence that has proved itself in delivering a need, a victory, a product: to lawyers who have won their cases, to a general who has mastered a campaign, to a businessman who has proved that his ideas turn into money; and most of all to his own kind, to the men who live with uncertainty—the politicians.

I suppose that the oldest of European lamentations about America is that this country pays exaggerated respect to the arts and skills of businessmen, in spite of the overwhelming majority of lawyers in Congress. It was a President of the United States who coined the greatly derided slogan that "the business of America is business." I have found it hard to get worked up about this phrase ever since I noticed —and I am picking my words as carefully as a cat picking the fish from the bones—that on the whole the most straightforwardly intelligent men tend, in America, to go into business. Not the most intellectual, or the most brilliant, or the most individual, but the shrewd and intelligent boys who in another country might go into civil service or university teaching or the law.

My own youthful suspicion of businessmen, as a human type or breed, was characteristic of people with my sort of literary education and background in the arts. (The only

expert training I ever had in anything was—under the guid-
ance of two wise men, E. M. W. Tillyard and Basil Willey—
the detective art of dating a piece of unsigned English prose
from the evidence of the syntax, vernacular, vocabulary,
style, and so on.) Let me tell you about my conversion. In
1942, at the worst time of the war for our side, I was
required to go off on a rather formidable assignment: to tour
the United States for four months and report back to Britain
on what the war was doing to the people of the United States
and their means of livelihood in most of the three-thousand-
odd counties of the land. I started in February, the day the
Normandie overturned and burned to ashes at her dock; and I
got back in July. I went South to watch the wartime drill of
the county agents in growing more and faster crops for the
Allies. I had the joy of watching the air force move into
Miami Beach and hearing a colonel explain to the stricken
hotel managers that the Air Force did not pay dollars for
suites of rooms but pennies for cubic feet. I met a man in
Rainelle, West Virginia, a dull and hoggish man except when
he talked about his trade, which was that of choosing the
proper lumber for the manufacture of heels on women's
shoes. I saw what the needs of the war had done to the
making of steel and the regrading of dates, to the tattooing of
sailors' forearms and the production of long-staple cotton for
parachutes.

What struck me before I was halfway through was that
few men in America are more stimulating to be with than the
first-rate man in an industry or a trade. I stress the word
"first-rate" because I soon noticed that when you want to learn
the fundamentals of a business—perhaps the fundamentals of
anything—you must go to the number-one man, to the expert
who is humble enough to have learned that the elements of
any subject are unveiled not at the start but at the end of all

your study. I recall still the panic that seized me on a visit to Houston, Texas, when I was asked to write on the effect of the Second War on the American oil industry, a subject I knew as little about as the effect of the Punic Wars on the manufacture of olive oil. I was sent at first to the public-relations office. Hopeless. They showered me with promotion literature which assumed you knew the elements of the business and meant to demonstrate that they knew them better than anybody. I moved up to the number-three man. He was middle-aged and firm-jawed and meant to impress me, always a fatal attitude for a teacher. He rattled on and on about water-terminal battles and freight rates and "allowables" and pro rata distribution, and he might have been talking about swimming-pool construction. When I told him I was lost, he pitied me and implied there was nothing he could do for me.

I now resorted to the one golden rule for a reporter at large in a strange state. I called up the state editor of the leading newspaper. Tell me, I said, who is the man in all of Texas who knows more about oil than anybody. He gave me the name of an old man whose credentials were easy to check on. His former subordinates and neighbors whispered about him in terms as reverent as a beginning novelist might use about Hemingway or a sandlot baseball player about Mickey Mantle. I went to see the old man, and right away he said, "What do you know about oil?" Absolutely nothing, I said. "Fine," was his comment. I sat with him for one day, and went over the fields for another; and in forty-eight hours he took me step by step over the history and practice of the industry. It was like sitting at the feet of Aristotle and having your mind rinsed out at frequent intervals with such drafts of common sense as "A play has a beginning, a middle, and an end." I went off on many more expeditions after that, and remember with pleasure the tricks of a couple of Irishmen growing spray orchids in an Oregon hothouse, or tramping out at night into the mountains of Arizona with an infrared lamp to spot strategic minerals embedded in the rocks like petrified tropical fish. From all these safaris and interviews I came to the tentative, but for me amazing, conclusion that the first-rate businessman in this country is more precise, more imaginative, watchful, and intelligent about his trade than 90 per cent of the writers and academics who despise him.

The war between these two bodies of men is a phony war, prolonged by people (which is to say most of the people on each side) who have little firsthand acquaintance with the professional problems of the other. If this is so, I hear the grumble rising, why wasn't President Eisenhower's the most scintillating Cabinet in American history, since Eisenhower had an admiration bordering on awe for successful self-made businessmen? Let me make a simple sententious distinction. A first-rate businessman is, saving some ghastly character flaw, always a success. But a successful man is not necessarily first-rate or, for that matter, second- or third-rate, either as an intelligence or as a man. There are many successful men whose intelligence is meager except in one department, that of making money. I truly believe that money-making is generated by a single lobe of the brain, while all the others slumber in a twilight sleep. It is a trick, like a gift for plumbing, playing chess, or successful adultery. I doubt you can transfer a first-rate man in any field to politics and expect him to be a shadow of his first-rate self. And here the brilliant business-man and the brilliant man of letters come together as deluded, and ignorant, outsiders. The trouble with politics is that it is not a special field; it is the whole of life, a continuous struggle to handle a dozen special and competing fields in the interest of the community. A politician is a man suffering from the ambition to assert power over the multiple interests of men with their own consent. Being in command of the situation is the end and purpose of the game, and it is seldom achieved.

So most of Eisenhower's captains of industry were abominable politicians. And so are most intellectuals who attempt it. To any bookish student of American politics, at any rate, I would say, that for every hour you spend on Laski's *American Democracy*, be sure to spend five minutes with James A. Farley or the elder Talmadge or the mayor of Memphis, Tennessee. Which reminds me of a sentence spoken by Clement Attlee, when he was ruminating the other day about the spectacular failure, as a practicing politician, of that same immensely learned Harold Laski. "A rum thing," were his lordship's memorable words, "he never quite seemed to get the hang of it."

31

THE INVISIBLE RULERS

Pity the President, any President, when he enters the third year of his office. It is going to be a rough time for him and a humiliating time for the people of the United States.

All Presidents start out pretending to run a crusade but after a couple of years they find they are running something less heroic and much more intractable: namely, the presidency. The people are well cured by then of election fever, during which they think they are choosing Moses. In the third year, they look on the man as a sinner and a bumbler and begin to poke around for rumors of another Messiah. By 1935, even the Supreme Court was up in arms against Roosevelt and the Congress was a camp of loyalists and renegades. By 1947, Harry S. Truman, the brave little gamecock who had amazed everybody by making great decisions, was once again "a haberdasher out of his depth." By 1955, Eisenhower was talking about being "President of all the people" and seemed indeed so far above the battle, or so baffled by it, that he had declined into a figurehead, *le President de la République*. And by Kennedy's third year, the New Frontier was not a firing line but a gag line. *The New York Times* gave the general complaint a pundit's touch by having one of its reporters ask the President if his administration had not "lost its momentum." All Mr. Kennedy could do was to fall into a philosophical frame of mind, enumerate the natural woes of the world and reflect that life itself is unfair, some men go to war, some do not, some people die, some don't.

Kennedy had good precedent for this sad reply. By the end of his third year, John Adams wrote, "If I were to go over my life again, I would be a shoemaker, rather." Jefferson was positive about only one thing: "No man will bring out the reputation which carries him into it." Lincoln felt that "if to be the head of Hell is as hard as what I have to undergo here, I could find it in my heart to pity Satan." What Kennedy said in private was a little more terse, not quite so apocalyptic, but it touched the nerve of the ache that sets in with the third year. Talking to a friend or two one evening when everything seemed to be going wrong—a Congress apathetic toward a radical civil-rights bill, thousands of promised schools unbuilt, medical care for the aged a fading promise, the Western alliance itself sagging—he said that when you are a Senator or a Congressman both houses look like debating chambers that are honestly competing with the President to do what is best for the country. "When you're in the White House," he said, "Congress looks like the enemy."

Hard words. But they were no different except in length and weight from those being written by political scientists and other learned idealists in books with titles like *The Democratic Deadlock*, which wondered whether any President will ever get more than a modicum of what he wants so long as Congress retains so much power that is not in the Constitution. They pictured the President as a pitiful Oliver Twist always begging for more, with no power to get it.

We're not talking here about the constitutional restraints: the two-thirds-majority rule, the right of the Con-

gress to override the President's veto, the power of the Supreme Court to declare null and void the law of any state that
violates the federal Constitution. These so-called checks and
balances have always been there. But more and more the man
in the White House, or so it seems to its inmates, is fettered
by bodies, by alliances, by certain little-known men who
constitute a court of invisible rulers. They are benign and
able men for the most part with no malicious intent; but men
who exercise to the limit their unwritten and immensely effective power. You hear little about them in the general lamentations over the character of a President or the character of the
Congress he has to fight. Of course, Congress itself, once it
gets its teeth into a bill, can prance and crash around like the
warhorses in the Bible. But I'm talking about the grooms and
stableboys who feed the beast or withhold the food they don't
think it ought to have.

There is, of course, the Speaker of the House, who can
be either a strong right arm to the President or a thorn in the
side. There is the Director of the Bureau of the Budget, who
can slice the grand designs of a whole Cabinet Department
into ribbons. There are the majority and minority leaders in
both houses. A weak majority leader can be less of a help to
the President than a strong opposition leader who happens to
be sympathetic to his side. We all saw how, in Eisenhower's
second administration, Senator Lyndon Johnson, a Democrat
of Texas, actually annexed the legislative power that the
President ought to command and bullied through some
impressive legislation—the first civil-rights act in a hundred
years, as an example—that the President was powerless to get
from his own party.

But I'm thinking rather of the men who run the committees of Congress. They are the villains, mostly unsung and
unrecognized, who take the stage in the third year. And they

are the beneficiaries of a simple, and seemingly unchangeable, rule of American government. Appointment to the standing committees of Congress is based on outstanding loyalty in the last election but more reliably on length of service in Congress. And by the same token, the chairmanships are rewards for even longer service. Since the South was for so long a one-party region, there is a disproportionate number of Southerners in charge of the vital committees. For the South sends the same men back time and again and in the fullness of time they come to run the committees. If they are patient, which Southerners have been learning to be for a century now, they can in their quiet way frustrate much bigger men and defy the President of the United States. A shrewd President knows this and suddenly acquires many Southern friends.

Consider, for instance, the House Ways and Means Committee (a body which is not even mentioned in an official guidebook called *Our Federal Government and How It Functions*). It was established so long ago as 1795. It has jurisdiction over all matters of public finance, tax bills, tariffs, and the like. It is a barometer of Congressional sentiment about the country's ability to pay its way. It weighs the chances of this bill or that and tosses back into the hopper anything that a majority is apt to dislike. But one man can, if he chooses, give both the committee and the Congress a lead by releasing to the floor a bill he personally favors. On the other hand, the President of the United States can fume and sermonize, but if the chairman of the House Ways and Means Committee is against the purpose of a bill, and feels averse to letting it be debated, he can bottle it up as long as he cares to. The first man, therefore, that a sensible President makes up to is this chairman.

For many Congresses now, he has been a mild, sealed-lip gentleman from Arkansas. If you have never heard his name, it is no sin. I doubt that one American in ten could identify him, and not one in a hundred thousand would recognize him. (American history is often one thing in the history books and another in the flesh.) The name is Representative Wilbur Daigh Mills. He is fifty-three. A lawyer, former bank cashier, former probate judge. A Methodist and a thirty-second-degree Mason. Two daughters, Martha Sue and Rebecca Ann. He first came to Congress in 1938 and he has been coming ever since. He works with no fuss and no publicity. Is the economy in a lull or a slump? He calls his committee into session. He orders up a flock of expert witnesses. When he has heard them all he will go home and think awhile and make up his mind. If he decides that a cut in the income tax is the proper remedy, he will phone the President, as the senior resident of a hospital might call an intern, and tell him he can go ahead and administer the medicine. The President will thank him warmly and rush to a television studio and wave the bottle in front of the 190 million patients and be hailed as Pasteur. And Mr. Mills will fade into his apartment and go to bed, happy in the knowledge that if John F. Kennedy of Massachusetts is the President of the United States, Wilbur D. Mills, Methodist of Arkansas, is the Confederate President, all the more potent for living in the shadow of the throne.

Let us look back to a more artful occasion. At Christmastime 1960, when Kennedy was basking in the sunlight of Palm Beach and the limelight of being President-elect, he called one evening a press conference on the terrace of his father's house down there. It is the time when an incoming President is looking for a Cabinet and shifting ambassadors; a time when he is reminded of many friendships and favors he had forgotten. With him on the terrace that balmy evening was a candidate for Secretary of State, a clutch of new aides, a roaming band of Secret Service men, and several other unidentifiables spreading themselves in one of the more serviceable shacks of the New Frontier. Standing inconspicuously to the side against a bush was a stocky, bald-headed man I could not place. I nudged a friend, a veteran of the White House press corps. "Who," I asked, "is the stocky guy?" "That," he whispered, "is the real Secretary of State." It was a pardonable exaggeration. He was John J. Rooney, Congressman from the Fourteenth District of New York, a man from Brooklyn, the son of immigrant parents, a Catholic Irishman. He was the chairman of the House Subcommittee on Appropriations for State. It sounds undramatic. But through him this subcommittee decides how much or how little the United States government shall pay its ambassadors, consuls, and officers abroad by way of expenses, entertainment, and the front that the United States puts up.

Standing alongside him under the palm trees was a much bigger man with a balloon of a bay window and blue eyes narrowed to a permanent squint. We knew who this was but we wondered all over again why he was there. He was Senator Kerr of Oklahoma and he had told us that he had to talk to the President about some business to do with the space program, for he was an influential man on the Senate's space committee. But the veteran at my elbow and I began to commune together like Holmes and Watson, and we decided that in bringing Senator Kerr and Mr. Rooney together the President knew very well what he was about. Kennedy, you may recall, was genuinely eager to change the American custom of appointing ambassadors who had to be millionaires simply to stay out of bankruptcy. He had advanced the revolutionary idea that perhaps the United States could at last afford very able ambassadors of modest means. Mr. Rooney might be the man to push this revolution, but Senator Kerr was the first man to convince. Because he was a powerful Senator and he shuddered in public every time he thought of an American ambassador pouring a cocktail for a foreigner. Senator Kerr was a Baptist and a teetotaler and was imbued with the conviction that even an adequate expense account for ambassadors would tempt the United States into sponsoring, on foreign soil, orgies unbecoming a simple, rude republic. Congress calls such allowances "representation allowances." Senator Kerr called them "booze allowances." We guessed, my friend and I, that the Senator might have space flights on his agenda, but he had booze on his mind. And so did the President. He was anxious to appoint two ambassadors—one to France, the other to India—who had little or no money of their own. The President-elect had his way. Mr. Rooney was given the signal to work on his subcommittee after Senator Kerr conceded that these were extraordinary exceptions which would not violate the democratic rule that by definition an American ambassador must be a millionaire.

Well, these are only a couple of examples that occur to me among scores of obscure men in Congress who can, if they choose, make the President appear very sluggish in living up to the crusading promises of the election that put him in. These are the road blocks and hurdles that do not appear along the shining highway of the presidency until they seem to crowd together in the third year of his term in the White House. No wonder that on the way there, he thinks of the presidency as a glorious privilege and a call to action; and that when he's sitting in his rocker he broods, as Jefferson did, on his succession to "a splendid misery."

32

THE FRONTIERSMAN

On a warm April night in southern Florida, in 1951, two United States Senators and a man from Missouri were asleep as guests in the house of a wealthy American statesman, in Hobe Sound, an exclusive strip of land on the ocean, fenced in from the plebs by towering Australian pines and highly cultivated bits of real estate with an asking price of about a hundred thousand dollars a lot. The three men, one from Georgia, the other from Missouri, the third from Texas, had been invited down from their legislative labors in Washington to rest and get in a little golf. They were to be called at seven.

However, just as the dawn was coming up over the sea and the blue herons that stand motionless in the neighboring lagoons, a telephone startled this silent house and it was answered by the man from Missouri. He was struck dumb by what he heard and he pattered off in his pajamas to the next room and tapped on the door. The only answer was the rhythmic snore of the Senator from Texas and the steady counterpoint, or drumbeat, perhaps, of the snoring Senator from Georgia, for he was at that time the chairman of the Senate Armed Services Committee.

The man from Missouri knocked harder and heard a groan and crept in. The chairman of the Armed Services Committee was asleep on his back, one sheet drawn up over his head, leaving a single closed eye on sentry duty. The Senator from Texas snuffled himself awake and elbowed up his leathery frame and asked in a few expressive monosyllables what the intruder thought he was doing waking people up before six in the morning. The man from Missouri simply said, "I just had it on the phone from Washington—Harry Truman's fired MacArthur." The Senator from Texas came upright, as on a hoist, and sat on the side of the bed and pondered the appalling news: that MacArthur, the hero of the Pacific war, the most Roman of all American generals, had been—as the order said—"stripped of all his commands." They whispered a few staccato comments and the Senator from Texas said, to nobody in particular, "So what do we do now?"

The visible eyeball of the Senator from Georgia rolled over the bedsheet and a high Southern voice came out from under. "Hitch up yo' pants, Lyndon Johnson," it said, "and let's get the hell back to Washington and get that investigation started or they'll have a posse out for us before noon."

It would take the ordinary citizen days to recover from the shock and to wonder what ought to be done. But the chairman of a Congressional committee sees most of life through the lens of his own specialty, and the immediate waking instinct of the chairman of the Armed Services Committee was to brace the President against the howl of the mob, to get to Washington, rap the gavel, and call the first witness. It was a sound instinct. Before the recriminations got started, the three men were back in the capital; and the Senator from Georgia began the famous hearings that took many months and, I believe, three million words to affirm the

judgment of the President of the United States and to confirm
the original prejudices, one way or the other, of its people.

This anecdote is very typical of Southern politicians, of
their wariness, their healthy respect for the shifts and terrors
of public sentiment, their relaxed assumption that pending
Judgment Day something practical can be done about almost
any catastrophe, from the loss of an election to an earthquake.

It came back to me the other evening when we learned
that down on the Mexican border, in Uvalde, Texas, a former
Vice-President of the United States had died. He was John
Nance Garner, called "Cactus Jack" after the burning and
barren landscape that weaned him. Of all public men today he
was the last link between the America of the Civil War and
the America of the nuclear age. He would never himself have
claimed the title of statesman, and, for that matter, he never
earned it. "An elder statesman," he once told Harry Truman,
"is a retired politician." He would not have claimed to
understand or sympathize with the trouble in the cities, the
missions to the moon, or the turn of American life much after
1934. Roosevelt's New Deal was the end of the road for him.
And when, at the end of Roosevelt's second term, he stepped
down from the Vice-Presidency, he went home to Texas and
swore he would never again cross the Potomac River. And he
never did. He was cashiered, you might say, by his origins
and his prejudices. The Depression overwhelmed him and
many more of his breed who had been raised to believe that
there was nothing an American couldn't face and overcome if
he rolled his sleeves and gritted his teeth and sweated it out.

Today this bluster may sound quite fatuous. But it was
a central conviction of the men who tamed the frontier, from
the Cumberland Gap to the American River. And John Nance
Garner was a fascinating faint echo of it. He was remarkable
not by any great gifts of mind or character but by his intense

typicality of one aspect of the frontier character: its fatalism, physical hardiness, cynicism, tooth-sucking humor, its humdrum pragmatism in the face of death, disloyalty, and disaster. A Texas judge like Garner demonstrated to perfection the quality once ascribed to W. C. Fields: "He had the greatest reverence for his colleagues, with the usual reservations and suspicions." It is easy to imagine him, a little quiet stoat of a man, hearing the shocked cries of the onlookers at the severed head of an Indian and glancing down and snapping out, "A flesh wound."

Garner was the son of a Confederate cavalry trooper, and he was born in a muddy cabin, one room wide—what they called in the Red River Valley a shotgun house. Almost all the neighbors lived on farms. The black soil produced cotton and the red clay soil produced corn, and there were little sawmills in the clearings of the shortleaf pine. This was 1868, only three years after the war was over, but not before the Apache raids were over in his part of the country. His horizon was alive with flying squirrels and timber wolves, and his life was bounded by what the farmers called "work-a-crop" parties, by planting and plowing, box-and-pie suppers and fiddlers' contests on Saturday night; and on Sundays by camp meetings, and the whole neighborhood chanting:

"I felt the old shoes on my feet, the glory in my
    soul,
The old-time fire upon my lips; the billows
    ceased to roll."

He was a small chunky man with slant eyes and he was neither pious nor studious. In his *Who's Who* entry, which he kept down to five lines, he put down "limited school advantages," and it was an understatement. But he learned poker from mustered-out soldiers, and it stood him in good stead in Washington, where he often in one year won more from his fellow legislators than the ten thousand dollars of his Congressional salary. He looked like a cross between a fox and a mole and had many of the more engaging habits of each. He somehow picked up a college education of sorts and at nights he started to read law. This was as practical a calling as any on a frontier which was riddled with army deserters, cattle thieves, claim jumpers, and strangers who came in and settled down to a farm on the general presumption of their neighbors that they had shot an uncle or sired an untimely baby someplace in Tennessee or the Carolinas. I well remember (the week, by the way, that Truman fired MacArthur) sitting at the bedside of a very aged lady in Alpine, Texas. She would have been about ten or fifteen years Garner's senior, but she talked with that intense concreteness of the very old when they are recalling their childhood and youth. She talked about the feuding families and the silent types who settled in the Davis Mountains; and she spoke with contempt of an expansive jolly man who came through in the 1870's, was full of praise for the bare landscape and said he meant to settle there for the reason that he liked the people and thought it was great farming country. Evidently, he had not shot or ravished anybody. "From then on," said the old crone, "he was a suspicious character."

There was a lot of preaching on the frontier, but it was reserved for Sunday meeting and left to one man, a professional. By weekday, you dealt with your fellow man, agile fly-by-nights, and rustlers and crooked lawyers and people who poisoned crops and dynamited wells. And from time to time there was an Indian raid. One of the first cases tried by the twenty-five-year-old Garner, when he was a county judge, was of a gang of men who had been systematically cutting down pasture fences. Barbed wire was a comparative novelty, an omen of the coming of law and order; it fenced off the open range and said, This land is mine. Marauders who liked to make the most of the chaos of the range burned pastures, cut the wire, and left warnings to anyone who replaced it. Garner, in this case, bypassed the finer points of the law. He simply turned the Texas Rangers on them.

In his early twenties, by 1890, Garner had moved four hundred and fifty miles southwest, but still in Texas, to Uvalde, which grows pecan nuts and harvests a fine crop of mohair from land that only a goat can thrive on. This was where John Nance Garner hung out his shingle as a lawyer. Pretty soon he was in the Texas legislature and in 1902 he went to Congress, a small farmer's, railroad-hating Populist who burrowed his way into power through the channels he knew best: the back room, the small office, the poker game, the little chat with worried men. All his life he distrusted orators, "crooners" as he used to call them. Politics was doing the best you could for the people you knew best; and that meant wheedling bills through a reluctant Congress. He was a tireless wheedler, and he once said that "a snort of bourbon is a better persuader than the Twelve Apostles." Whenever a sad man came to him complaining he was getting nowhere with a local bill he'd sworn to sponsor, Garner would shuffle him off to his small office. "Come," he'd say, "let's go and strike a blow for liberty."

Such new forces as organized labor were as strange to him as space men in science fiction. And labor reciprocated, in the words of the miners' John L. Lewis: "He is a poker-playing, whiskey-drinking, labor-baiting, evil old man." The Vice-President couldn't have cared less about this kind of attack. The vice-presidency itself he thought a mistake, a high-falutin step into the robes of power, not power itself.

"It's an office," he said with much truth, "that ain't worth a hill o' beans." At a later time, he warned his fellow Texan Lyndon Johnson not to take the second place on the ticket: "It doesn't amount," he said, "to a spit in a pot." Roosevelt, who called him Mr. Common Sense, was always asking him for the truth about his chances of getting a bill through Congress. Garner never flattered or kowtowed. "Captain," he said, "do you want it with the bark on or off?"

Until he was ninety, Garner attributed his great age to bonded bourbon, and then after he was ninety to swearing off it. The other night he took a fever, went into coma, and died, on the verge of his hundredth year. I was about to say there is nobody left who is like him. There is one man. Lyndon Johnson is like him.

33

TOPIC A: 1954—
THE COURT AND
THE NEGRO

When I first went South, I was in the South but didn't know it. I was on my first visit to the home, and the home country, of my first American college friend, who is now a doctor in Maryland and was brought up on the edge of a beautiful valley outside Baltimore. (Today only a couple of golf courses hold the landscape against the encircling postwar suburbia and a maze of freeways.)

This man holds a special place in the history of my friendships because in the early 1930's he was a tolerant and amiable teacher about all things American. He instructed me in the wry, and often barefaced, realities of city and state government. We had a common interest in jazz and maintained it against the prevailing conviction of ninety-nine college boys in a hundred that Ellington, Louis Armstrong, and other combinations were "dinge stuff," that is to say a minority fad indulged in by Negroes. He had an affectionate knowledge of the local trees and flowers and first showed me something of the variety of American oaks, and introduced me to the pink and white dogwood and the Maryland golden aster. He was also responsible for my first taste of crab cakes and terrapin stew and for easing me into the pleasing custom, on hot summer nights, of spreading a newspaper on a table on the back porch at midnight, slicing a watermelon into quarters, and lolling back and burying your face in a quadrant till you came up for air with a drooling sound and paused to spit seeds at the moths.

Many of these pleasures came our way through the stealthy solicitude of Miss Minn. Miss Minn was the cook, first maid, second maid, laundress, nurse, cleaning woman, mother confessor, and hub of the household. She was the first Negro I ever knew and to this day is a great mystery. Even twenty years ago she admitted to no age. She was rumored to be a grandmother, though she never seemed to know how many times. She was not so much an employee in the house as a presence, like a clock that never tells you it's there until it strikes the hour. And hours would go by without any thought of Miss Minn, for she made no noise at all until you began to search for a newspaper or felt hungry or thought aloud that a glass of beer would be just the thing. At such times she would amble through the room or the garden like a forgotten ghost, accidentally bearing the newspaper or a tray with two beers. She was never called and was never out of reach, giving the impression—whether you were upstairs or downstairs, in the garden or the kitchen—that the house was loaded with Miss Minns.

She had no politics, no grievances and—I almost said—no life of her own. But much of the raillery and lazy banter that went back and forth between the family and Miss Minn was about another existence, the echoes of which drifted to us from the edge of our world and the beginning of hers. It was —to us—a very vague, timeless world that sounded, from the hints she dropped, like the libretto of a low-life opera, in which husbands came and went, forgotten sons turned up from distant places, stayed over a carefree weekend and con-

sumed festival meals of snapper turtle, whole crabs dunked in
beer, steaks as big as doormats, and then left and showed up
again a month or a year later as buck privates, or on
crutches from a car crash, or with a new wife and two
children. Miss Minn never went into this side of her life for
more than a couple of sentences and I honestly don't know
when she managed to live it except on certain weekends,
when she was off and the family was reduced to camping out
of the icebox. Her own style of talk conveyed that these sons
and lovers and erupting relations were creatures of the imagination who flitted like elves or stray animals through a shadowy forest.

Miss Minn had been with my friend's family for thirty
years and expected to die with them. She is the last of an
ancient breed. I don't believe that if you put the question to
her she would have had any notion what you meant by "the
Negro problem." She might have asked, "Which Negro?"
For all her vaguely suggested problems were about a particular person in the here and now. To me, a new arrival in the
country, Negroes were at once a rooted part of the landscape
and a fascinating novelty. The "white" and "colored" signs
on the doors of waiting rooms, toilets, and the automatic
retreat of colored people to the back of buses and theaters
were a shock, but this was the Americans' country and maybe
they knew best.

If this sounds callous now, let me say that the mass of
people at any given time are rarely better than their lights.
And I picked up the attitude of my friends, which in the
North was one of lumping the Negroes with poor people
everywhere and overcoming the unconscious discomfort of
this attitude by praising with particular warmth any Negro
who had pulled himself out of the morass of his race with a
special talent: a Negro pianist, dancer, poet.

My friends in the South had a quite different feeling. The Negroes were close to their lives, the essential servant, handyman, labor pool, but also confidant, childhood friend, licensed clown, grumbler. The great mass of Negroes who grew the cotton and tobacco and plowed their squalid little farms were off there somewhere over the horizon. Their lot was wretched but we didn't think about it too much; the legend was passed down from generation to generation that they could put up with squalor much better than us (they had to) and that they mostly maintained a happy-sad temperament with bouts of fine singing.

The experience of the South was to come later, but Maryland is of the South if not in it, and just now I might have been talking about the Miss Minns of Louisiana or Alabama. I wasn't aware of this at the time, and the distinction between the North and South didn't come up until one night we were cruising around the countryside in the north of the state and I happened to remark to my friend that there were no Negroes around, in any of the small towns where I had seen them by day. My friend said, "No? Let me show you something." He turned down a side road and circled back to town, and just where the open country was planted with the first outposts of the suburbs he stopped the car, and where four roads met he beckoned me to a tree. Nailed to a fence was a wooden board and on it had been crudely painted: "Nigger, don't let the sun set on you here."

We were very close to the northern boundary of Maryland; we were, in fact, standing at the Mason and Dixon line, which divided the slave states from the so-called free soil to the north before the Civil War. This imaginary line is named after two English surveyors, Charles Mason and Jeremiah Dixon, who in 1767 settled an old colonial boundary dispute by defining once for all the southern border of Pennsylvania.

This is a precise explanation, but to any American you might stop on a street today, the Mason and Dixon line is the division between two Americas, two worlds, two social systems.

Maryland was neutral in the Civil War. It is a border state. Many industries and customs are Northern, but once you get south of Pennsylvania, the vowels are slurred, the voices are less strident, the coats come off in the summertime, the Negroes are everywhere, and the white man is boss. He is, with shuddering exceptions among the poor whites, a more indulgent and considerate boss than the more vocal Northern liberals could ever be. They like to storm about the smugness and insensitivity of the Southerners, but they do not often get within hailing distance of a Negro they might help or take for a friend. Perhaps one Negro is the wrong unit, because self-conscious liberals and literary bohemians have regularly made a point of cultivating any pet Negro who is foolish enough to stand in as a sop to their conscience.

Now of the many Southern words that reflect the separate life of the South, none has been more taken for granted than the word "segregation." I know Southerners who have been brought up to give time and money and pride to the legal protection or the neighborly defense of the Negroes who work for them. Their children and the local colored children are close playmates (in a way that Northerners rarely are) up to the age of puberty. But if you ever suggested that their children should go to the same school as the Negroes, they would throw a fit. Well, they're going to throw a fit.

For, as everyone has heard by now, the Supreme Court of the United States has just handed down a judgment[1] that I should think is going to cause the most revolutionary change in American social life since, eighty-six years ago, the Court

[1] On May 17, 1954.

decided that Negroes were American citizens like any other and were entitled to the equal protection of the laws of the United States. The country was saved from the thunderbolt that has just descended on it by a reservation that the Court made: The status of the Negro was to be equal "but separate."

But today the Court recalled the famous phrase of an old judge who defended that earlier ruling. "The Constitution," he said, "is color-blind." So it is, but the people who hope to live by it are not. And in the Southland, whose sad and profound culture antedates the Constitution by nearly a hundred and fifty years, many generations of Americans have been brought up not necessarily to believe that the Negro is an inferior human being (no Southern Catholic, I hope, would be brought up to believe any such thing) but to believe with Abraham Lincoln that "the physical difference between the white and black races (I believe) will forever forbid the two races living together on terms of social and political equality, and inasmuch as they cannot so live, while they do remain together there must be the position of superior and inferior. . . . I am not, nor ever have been, in favor of making voters or jurors of Negroes, nor of qualifying them to hold office, nor to intermarry with white people. . . . I, as much as any other man, am in favor of having the superior position assigned to the white race."

That was spoken nearly a hundred years ago and it is, no doubt, unfair to Lincoln to imply that he would feel the same way today. But it is not ridiculous to think so. Millions of decent—should we now say "otherwise decent"?—Americans think and feel so, in the South and far from it.

It is hard in a few minutes to take up this challenge to the instincts and traditions of a whole region without doing its people a clumsy injustice. From much travel—and stopping

—around the United States, I have to say that I respect more the considerate relations that many Southerners have with the Negroes around them than the glib "social consciousness" of Northerners and Westerners whose daily life has a guaranteed immunity from Negro problems, either because there are few of them around or because they exist conveniently in some tight, slummy corner of the big city. It is one thing to talk about equality in New York or Oregon and live it in Alabama, where one person in three is colored, or in Mississippi, where there are one million whites and one million Negroes.

So, in the South, and in the Deep South most of all, the mere force of numbers is a threat, if only in the minds of men, to the political and social dominance of the white man. When people, even the gentlest people, fear that they might be terrified or intimidated, they tend to take terrifying precautions. I am not thinking of the understandable misgivings of those Southerners who remember, through the books or through a grandfather, the Negro soldiers who patrolled the beaten South or the state legislatures run in the main by Negroes. I am thinking of something simpler and more universal. In the places where there are many Negroes the black man is invested with the force—the threatening force—of a myth. The daily experience of white people may deny this myth but in their secret heart it has great vitality. It is an image of a black man who is a little slow in his wits, terrible in anger, and above all potent (there's the rub). The scientists have proved this to be nonsense, but, even after a Supreme Court decision, human beings trust their intuition more than the demonstrable truth that their intuition is moonshine. Some of this fear of the Negro may be only the cover-up for the guilt the white man feels for the way he has treated the Negro. But I think the central fear is something else, a fear so embarrassing that white mothers whisper it to each other and intellectuals fretting over "the Negro problem" will not deign to consider it. It is summed up in the old folk question, muttered behind the palm of the hand: "Would you want your daughter to marry a *N-e-g-r-o?*"

The revered Lincoln saw only one solution to the problem of the Negroes' suffering: colonization somewhere in an unsettled land. The late, detested Senator Bilbo of Mississippi saw two possible solutions: "Separation or Mongrelization." At the moment, it would be difficult to advocate or argue these solutions and be taken seriously. But it seems to me, at least, frivolous and superficial not to face the fact that after a generation or so of mixed schooling, social barriers will tumble, young people will pick their friends for themselves, they will fall in love, as they do everywhere, with the girls and boys around them.

This is a consummation which is at present being devoutly ignored. The traditions of American life are strong enough, *so far*, to make intermarriage prohibitive in the thirty-one states where white and colored do go to the same schools. Oddly, it is in the South, where the races are separated in school and church and in theaters, that the Negro is woven deep into the texture of society. And it is in the South that the test will come of whether the white man can live and work with the black man as a social and political equal and create a new kind of American society which has at last relaxed the powerful tensions of three hundred years. In the exhilaration of the Supreme Court's trumpet call, we should not, I think, expect too much of the whites, now or later. We can only say that to proclaim the attempt at a new American society should give tremendous pause to the racial propaganda that rages over Asia. If it works, 1954 will come to be a date in history as momentous as the year of Magna Carta.

34

TOPIC A: 1963—
THE DEEP SOUTH

When the Supreme Court of the United States decided nine years ago that black and white children were going to have to go to school together, and that the great change should be made "with deliberate speed," we looked to the Deep South for trouble, and we got it. For it is down there that the Court was challenging not a social truce but the roots of a separate culture. All morals aside, it is a perilous thing to try to order people into a new way of life. And since then, it is the Deep South that has called off the names of the battlefields of the Second Confederacy. Little Rock and New Orleans and Oxford and now Birmingham in Alabama.

Once again, a letter from America must be a letter from the Deep South. I sense a rustling sound, a fidget of embarrassment. What precisely, you whisper, *is* the Deep South? A good question. It is the long sweeping arc of states stretching from South Carolina around the Gulf of Mexico to Texas. Before the Civil War it was called the Cotton Kingdom and it produced the crop with Negro slave labor on plantations. When that system broke down, sharecropping and a tenant system replaced it. The depression and the invasion of Britain's textile monopoly by Egypt and Japan and others, and then the development of synthetics, played havoc with the cotton industry. And the Deep South labored through the Depression to vary its crops; and since the Second War it has developed textile industries and electronics research, and pockets of it work on the space industry. But it is still the land that supports or defeats the Negro. In the cities, he still works on the lowly jobs and lives in the rotting parts of town.

More to the point of this sketch of the Deep South is the great, and I'm afraid reluctant, change that has come over our own attitudes toward the Negroes and this, their most indigenous province. By "our own" I mean the attitude of what you might call the uninvolved onlooker: the American of the North and Midwest and West and, for that matter, the visiting foreigner, the European newspaper reader.

Thirty years ago, when I first began to explore the South, a liberal was liberal about other things than now. He was in favor of a federal conservation program and hydroelectric power and public works, and he was against Hitler. The Negro might touch his concern but not his program. The interest of even the most liberal Englishman, say, was in the music, the vernacular, and the general pathos of the Negro. On a drenching summer afternoon, I remember in a cotton field in Alabama a fat and sweating colored girl stretching her back and letting out a powerful contralto voice, singing, "Go down, ol' Hannah, don't you rise no mo'." In the scruffier parts of the towns, a white man could sit in dark corners of saloons and feel deeply fulfilled while a bent-over pianist beat out the unchanging twelve bars of the blues. Down in New Orleans at sundown you could walk along Basin Street and indulge a reverie or two looking up at the broken transoms of the old sporting houses, the domain of Josie Arlington and the "Countess" Willie Piazza. And a little later on you could sneak along Rampart and Bienville streets in the hot night, skip over a rat slithering along the gutter, and hear half-naked black girls crooning from behind the latticed doors of their one-room cribs: "I ain't good lookin' and my hair ain't curled, but my mother taught me some'pn gonna carry me through this world."

The Deep South simply reinforced with the adjective the deep troubles of the South. Round its whole twelve-hundred-mile curve down through the Carolinas and all the way around to the bayou country of Louisiana there was no doubt you were in a depressed part of the world. It was the job of many devoted Southerners, scrimping out-of-work writers, to write up the lives and the griefs of the Southern farmer, white and black, in the set of guides to the states put out by the federal government as a relief project. (They still remain the best guides ever written to the life and landscape of the United States.) This army of New Deal writers probably had much more influence than we guessed at the time in shaking the well-meaning onlooker out of his trance over the myths of the South. If you had lived in the North in the 1920's, you were as likely as not to accept the assumption of the Northern literary rebels that genteelness in the literature of the North was preposterous but gentility in the life of the South was the real thing. It was clearly not so. There were a few shaky but appealing ruins of the plantation tradition. There was an elaboration of courtesy. But the carpetbaggers had overrun the land and white merchants and poor whites had seized and exploited it. And their sons and grandsons had turned into a pretty hard-bitten plutocracy, retaining and enforcing the worst superstitions of their forebears. By the 1920's the South also stood for lynching and the Ku Klux Klan and the bigotries of the most primitive nonconformists in the Western world. If this is all difficult to imagine in the abstract, all you have to do to bring it to hideous life is to see it particularized in the rulers and the ruled of a single fictional county in Mississippi. It is William Faulkner's tragic theme.

Thirty years ago, Faulkner was only just beginning. But wherever you went through the South, if you kept your eyes and ears open, you knew you were passing through a ruined kingdom. The myths, even in the moment you discovered them, were worm-eaten. But in those days the traveler did not try to analyze these things politically. If he was so inclined, the New Deal had conveniently shouldered the burden of the poor. There was the Civilian Conservation Corps for idle boys, and the W.P.A. setting hands of any color to work on bridges, highways, post offices. The vast eroded valley of the Tennessee River was to be watered into rich harvest again by a great new dam, one of the biggest hydroelectric projects in history. When that the poor had cried, Roosevelt had wept. It was a very satisfactory state of things for those of us who felt humane but had a foreign background, who were artistic connoisseurs of someone else's tragedy.

The New Deal was, in fact, if only we'd had the gumption to see it, a menace to this attractive view of the lowly. On his next visit to New Orleans, for instance, our Englishman would find the whores' cribs destroyed, the last Basin Street transoms pulled down, and the street itself an anonymous block of a federal housing project. These rousing acts of social reform seemed almost to interfere with the two characteristics of the South that most fascinated the traveler: the drugging appeal of the landscape and the exotic appeal of the Negroes. The lawns and columned porticoes were never far from tangled swamps with odd flowers. The bloody sunsets outlined tall rigid pines and barefoot boys holding crude sticks over streams and hoping for catfish. And always drifting against the sky were the long gray-white tufts of Spanish moss on spreading live-oak trees. The live-oak was indeed a creepy symbol of the South, for in the sunlight and at a distance it was a majestic sight, and the Spanish moss trailed from its branches like the plumes of a jousting knight. As you got closer, the knight was slightly flyblown. In the twilight the moss was a gray fuzz, of the sort you find under beds, and you saw that it was a parasite clinging to the outline of a healthy tree.

When, next Saturday, the President goes to recall the great innovation of the Tennessee Valley Authority, he will no doubt talk about the green and liberated land. But it is astonishing that we look back on all these things I've talked about and that we hardly guessed what they would come to mean after a war in which we boasted around the earth about the equality of American life, and the Declaration of Independence. We never guessed that the colored man everywhere would fool us, and read it. We went on applauding the colored delegations that swarmed into the United Nations. As the earliest rebel against a colonial power, the United States gave almost ritual applause to every new nation of Africa and Asia. She thought it was, like her own revolution, a revolution of colonials against absentee rulers. She did not notice in time that it was also a revolution of the colored man against the white. And now, in the farthest reaches of the South, ordinary white people, not much more stubborn or vicious than you or I, are resisting this great convulsion. They are talking about "states' rights" while the Negro is talking, *for the first time*, about being an equal man in his own country.

The impulse of the decent, but still uninvolved, onlooker is to jump from one extreme to the other. Into moral righteousness most of all. It makes you feel cleansed and exempt from responsibility. Somebody else—*they*—did it. It solves all the complexities at a stroke and keeps the liberal secure in his strong feeling that even if he does nothing, he is at least touched.

But there is a practical question being asked, I don't doubt, by hard-headed people, not only Southerners (wait till we hear from Roosevelt's swarming fans, the working-class city immigrants who paid off the mortgage and own a house with a garage). The practical question is whether we are inching along toward a view of the Constitution which its authors took only in a flight of oratorical fancy. When the Founding Fathers wrote "all men are created equal" they meant without any doubt all white men. The Negro means all men. We are now, and I think rightly, turning that phrase into a moral principle. But to turn it into a fact of American life is going to involve this republic in a turmoil the like of which I doubt it will have seen since the Civil War. And, to come down to the present tactics of resistance, it is going to involve the South in many more forms of renunciation than the segregated theater or school or lunch counter: in the renunciation of a way of life which is its own and which, as Faulkner, Caldwell, Tennessee Williams, W. J. Cash, and William March have amply shown, lies deeper than court orders or police regulations or freedom marches.

35

TOPIC A: 1965–
WATTS

By the grace of God, but not I'm afraid by any other agency in sight, the gutted suburb of Los Angeles at last shook itself out of the stupor of fear and hate that overtook it once the fires were out and the ten thousand troops of the National Guard moved in. It's an awful lot of troops for a suburb no bigger than the seventy or eighty others of that vast, brash, and most modern city. I heard, and can well believe, that there was a chilling moment on the Sunday or Monday night when it occurred to somebody in the Governor's office that if Watts had sparked another riot of this dimension elsewhere in the state, or two others of half the size, there would have been no more National Guardsmen left. The mere rumor that this was so could have triggered pandemonium in every Negro quarter of every city in the state that had its share of tough guys on the loose.

The first deduction is that such people started it, though we are learning with every new stage of the Negro revolution that our earlier assumptions were false. But suppose that it was such people. How were they able to rouse, within an hour or two, the teen-agers and the middle-aged and some of the harmless old into a frenzy of beating and looting and burning? The scale of the violence in Watts bears no relation to its physical condition. It is a place that many slum dwellers, in the old cities of the earth, would gladly settle for. The houses may be frowzy now, after thirty years of neglect and the desert dust settling, and ill use and smog and the paint scaling off in the sun. But they are small bungalows on their own half-lots, with bathrooms and bedrooms and some with little lawns and back yards and garages. The people who built these houses in the 1930's never figured, any more than the rest of us, on the tripling of the automobile population or the human population either. So that the streets bulge with motorcars, a good many, you can be sure, stolen and replated.

Or, we look at the record of the state. It is not perfect but it is not feckless either. It did, only a year ago, pass a law —by the overwhelming will of the majority, we ought to say —legalizing segregated housing or, in more artful language, upholding the citizen's "right" to choose his neighbors when he sells a room or a house. But southern California has done better than most states in revamping bad neighborhoods and putting public money into Negro welfare. It never had a poll tax. It never had predominantly Negro sections until the Second War, though it has long had Mexican sections in the south and Chinese quarters in the northern cities. Its schools were integrated long ago, not by decree but because since the old Iowa farmers were conned into settling in paradise after the First War, California has been the new melting pot, open to all comers with an automobile and a down payment. Some people would say that California has been a truer melting pot of the races since the Gold Rush than New York was when the hordes from central Europe came in in the early 1900's.

But these are now dead and irrelevant arguments. The safest bet you can make in these new and dreadful summers is that only the rural Midwest and Vermont (which has almost no Negroes) are safe from the threat of riots. They can happen any day, any week, any summer month in any Northern city you care to name. "Northern" was not a slip of the tongue. We are just beginning to learn, with much bewilderment, that the chances of open violence are greater where the Negro has superior legal and social equality but doesn't have the money or the jobs or the housing he would like. A sociologist at the University of Pennsylvania put his finger on the irony that hurts: "The history of revolution shows that when conditions get better people become more openly dissatisfied. The disparity between their lot and that of others becomes more evident. It is not accidental that rioting is occurring *after* the civil rights legislation."

This is the puzzling part to most people and the wounding part to President Johnson, and the civil-rights leaders, and the young students who go South to join the marches, and the former Attorney General Robert Kennedy and his successor Nicholas Katzenbach who did so much to start the slow landslide of civil-rights legislation moving through the Congress. Of course, not every Negro is going to get the vote this year or next, or share a white schoolteacher good or bad, or move into a new house or be offered a white-collar job. Vast numbers of whites, by the way, are not going to get these things either. The simplest mistake that goes bounding through much testy criticism of the United States is to believe that the Negro is, if not in chains, everywhere subjected to a special and shameful code of legal humiliations not shared by white people in the same dumps of society. In the South, until lately, this was true; and it is still true in great reaches of the Deep South. But down there too the federal government has shown energy and even bravery, sending its registrars and marshals and FBI agents and gallant anonymous clerks into the diehard ditches of segregation. So while the Southern

Negroes are slowly, too slowly, acquiring the roots of citizen-ship—the ballot, the right to sit on juries, the right to a friend at court, the right to run their own towns—the North, which has had these things for generations, explodes in an ecstasy of rage. Against what? Against law, property, public order, and their guardians. It was much the same story, the same week, in Los Angeles, in Chicago, in Springfield, Massachusetts.

The Los Angeles rioters, having taken their fill of liquor and television sets and groceries and furniture and cameras and cash registers and motorcars, turned then to the people of whom these luxuries are the symbols—to the owners. Not literally to the owners, though I believe there was lots of damage and resentment against absentee landlords. I mean the property owner's surrogate: the white man. They roamed after white men and thrashed light-skinned Negroes by mis-take; and the fact that they beat up white people as poor or shiftless as themselves is not an accident but an inevitable incident of what had become a symbolic act of rage against the white man.

Let us be clear about the kind of Negroes we have in mind. We are not talking about decent Negroes hungry for a decent house and a place in society. We are not talking about the people who long for a vote or a seat on a jury, the precious rights of first-class citizenship which—ten years ago—we thought would equalize and settle everything. We are talking about people who long for a television set, a case of bourbon, a girl, a cool car, and a wad of folding money. (It might come out that against all our preconceptions we are talking about decent, even educated, Negroes who do long for both the jury seat and the pleasant house and a job.) Anyway, there are living in Watts the appalling number of five hundred crimi-nals out on parole; and what a relief it would be to clinch this discussion with the certainty that *they* started and led the riot. I'm sure they were in there. And they must at all times form a ghastly elite corps for the young unemployed (twice the white rate), the bastards (one in four), the Artful Dodgers by the thousand who thus have five hundred Fagins to instruct them in everything from petty thievery and drug addiction to the manufacture of Molotov cocktails.

But we still have to remember that something very like the Watts riots happened in Rochester, New York, and Springfield, Massachusetts, to the confusion of their sober citizens. It is risky to find in any social upheaval a single cause. But there is one that is blatantly there for all to see, which no sociologist would deign to bring up. I believe the seed of this anarchy, and it is nothing less, is in the poor Negro's envy not of the white man's vote or his education but of the white man's fancied wealth and the baubles it buys. Whatever Watts lacks it does not lack television aerials. And I suppose if you sit in a mean room all through the day beside a litter of listless children and a worn-down mother (the chances of a father in residence are only three in four) and you keep seeing the svelte girls in the automobile and cigarette ads, and the young white Apollos, and the glowing families with the new washing machine, and the house in the pines just secured by a loan from the silvery-haired saint in the friendly bank—I suppose you come to believe that this is the way the whites live night and day. They have everything: the vote and the clean jobs and the education—if you're interested—but also the goodies and the money and the golden girls. It is a kind of pasteurized, idiot version of the old European belief that all Americans are rich.

Last year I saw some of the looting in Harlem, and the same signs were unmistakable in Chicago and Springfield and

Watts. The envy satisfied in the moment of seizing a useless luxury, but one that is the short cut to the good life, which is not coming soon.

I said earlier we could list forever the good reasons why this should not have happened in Watts. The police and the psychologists and the sociologists and the politicians have suddenly been falling over each other to amass a pile of reasons why it should: the illegitimacy, the heavy unemployment, the school dropouts three times as bad as the whites, the crime rate four or five times as bad, a steadily growing population of young, idle, corrupt Negroes already beyond the reach of appeals to citizenship and beyond much interest in liberty or education but only in their shining fruits and showier symbols.

I don't know if it will have helped much to isolate this tragic strain of envy, the most dangerous social form of twisted ambition; or to have mentioned the pimping role of television, with its ceaseless tantalizing exposure of the white man's dainties for sale, or perhaps for looting if you run, don't walk, to your nearest department store. But these things get no mention from the city fathers who moan about morals and pray for more federal funds.

Since the banning of commercial television is the blessing least likely to fall on these United States, what the people of Watts need at the moment is a full-time birth-control program, the safe return of some of those parolees to jail, a couple of churches, a hospital and a social-service annex, a public-works project, six playing fields, a regular bus service, and an army of colored men on the police force.

V THE VIEW FROM THE WEST

36

THE WESTERN MYTH

We were sitting around a New York living room on a hot night, a half dozen of us, the guests of a literary critic married to a woman who had been a war correspondent in China in the Second World War. Nobody else in the company had ever been in China and we listened with obedient interest to the wife's tales about the old regime in Peking and the new. Our host remarked that wherever the Chinese were going, he was grateful to have a souvenir of where they had come from. He reached forward and gently touched an ornament, a small piece of pottery, the likeness of a horse made in China a century or so before the birth of Christ. He fingered this statuette and remarked that like most Westerners he had to take the value of such a thing on trust. He didn't know whether it was a rare or a commonplace thing. But he preferred to believe as he touched it that it had been fashioned many, many hundreds of years ago. This set off an argument about the motive behind the collecting mania. Most of us agreed that people who collect first editions of old books are more interested in the bindings than the contents; the very devoted collectors will even insist that the pages of a famous book be uncut. I myself own a three-volume Boswell's *Life of*

Johnson, which I bought at auction for less than twenty dollars. It was a second issue of the first edition, and the pages are conveniently cut, on the assumption of the innocent bookbuyer that they are easier to read that way. This bargain came up immediately after the auctioning of a *first* issue of the first edition of Boswell, pages uncut. It sold for, I recall, about six hundred dollars.

Our host was sympathetic to this discrepancy. When he handled the Chinese horse, he said, or saw a letter written by Dickens or Lincoln, say, he felt himself to be a small link in the human heritage. He believed in that moment in immortality. I appreciated the idea but not the sentiment. The others nodded and were silent. He must have sensed the general politeness. "Come now," he said to me, "you surely have something that gives you the same sort of small thrill."

Then I remembered something. "Wait a minute," I said. "There is something that I would hate to lose." Ah, said our host. He guessed I owned some relic of William Pitt, or Tennyson, Gladstone perhaps, some equally distinguished part of the English heritage. "No," I said, "it is a check drawn on the Nevada Bank of San Francisco. It says, 'Pay to Wells, Fargo and Co, Two Hundred Dollars and fifty cents.' It is dated in May 1887 and it is signed by Adolph Sutro."

The assembled company, being what they call a sophisticated group of New Yorkers, was less than thunderstruck. Our host was frankly shocked. "And who," he asked, "was Adolph Sutro?"

It was my turn to be shocked. I outlined the Sutro story. San Francisco, I said, as even my host must have heard, had been a frenzied place in the early 1850's on account of the Gold Rush, but by 1854 the boom was sagging. In February 1855, there came a disastrous day, known as Black Friday, when half the banks of San Francisco failed. Millionaires who had been grimy miners three years before took off for South America and left hundreds of thousands of dollars in bad debts. Others quietly shot themselves. They had gone from shirt sleeves to shirt sleeves in three or four years.

Four years later, silver was struck in Virginia City, Nevada, in what was to be known as the great Comstock Lode. Once again the fortunes poured into San Francisco, and once again an express company, which had made its name receiving deposits, making loans, shipping gold to the East, was in business again. The name of the express company was Wells, Fargo. But again, in the middle sixties, the precious stuff gave out. The Comstock Lode was evidently drained dry of silver. It was now that a poor German Jewish immigrant, one Adolph Sutro, conceived the idea of "deep mining": of building a tunnel that would run far under the Comstock Lode, drain the flooded shafts, and extract the invisible, unreachable ore. The lode had already been monopolized by a famous ring of mine owners who were thrown into alarm by this proposal, all the more because they suspected that Sutro might have something there. They first ridiculed his idea and then schemed to annex it. He was after all an ignorant immigrant of a sort easily put down by native Westerners—that is to say, by other immigrants from Europe or the Eastern states whose California roots went back all of one generation. But this poor German fought back and bested the monopoly and at last built what you may today examine as the abandoned ruins of the Sutro Tunnel.

The polite New Yorkers were enthralled, not, I am sorry to say, by the story but by the absurdity of a native Englishman's thinking that this was interesting at all. I was warmed up by now and hoped to excite them out of their apathy by saying that you can still walk on the verandah of one of the mansions bang up against the mines where the silver barons and their friends would duck out, during some big ball, and look across to the tunnel only fifty feet away to oversee the Greeks and Chinese and Yankees dredging up the shiny stuff that made the ball and the banquet possible.

Our host spoke up. He said he was ashamed (though not much) to say that he himself had no interest whatsoever in the history of the American West; but even if he had, he could not conceive how anybody raised in a country where you can take a bus ride along the route of Chaucer's Canterbury pilgrims could have the slightest concern about a check written by an obscure German immigrant only sixty-eight years ago. To me, I had to confess, this check was a testament, an echo, of the great age of Nevada. Put it to your nose and you can almost smell the characteristic smell of the desert after rain. Shut your eyes and you can see Mark Twain running a newspaper only a few blocks away from Sutro till he was drummed out of town. Chaucer, I allowed, was fine and dandy but if you were born in a country where your local church was put up before the Spanish Armada, the difference between five or six hundred years is not very impressive. Whereas the charm of the American West to a European is the fact that in the memory of people still living the West has replaced the age of the warrior barons with the age of the air-conditioned lunch counter and the jet plane. I have talked to men who remember Kansas and West Texas and Nevada when they were at the stage of civilization Britain knew not long after the Middle Ages. As late as 1870, any place the railroad ended, the Middle Ages lived on. Today, it is the mid-twentieth century there as surely as in New York or London. I had talked, I swore, only twenty years ago, to an old man who remembered Wild Bill Hickok. It was like meeting an Englishman who had spoken with Robin Hood.

As a final limp exhortation, I said that my check from Adolph Sutro was a link with the Crusades.

The name of Hickok roused the company from its genial torpor. Had not President Eisenhower recently said something about him? Indeed, he had. And in the excellent cause of rescuing an American hero from the slander of his recent reputation. The President was, at this point, reacting rather late in the day, I must say, to the technique of character assassination so brilliantly practiced by Senator Joseph McCarthy. The President was evidently disturbed by it, though he would not go so far as to mention names or bandy indictments. He had made a speech warning his countrymen that no American could go on being proud of his heritage unless he maintained the code of James Butler Hickok, which laid down that a man must always be permitted to meet his enemy or his accuser face to face. To most of the audience, I don't doubt, the name of Hickok was a rattle of gunfire from an old Western. To President Eisenhower it was a strong and indestructible memory from his own boyhood. He was a boy in Abilene, Kansas, where the cattle from the Chisholm Trail went aboard, only twenty years after Hickok was sworn in as marshal and told to clean up the place. A succession of weak or conniving marshals had been shot or run out of town. And then, we are told, there appeared this lanky six-footer who established a different reign of terror by throwing up a coin and denting it with a bullet before it hit the ground; who moved in on a brawl, shoved the antagonists aside, grabbed somebody's hat, skimmed it high across the room, and riddled its rim with bullets fired in a rotary motion that kept the hat spinning in the air. However that may be, it was attested that Hickok had killed forty-three men before he came to Abilene. The manners and mores of his new town compelled him to the duty of shooting about sixty more. "Talk about a rule of iron," said the mayor of Abilene, "we had it."

There is, however, a long stretch of fantasy between the fact and the legend. Hickok was not such a gentle, perfect knight. He never used his bare hands. His bravery, the less impressionable recall, was "of the cruder kind that relies on hardware." But it seems to be a fact also that he made a point of never shooting even the lowliest deadbeat from behind. It was a boast of his, and it was his undoing. When his fame spread far and wide he gave up his buckskins and he took to a Prince Albert coat, check trousers, and pearl-handled revolvers, and he let his hair coil modishly around his shoulders.

But, as with many another desperado, the legend is tougher than the truth. It is a brave element in the national memory, a sign of the persistence of idealism in ordinary folk, that in spite of recorded history people do not like to forfeit the idea of Hickok as an American hero. He has also enjoyed, we should remember, the privilege of being played in the movies by Gary Cooper. So he is now a symbol of the heroic encounter, of the classic American ritual in which the dusty street is cleared, the marshal and his enemy retire in good order and reappear at high noon walking toward each other with the dramatic precision of ballet dancers, till they are close enough for one of them to be quick and the other dead.

In his latter days, Hickok got so taken with his glory that he allowed a play to be written around his life; and he went on tour as the star of it. And then, in 1876, he came to Deadwood, South Dakota. His lifetime boast of looking an accuser in the eye was too much for an envious, cross-eyed drunk named Jack McColl. On the afternoon of the 12th of August, 1876, Hickok was playing poker in the saloon with his back to the window. He was holding a hand of aces and eights. He did not see or hear McColl creep in by the door. He was shot in the back of the head and he keeled over and came to rest with his fingers splayed holding what forever afterward has been known as "the dead man's hand."

Maybe my friend's horse was not made in China a hundred years before the birth of Christ but in New Jersey a year before the inauguration of Eisenhower. Perhaps my Adolph Sutro check is a fake. Hickok was no better than he ought to be. And President Eisenhower's tribute to his manliness may have been an appeal not to the fact but the myth. If so, his instinct was sound. History, somebody said, is not what happened but what the people think happened.

37

JOHN MCLAREN'S FOLLY

The idea that San Francisco is a beautiful metropolis, if not the most beautiful big city in America, is one to which, I should think, most Americans and all San Franciscans are delighted to subscribe. I hate to crab our conversation at the start, but it seems to me that the appeal of the place is its cozy, small-town quality, which a huge bay and nine rambling hills cannot convert into a metropolis. San Francisco is not a beautiful city any more than a homely girl standing on a beautiful mountaintop is a beautiful girl. There is a plain reason for this, and we will examine it and then pass on to something of which the San Franciscans, or more accurately the Scots, have a right to be proud.

The city, as everybody knows, was destroyed in what historians and visitors call the earthquake of 1906. There is a firm superstition among the natives which makes them refer instead to "the fire." San Francisco, like much of northern and central California, sits precariously on the rim of a geological fault, the San Andreas fault. On the morning of April 18, 1906, the fault gave a strenuous heave, and certainly there was an earthquake, the most damaging that has been known in North America in modern times. But whether you have in

mind the enormous shudder, or the devastation of the subsequent fire (which had Enrico Caruso running out of the
Palace Hotel screaming, "It is worse than Vesuvius!"), the
truth is that the center of the city was totally demolished. Its
rebuilding came at an unfortunate time—I mean unfortunate
in the history of domestic architecture, either domestic or
foreign. After a century of peace in Europe, and forty years
of it in America, it was a comfortable, smug, and earnest
time, relieved by heavy whimsy in the arts, and these qualities
were reflected in laborious and whimsical ideas about beauty
in brick and stone. Accordingly, San Francisco is dense with
thousands of the most clumsy, formidable, comical ginger-
bread houses and hospitals and other public buildings you can
imagine.

The great thing about San Francisco is not its parts but
the sum of its parts seen from a long way off. In other words,
the precious thing about it is its site. Like the plain girl
standing alone on the beautiful mountaintop, its outline, its
profile, has a dignity and charm which only rarely belong to
any of its lesser attributes. The city itself is hillier than
Naples, more intimate than Hong Kong. It is founded and
spread over nine great hills overlooking a fine bay, and in any
city that ever knew ice or snow it would have been an impossible hazard to life and limb to build houses over the hills and
have streetcars or automobiles run up and down them. But
San Francisco has had a flurry of snow twice, I think, in forty
years; and though its nights are very often cool and clammy,
the thermometer does not drop below freezing and not often
into the forties. In fact, San Francisco has one of the nar-
rowest ranges of daily temperature, winter and summer, of
any city in America. So the buildings topple all over the hills,
and the streetcars are pulled up by cables running through
slots in the middle of the roadway, and the first necessity of

an automobile is flawless brakes. When you park your car on a slanting street, you must turn the wheels to bank against the sidewalk curb. If you do not, you get a ticket. You drive very often straight at the sky and when you come to the crest of a street that crosses a main thoroughfare you have to pause at an angle of thirty degrees or so until the crosstown traffic lets you nudge your way over the hill before you plunge down a block or two and begin the next ascent. The steepest streets have steps cut into the sidewalk, and the tourists goggle at the hills and giggle at their own attempts to walk up and down them. But the residents pant and pause at half a mile an hour and totter down a house-lined mountainside to do their day's shopping. This gives the place a solemn but rollicking air.

The land breezes are very dry and the ocean winds very clean. So it is a sparkling city much of the time, except when the fog from the ocean comes sliding in as solid as a freight train, except especially in the foggy, cold days of July and August. Until the Second War, when industry began to disfigure the whole littoral of the bay, smog was something that God in his wisdom had visited only on the vast, blowsy city four hundred and forty miles to the south—the city of the angels (a misnomer if ever there was one): Los Angeles.

Seen from any distance in the late afternoon of one of its crystalline days, San Francisco is a white city rolling over these great hills, and certainly it is unlike any other city of the United States. It is also a place of succulent and rare vegetation. And this is the miracle of the place that I want to talk about.

When San Francisco was founded, in the mania of the Gold Rush, it was nothing but a collection of huge sandhills overlooking on one side a great inland bay and on the other the Pacific Ocean. The earliest prints—I'm thinking of the fine ones they made in the 1850's—show fleets of decorative sailing ships in the harbor but not a tree in sight. Soon the Nobs—the makers of the earliest gold fortunes—built large houses on the highest hill, which was consequently known, and still is, as Nob Hill. Like the others it was a mountain of shifting sand. And when the winds blew in from the Pacific, the mountains appeared to move inside the orbit of their outline. It was like the Sahara in a storm, and the people staggered blindly up and down the hills holding handker-chiefs over their mouths and noses. The more chic residents patronized a shop started by a Frenchman (it is now a pros-perous store) and bought from him one of his first products: a cotton-gauze mask intended to protect you from the suffocat-ing fogs of blown sand.

This was accepted as a fact of life for twenty years or so. Then the city fathers had an agreeable new idea. They had by now acquired the essential amenities of a city—a red-light district, pretentious houses, a concert hall, and a police force, in that order (after some violent years in which the most responsible citizens, outraged by the rapine and murder that infested the place, took the law into their own hands as a committee of vigilantes). Now the city fathers thought that they would have a park. This would be rather like Holland thinking it ought to have a mountain. It was plainly an impossibility.

Nevertheless, the city council set aside one thousand and seventeen acres of high flat land near the ocean which was, most of the time, a windswept desert. The fathers labored to plant seedlings and flower beds but found that they promptly choked and died. After three years of this noble experiment, the daily newspaper of a small town in a grassy valley to the north wrote a chuckling editorial: "Of all the elephants the city of San Francisco has ever owned, they now have the heaviest in the shape of 'Golden Gate Park,' a dreary waste of shifting sand hills where a blade of grass cannot be raised without four posts to support it and keep it from blowing away." It was almost literally true. In the seventeen following years they had managed to plant and hold—with many sorts of structural braces—a thin forest of trees and some grassy spaces on the eastern, the leeward, side. In 1887, the park commission, still regarded as a bunch of visionaries, appointed a new superintendent, a Scotsman, John McLaren, a young landscape gardener, then twenty-nine years old. The commission gave him, with his assignment, a prescription in the following gaudy language: "Mr. McLaren, we want you to make the Golden Gate Park one of the beauty spots of the world." An English visitor to the city took home this sentence as a prime example of the Americans' gift for windbag rhetoric. But young McLaren was neither boastful nor amused. As he received his certificate of office, and as thousands mocked, he replied: "With your aid, gentlemen, and God be willing, that I shall do."

His first task was not to move mountains but to arrest them. And for that he needed what San Francisco did not have, a steady source of fresh water. Even then the salt water of the bay backed up and percolated all the surrounding land. McLaren did not ignore this disability but he fought it for a year or two. He was a Scotch type familiar to most of us, a rather grim poet of a man with the singlemindedness of a mule. He would often, as he later wrote, "go out into the country and walk along a stream until I came to a bonnie brook. Then I'd come back to the park and try to reproduce what Nature had done."

So he started out with what you would expect a Scot to start with: barley. It normally grows fast and dense. But not in San Francisco. He turned to native lupine. Same thing.

Then he recalled the tough beach grass of Scotland, and it was the first plant to put down rapid roots and grow, on top, fast enough to give a green fringe to the dunes which the blown sand could not bury. Then he looked around for a couple of species of trees, one to hold the contours of the sand, another to build up soil as well. He found both in Australia and imported them: the tea tree and the Australian acacia. Eucalyptus, the gum tree as Australians call it, came from there too and did pretty well, though it had a habit, and still has, of blighting the growth of anything within its shade. From the nearby valleys and the canyons of the peninsula he brought in two of the loveliest of the small trees of California, the manzanita and the madrone. I make it sound as if McLaren were a slogging, purposeful type who knew what he wanted and got it. In fact, for several years he seemed to be undertaking a missing labor of Hercules. His task had its satisfactions but its despairs also. One time he planted a thousand trees, and a few months later they looked like the markers for new-formed sand dunes. He dug them all up and he tried again, and again. Fertilizer was a constant problem. It cost a lot of money to ship in from southern California, and his original budget was slimming fast. So he asked the mayor if the sanitation department would collect and deliver to him the horse sweepings from the streets. Without too much publicity it was done.

One of his faults, as a public official, was that he was immune or allergic to political finagling—something that any man who wants anything from those in power must learn to accept and exploit. He would no doubt have been horrified at Franklin Roosevelt's remark about a big-city mayor, a gruesome character but a Democrat, from whom Roosevelt expected a landslide of votes in a crucial election. A squeamish member of the Roosevelt team was afraid that mayor was too crafty to depend on, and anyway he was, the man said, "a son of a bitch." "Yes," said Roosevelt, flashing his most endearing smile, "but he's *our* son of a bitch."

Young McLaren, on the contrary, would not truckle or hire or pay patronage to influential men he disliked. The police superintendent was one. And after some rude rebuff McLaren found three of his proudest trees had been hauled away overnight by the police from in front of their station house. John McLaren summoned his staff the same day, had the new cement shoveled away, and planted three new oaks. They stand today in front of the San Francisco police station.

But as he asserted himself, and the park began to grow into a visible thing of beauty, the San Franciscans came to think of him as a precious city asset. It was a time, remember, when rich men expected to die in their fifties and accordingly retired at forty to live it up a little before the end came. Sixty was then the rather late, but compulsory, retiring age of all civil servants. But when McLaren got there the people of San Francisco insisted that he stay on. And when he was seventy, they insisted again. After that he was given a perennial waiver of retirement. And he died, still the superintendent of the park, at the age of ninety-five, in 1943.

Long before that time the Golden Gate Park—with its lush meadows and artful wildernesses, its sheep pastures and Japanese tea garden, its peacocks on little lawns, its waterfalls and great evergreen forests, its protected buffalo and deer, its five thousand varieties of plants, its daisies from South Africa, cypress from Kashmir, abelias from the Himalayas, its hundred-odd types of conifer, its rhododendrons from Tibet and Siberia, its playgrounds and its foxes, its dozen lakes and its myriad blackbirds—it had become indeed what McLaren promised to make it. Certainly, in my experience, the most beautiful entirely created city park.

I thought of John McLaren this week because he was doing his damnedest to hold the first trees just at the time, around 1895, when a dozen other Scots came over to teach Americans the game of golf. The United States Open championship was held in San Francisco last week, and the great bane of the big hitters was the trees, the forty-three thousand cypresses and pines and eucalyptus planted in John McLaren's early time and tended, at one time or another, by him. Arnold Palmer, the most heroic of the new breed of America's millionaire golfers, lost the championship by driving constantly into the fronds of a great overhanging cypress. His collapse and his tragedy could all be put down to Scotland. You could say that one Scotsman gave him his living and another took it away from him.

38

THE NEW CALIFORNIAN

It had been one of those rancid weeks of the Eastern summer, with the temperature in the high nineties, and the streets like ovens, when the sweat gets in your eyes and the newspapers feel like dishcloths. Happily, I had to go to California, to Los Angeles, where they were sympathizing aloud with all those people—and there are not many—who haven't had the sense to move to California. Los Angeles, after all, had invigorating temperatures in the eighties and was stimulated by its healthful smog, a thick steaming yellow layer formed by the sea mists moving in on the industrial smoke of that thriving huge city. It produces a foretaste of the special hell which, a recent survey warns us, will suffocate us all by about 2000 A.D. I expect, myself, to have suffocated in the ordinary course of nature by then. But the young, tanned, long-legged, heedless Californians don't believe in population projections or the existence of hydrocarbons and nitrogen oxides in the air. They have no knowledge and no fear, and perhaps it is the best way to go.

I stayed with a friend who has just built a house on the top of the rim of the mountains that form a bowl in which sits

Los Angeles. He himself is just above the smog line, so that
on clear days you can see forever; but on most days you can
watch, or imagine, the quarter of a million workers on air-
craft and space equipment stewing in the San Fernando Valley. He is fairly new to California. So he is, like all such, a
professional Californian. They are a particular human breed,
much touchier than the oldest resident about the usual com-
plaints—the peaches the size of footballs that have no taste,
the roses the size of grapefruit that have no smell. With such
a man you do not discuss what is good or bad, what is awful
and wonderful about California. It is all miraculous and it
will go on forever.

We drove directly from the airport to his house, first
whizzing twenty miles along the freeway buckled in our seat
belts and slotted in one of the eight lanes of the highway. We
came off it and went winding up a two-lane spiral till there
was nothing above us but the burned-out shrubbery of the
mountains and beyond that the sky and a wheeling buzzard or
two. Along the way he talked about what other people might
think of as the problems of living in California but which he
—a boy from Missouri who had lived most of his life in
Chicago—called rather the joy of building his little gray
home in the West. "You know something," he said, "there's
nothing like it out here. Nothing. You wait and see."

I did not have to wait long. I saw a whole mountainside
plowed away, or rather sliced away, and the slice deposited in
the valley below and pressed down by an armored battalion to
provide a stable bed for a "development" of three hundred
new ranch-type "homes," what we used to call bungalows. It
was not a pretty sight and he conceded that "we're doing
something about these raiders. We've gotten together, one or
two of us around here, and formed a protective association.

We've done a bit of lobbying in Sacramento and we hope to get the state in on this thing, declare this section a state park or forest or something."

We wheeled around the face of a mountain veined with firebreaks and passed a new firehouse. "That's another of our little projects," he said. "Costs like the devil but it makes you feel a little easier nights." We swung up and down and plunged into a long curving driveway and came to his—I almost said garage—to his carport. (A low bridge in California is not a low bridge; the signs say, "Impaired vertical clearance.") He thinks of shoving this two-car garage back into the mountainside and extending the present patio to provide for a tennis court. Meanwhile, he showed me a small decorative wall high above the house with a carpet of thick vines between it and another wall of the same design—a sort of Regency, Greek-key motif. "Very pretty," I said.

"Hell, that's not décor," he said, "that's protection. Those are fire walls. And the vines, too; they're not very decorative either, but they burn very slow and give off lots of smoke, so you won't be caught napping." This reminded me that I had got up at four a.m. his time and had a five-hour flight, and I was going to suggest a nap but thought better of it.

I met his maid, a smiling German girl, and when she'd gone away he whispered to me that he'd insisted she take driving lessons. Although I've known California for over thirty years I didn't instantly get the connection. But it was very firm to him. "You don't think I want a girl marooned here in the middle of the night—trapped by a forest fire. She doesn't think she's a very good driver but I told her just so she can get out and down the mountain."

We next examined the automatic sprinkler system he has installed in the bushes above the house and around the small garden. "Goes on," he explained, "whenever the ground heat rises above a certain temperature." The sort of precaution that more of us should take. At any rate, he told me I could relax, and anyone who has seen a California fire gobble up the tinder of the mountain brush should be grateful for this reassurance.

"Well," he said with a cheerful change of tone, "how about a dip?" He indicated the kidney-shaped pool and its glimmering turquoise water. I motioned to unbutton a shirt. "Hold it!" he commanded, and just in time. Because there was a pleasant young man walking toward us from the hillside and he had in his hand a long pipe like a giant vacuum cleaner. He started to dip it in the pool. He was filtering the water and clearing off a light scum of leaves. My friend groaned. "I tell you, trying to keep this pool clear. God knows what it costs by now."

By the time the young man had finished his filtering we were pretty burned up by the sun, which you might think is the whole idea of southern California. "No point," said my host, "sitting and sweating out here; let's get inside where we can breathe right." We went in through a glass-paneled door and sat in his large circular living room and breathed right. He walked over to a thermostat on the wall and flicked it with a fingernail. It let off a minute fizzing sound like a small escape of soda water. "That'll be better," he said and indicated that he had set the air conditioning at seventy. It was dry and cool. So now, what? The sun was blazing away but sinking fast. Obviously, it was time to think of a drink. This is always a very delicate moment in the joust known as status seeking. It is entirely possible that Californians by themselves drink nothing but beer or distilled barley juice. But the visitor feels compelled to act for a time like his picture of a "typical Californian." So, even more, do the new Californians. Anywhere else on earth you might say Scotch or a martini. But it is part of the California legend, accepted without question by all Easterners, that Californians change the fashion in drinks about as often as they change their playshirts. I well remember, about ten years ago, when another new Californian casually suggested a "bullshot," and I looked at him as if he had suggested an elk or a buffalo. A bullshot was just then coming in in California and would, in the normal course of time (about two years), make its way to such outlying provincial capitals as New York and Washington.

"You honestly don't know what a bullshot is?" my friend asked in amused astonishment. "How about Vietnam?"

"That I've heard of," I said.

He explained, like a doctor telling a small tot how to swallow an aspirin tablet. "Just beef bouillon with a slug of vodka." It is one way of taking soup and getting plastered at the same time. So now my new host made a suggestion or two —"A screwdriver, mountain mule? How about the Thing?"

"How about," I said quickly, "a bullshot?"

"Sure," he said, "why not?" and his expression conveyed that he was not the type to jeer at a maiden aunt who sticks to her gooseberry wine. He made the Thing for himself, and I'm not going to give away *that* recipe, not before it gets served in the White House. He handed me what I would call a tureen but what he assured me was listed in the catalogue as a "party goblet." It contained about a quart of bullshot.

He stretched himself and leaned over to a large jewel box, which might have been a monster cigarette lighter equipped for a man who was going to sit and smoke himself to death without moving. It was a cigarette lighter. It too fizzed and ejected streams of invisible gas, but no light. He picked up a miniature Bible. It was also a cigarette lighter. More fruitless clickings. I thought it was time I did something to restore the prestige of the East. "Remember George Kaufman's line about cigarette lighters?" I yawned.

He was now juggling cigarette lighters the way a Japanese salesman handles transistor radios. "No," he said, "what did Kaufman say?"

"He said that if matches had been invented after lighters they'd be the sensation of the twentieth century."

"A great line," he chortled and went off to the kitchen for a match. At last we sat and sighed and hugged our drinks. "God!" he cried suddenly and quietly, weary beyond telling. He looked across the pool to a fringe of lawn encircled by a short wall which stopped you falling down a bank of vines and the mountain. "Look at that miserable grass! Nobody knows de trouble I seen with that grass."

I peered into the declining sun at the frowzy lawn. "It does look a little beaten up," I said.

"Not beaten up," he snorted, "eaten up."

I was about to ask by whom or what, but at that moment something popped through a hole in the wall, bounced on the lawn, jumped up on the wall, and sat facing out over the valley with its back to us. It looked like one of those gargoyles gazing out over Paris, but knowing a little about the exotic fauna of California I guessed it might be a mongoose or possibly a miniature kangaroo.

"Damn squirrels," muttered my host, "they nibble away everywhere." He reeled off a whole seed catalogue of grasses he'd planted and torn up. "But it does no good, we're just overrun with opossum and skunks and squirrels and muskrat, and the goddam deer come roaming in at night. But gophers. Gophers are the worst. Just look at those holes!"

Through the orange haze of the sunlight I could just see

what he meant. It was not so much a lawn as a chewed-up, rudimentary putting green. He marched off into his bedroom and returned with a rifle. He gingerly slid open the glass doors. He sat just inside the room, and while he was loading the rifle he flicked what I thought was another cigarette lighter, but it was something else this time and the television set whooshed on. A sheriff or a rustler was galloping through a canyon and letting off cannonades of rifle fire. My friend lifted the rifle from his lap and looked toward the lawn—an alert, suburban Hemingway. A gopher stuck its head out of a hole. My friend sighted and banged away. From the telly came an answering blast of gunsmoke.

"Yes, sir," said my friend, "it's a great life out here."

"You can say that again," I said. He said it again.

39

CALIFORNIA:
A FORETASTE OF
TOMORROW

There was a time—and it seems a lifetime away though it was no more than ten or fifteen years ago—when I used to go to California every spring for rest and pleasure and for the special excitements of the West.

If you come from the Eastern states, or farther east still, from Europe, going west is a continuous journey of suspense, from the moment you are over the Appalachians and know that the Atlantic has gone for good. In the Midwest, the sky is a little wider, and the prairie is a kind of sea all its own; so much so that in the wheatlands of Kansas you get the illusion of great heaving yellow swells, and the silos float by like battleships on the horizon. After that, the promise of the West is closer still, and at some point—in my experience it is most dramatic going over the last tilt of the Edwards Plateau in West Texas—the land crumples into majestic folds and you see ahead of you, thirty or forty miles ahead across a sunken plain, the rising foothills and beyond them the several carved-out layers of the Rockies. You are entering what the French call *le Far-Ouest*.

Everyone who is not a dolt feels the romantic lift of going West, and all of us—Americans as well as Europeans

—have been conditioned by the history and the folklore of the Indians and the pioneers and the Argonauts and the homesteaders, and later on by the first air-mail pilots and even by the Okies. And now by the letters back home of Second World War veterans who left the dismal neighborhoods of Pittsburgh or East St. Louis or Chicago or wherever to train on the California coast or sail to the Pacific from there—and who swore they'd go back for keeps and did. If the appeal of the Far West is a romantic illusion it's one that's well nourished by the experiences of the first white people who made the crossing from East to West.

If you get hold of an old map, or one with enough early place names still on it, you can relive—in comfort—the ordeal of the Forty-Niners by letting your eye jump from the way stations they stopped at and named. The first outfitting post, where the railroad and the steamboat ended, and where they picked up their oxen, mules, axes, bags of flour, and bacon for the two-thousand-mile walk to California, strikes the first clarion note with the name Independence, Missouri. For the obvious reason that they meant to stay alive, they followed the rivers, and consequently the sequence of place names they left behind indicates either a preferred route or a good place to rest (Sweetwater, Willow Creek, South Fork). Now they crossed the Great Plains and in time the Rockies, and the names are a little more dour (Bear Trap, Hole-in-the-Rock, Battle Mountain). Then on into the Nevada desert, where the Humboldt River went into the ground and there was no water, and exhausting heat for forty-five miles. You can still go through places that have no more to mark them as towns than a gas station, the skeleton of a rotted house or store, and whose names memorialize the worst passage of the Gold Rush families: Alkali Swamp, Lost Mule-shoe, Dead Man's Well, Endurance. But if they still had their oxen and their children and they'd survived cholera and dysentery they came into lush grassland (Happy Creek Station); and they could be cheerful for a while before the long climb up the Sierras and the prospect of a snowbound winter or the temptation of cut-offs that led to desolation and death. At last, for about two thirds of the thirty thousand that tried it, there were the western foothills and deep meadows again and roaring streams and the distant sight of the Coast Range. And the feeling that the worst was over. Here, along the creeks where the gold was—sometimes—the camps erupted in hysterical or bitter place names: Brandy Gulch, Humbug Canyon, Knock-'Em-Stiff, Rich Bar, Poverty Hill. And those who got to the Coast and looked out on the Pacific shore named two towns that are now pretty indistinguishable from most other free-way suburbs. But the names are there: Crescent City and Eureka.

My point is that even today when you tumble down the Sierras foothills to the west, you feel that the ocean and the end of the journey is there. And it is the place where today twelve hundred permanent settlers every day cry—Eureka! They made it.

I began by saying that as late as a decade or so ago it was possible for a foreign correspondent to go to California for recreation solely, and feel no qualms. In line of duty, if I was not technically on holiday, of course I had to write pieces, and they were usually about the history, the landscape, the physical pleasures of the state: the lupines and other wild flowers smearing the mountains in April, the redwoods, the Spanish missions. Once I remember making a big thing of the fear that an indigenous bird, the California condor, was dying out. And, of course, you could always write something about Hollywood. But roaming around California on company time, so to speak, always encouraged a little guilt, a wobbly feeling that your editor was tapping his teeth in darkest Manchester and hissing, "This is all very well but isn't it time he was getting back to the real America?"—to Washington and the industrial East and the grouches of the Farm Bloc, and the South converting from one-crop farming to a range of crops and challenging Massachusetts and Britain in textiles? And what was *The New York Times* saying? And which Republican candidate was going to be picked for the presidency by the really influential men, by the Eastern Governors and the Midwest diehards and the New York banks and the big men in Pennsylvania?

Well, there has been no more drastic shift in American history of the last hundred years than that from the old California to the new, no more decisive transfer of power than that from the East to the West. Power, and money. No roving reporter need any longer feel guilty about rattling around California. The huge place—it is still roughly eight hundred miles long and two hundred and fifty miles wide—is seething with stories, and I don't mean travel tidbits or local color. It would now be possible, in fact it would show foresight and good judgment, to base yourself in California and report nothing but the most pressing national problems of the United States.

In 1940, this state had just under seven million people. Today it has nineteen million, over five million of them students. It has become—with New York—one of the two great prizes to win in any national election. It is the most populous state, and this old bucolic stamping ground is second only to New York in manufacturing. Only twenty years ago, the professional Californian (who can be as trying as the professional Southerner) used to boast that half of all the lettuces comsumed by Americans—think of it!—came from the Salinas Valley. One small town near Monterey still has an electric sign arching over the highway. It says, "Welcome to the Artichoke Center of the World." It is true, but the ceremonial advertising of it is a hangover from the days when California boasted about its citrus fruit, the movies, the climate, and its happy retired population because it didn't seem to be able to lay claim to much else. (Though, even forty years ago, its two biggest industries were tourism and petroleum.)

Its politics have always been something that nobody cared to explain at length. I don't mean they were particularly corrupt, even when they were dominated by a single railroad. But they were and are very complicated. Lord Bryce, I think it was, writing back in the 1890's, said that there were four main variations of democratic government: the British parliamentary system, the American federal system, the French assembly system, and California politics. Of these, he added, "that of California is the most complicated."

So California has always been rich in local color and local conflict. But until the Second World War it was an outlying kingdom on the Pacific Coast: beautiful, self-conscious, self-regarding, its old miner's passion for gambling adapted by quacks and immigrant evangelists into short cuts to riches or salvation. A place out of the mainstream of American business and American power. The day came when California was called upon for a special contribution to the war. It had been shipping billions of pounds of fruits and vegetables and petroleum, and it came to devise the K-ration for guerrilla fighters. But when Britain was begging for all the ships' tonnage that an ally could provide, it seemed to Washington that the labor of New Orleans and the Gulf Coast and the old-line West Coast shipbuilders was not enough. There appeared a man. And if you are to attribute the turn in California's fortunes to any one man, Henry Kaiser is that man. He was a new type, an industrial-mass-production expert. A producer of what? That was beside the point. You name your needs and he would supply them. He made the absurd promise to mass-produce ships. The traditional ship-builders, the old Scots and their San Francisco cousins, laughed at a man who talked about "the front end" of a ship. Roosevelt was an old navy man too, but he didn't mind what you called it so long as you delivered. Well, Kaiser promised to deliver one ship, one Liberty Ship, a day. And did. He came to be irritated by the slow business of getting steel from the Great Lakes, two thousand miles away. California, he announced, must have its own steel factories. Where, I remember asking him, would he get his ores? "We'll mooch around out here," he said, "and find them." He found them in Utah. The steel factories rose, and soon the airplane factories were out-employing the movies and the clothing manufacturers and the fruit packers and the insurance companies combined.

I sit here on the crest of the hills and look west to the monster city of Los Angeles—forty miles wide, is it?—which is already a prevision of what all our cities, here and abroad, are likely to become. And I look east, down into the San Fernando Valley, which in the late 1940's was a romantic relic of Spanish California, with its small, dusty, red-tiled towns, and its corrals and ranches and its noble battalions of eucalyptus marching between the mountains. Bing Crosby had a popular song dripping with nostalgia for old California: "Make the San Fernando Valley My Home." One million, one hundred thousand people have since taken him up on it. Today, a couple of hundred thousand of them work on a fat slice of all the contracts of the space industry. Down the coast to the Mexican border you can spend days and nights visiting research institutes and "think tanks" in everything from weather forecasting to nuclear war strategy, the future of

light metals, landing on the moon, the plotting and shape of
cities on the ocean bed. The serious purpose of some of these
doubledome colonies is often questioned by visitors—visiting
Europeans, naturally—who find it painful to believe that the
native habitat of Shirley Temple and Aimee Semple McPher-
son can house pioneers in anything other than fake religions
or a new color process. Naturally, there are phonies abounding, but so there are in any new specialty.

It is the human growth of California that makes it now a
microcosm of the United States in the last third of the twentieth century, and a bubbling test tube of its most characteristic problems: of education, of budget balancing, of public
welfare, of race, of crime, of city management, of housing, of
pollution. In its cities and bulging small towns, California
began to face a decade ago the kind of social ordeal that is
now causing anguish all over. This challenge, mated to the
wealth of its new resources, is what has provoked its advanced
technology, attracted inventive people and new materials and
management techniques and Nobel Prize winners, and the
new people doing the new work in biochemistry, astrophysics,
and the planning—if planning is any longer possible—of the
modern city. The most serious threat to the old authority of a
university comes from California. The most voracious need
for new schools. The most flagrant types of criminal youth.
The most insistent demands of the medically indigent. The
most vocal opposition to Vietnam. The most haunting fear of
racial war.

It used to be said that you had to know what was
happening in America because it gave us a glimpse of our
future. Today, the rest of America, and after that Europe,
had better heed what happens in California, for it already
reveals the type of civilization that is in store for all of us.

40

A BAD NIGHT IN
LOS ANGELES

It does not seem nearly so long ago as thirty years that the trade of the foreign correspondent caught the fancy of the Hollywood producers. And for good reason. Hitler was on the loose, and Europe was crackling with crises and atrocities, and some of the best American reporters of the time—John Gunther and Vincent Sheean and Ed Murrow—always seemed to be on hand. They came to look like heroic agents of the American people, who were fascinated and repelled at long distance by the violence of Europe and who, I must say, indulged a good deal of self-righteousness in parroting the ancient American lament about "old, sick Europe."

Well, I was saying, the foreign correspondent was in vogue. And soon Hollywood created a romantic stereotype of him. First in the Boy Scout version of Joel McCrea in a trench coat, then in the subtler variation of Bogart, who acted so tough and seemed as tricky as Goebbels but who—for all his smoker's cough and his cynical appraisal of passing females—was secretly on the side of all good men and true.

This attractive stereotype was not only larger than life but luckier than any journalist living or dead. He followed unerringly in the tracks of dictators and tipped off foreign ministers marked for *Anschluss*. He was behind the curtain when a king signed an instrument of abdication. He knew the man who shot the prime minister. He decoded the vital message that gave the date of the invasion. He was always where the action was.

In life, it is not like that. Only by the wildest freak is a reporter, after many years on the hop, actually present at a single accidental convulsion of history. Mostly, we write the coroner's inquest, the account of the funeral, the reconstruction of the prison riot, the *trial* of the spy, not the hatching of the plot.

On the night of Tuesday, June 4, 1968, for the first time in thirty years, I found myself, by one casual chance in a thousand, on hand: in a narrow serving pantry of the Ambassador Hotel in Los Angeles, a place that, I suppose, will never be wiped out of my memory as a sinister alley, a Roman circus run amok, and a charnel house. It would be false to say, as I should truly like to say, that I am sorry I was there. It is more complicated than that. Nothing so simple as a conflict between professional pride and human revulsion, between having the feelings and having to sit down and write about them. Yet, because I saw it for once not as an event to comment on but as a thunderbolt assault on the senses, my own view of the whole thing, now and later, is bound to be from the stomach up to the head. Visceral, as we say. I don't imagine that if your hand falls on a live wire you are in any condition to measure the charge or judge the sense of the public safety regulations or moralize about the electric company's dereliction of duty.

So my view of this miserable episode is probably strange and I ought not to ascribe to anybody else the shape or color of the opinions that floated up later from my muddled sensations. I warn you about this, because I feel unmoved by some ideas that others feel strongly, and on the other hand I have some fears that others may not share. So, since this is a more personal talk than I could have hoped, I had better tell you how it came about.

On that Tuesday afternoon, I was in San Francisco, on one of those jewel-like days that are revealed when the wrapping of the morning fog has been lifted. I had no great urge to fly to the vast spread of Los Angeles. On the contrary, I had hoped to spend the day padding down the fairways of the Olympic Club, which run like cathedral aisles between superb stands of cypresses. But it was election day, and Los Angeles is now the hub of California politics, if only because— of the fifty-eight counties of California—Los Angeles County alone accounts for 48 per cent of the vote. For the purpose of an election dateline, San Francisco, four hundred-odd miles away, was not much better than New York City. So it had to be done. I was going to have to report the general atmosphere of the winner's camp and the loser's.

I had seen scores of these election-night entertainments. They are amiable but blowsy affairs. But to give me a fresh view of a ceremony that had staled by familiarity, and also to make some compensation to a hostess who had offered me a bed, I had asked her if she would like to mooch around the town with me and see what we could see. She was agog with anticipation, for just as a foreign correspondent thinks a movie actress must have a fascinating life, so a movie actress thought a correspondent's life must be glamorous in the extreme.

So, high in the Santa Monica hills, amid the scent of the eucalyptus and the pepper trees, we sat for a while after the polls closed and waited for a sign of the outcome. You don't have to wait long in these computer days. The

Oregon result was exactly predicted by the Big Brain twelve
minutes after the polls closed, when the returns already in
were less than one per cent. Somehow, the Brain was having
more trouble with California. Party politics are, for various
historical reasons, very loosely organized in that state, and,
for one thing, its northern end tends to contradict the verdict
of the south. So when the early returns from the north showed
McCarthy in a commanding lead it proved nothing. Los
Angeles County, with its heavy working-class vote and its
swarms of Negroes (or blacks, as we are now more respectfully meant to say), and its Mexican-Americans, was fairly
certain to go heavily for Kennedy. Pretty soon, the gap between McCarthy's tally and Kennedy's began to shrink and
it became clear that, saving a miracle, McCarthy would not
be able to withstand the avalanche of Los Angeles votes that
began to move in for Kennedy. The computers were silent,
but the writing was on the wall.

Just before eleven, then, we took off for the McCarthy
hotel, and there was no doubt when we got there that the
college boys and the miniskirt girls and the wandering poets
and the spruced-up student leaders and the chin-up McCarthy
staff were whistling in a graveyard. There was a rock band
that whooped it up all the louder to drown out the inevitable
news. They would pause awhile, and another ominous sta-
tistic would be flashed, and an m.c. would shout, "Are we
downhearted?" And the ballroom crowd would roar its defiance of the obvious.

The Ambassador, a comparatively venerable hotel miles
away on Wilshire Boulevard, was the Kennedy headquarters.
And that was the place to be. We took off, and so did lots
of other people, so that when we turned into the long driveway we lined up behind scores of cars containing all those
sensible people who love a winner. At last we got into the

hotel lobby and a tumult of singing, cheering, and happy hobnobbing. Election parties give out innumerable tickets and badges to keep out the rabble, but no one is more aware than a winning candidate that on such occasions the rabble are the people. So you can usually drift with the multitude and nobody asks for a credential.

It was not so at the Ambassador. Guards and cops blocked the entrance to the ballroom, and I doubt that a passport and a birth certificate and a personal recommendation from Senator Kennedy could have got you in. My own general press credentials were useless. The lobbies were too packed to lift an elbow and too deafening to talk in. My companion and I screamed at each other through the din of all these happy people and we decided that the whole safari had been a mistake. We turned and started down the corridor for the outdoors and for home.

On our left, about fifty feet along, was another door to another room and a pack of people trying and failing to get through. There was a guard shaking his head continuously and pushing people back and behind him a young Kennedy staff man turning down everybody. This man shouted over the bobbing heads, "Mr. Cooke, come on, you can get in here." We were folded in through the mob and emerged, as from a chute, into an open place: a cool, half-empty room, a small private dining room of the hotel stripped and fitted out as a press room. There were two newsmen I knew and a radio man untangling cables, and a swarthy photographer in a sweatshirt locking up his cameras, and one or two middle-aged women and a half-dozen Western Union girls, and a fat girl in a Kennedy boater, a young reporter in a beard, and, I guess, his girl.

It was a perfect private way through to the ballroom. But one of my reporter friends said, "You don't want to get in

there. It's murder in there. Anyway, Pierre"—Pierre Salinger
—"has promised that when Bobby gets through his speech
he'll come through into this room and talk with us." It was
an unbelievable break. We sat down and had a drink and
heard the telegraph girls tapping out copy and tried not to
wince at the television set in a corner that was tuned up to
a howling decibel level.

A few minutes later the television commentators gave
way to the ballroom scene, and Bobby was up there with his
beaming helpers and his ecstatic little wife, and he was thank-
ing everybody and saying things must change, and so on to
Chicago. It was about eighteen minutes after midnight. We
were standing outside the swinging doors that gave onto a
serving pantry he would come through on his way from the
ballroom to us. These doors had no glass peepholes, but we'd
soon hear the pleasant bustle of him coming through greeting
the colored chef and various waiters and bus boys who had
lined up to shake his hand.

Then. Above the bassy boom of the television there was
a banging repetition of sounds. Like somebody dropping a
rack of trays, or banging a single tray against a wall. Half
a dozen of us were startled enough to head for the swinging
doors, and suddenly we were jolted through by a flying wedge
of other men. It had just happened. It was a narrow lane he
had to come through, for there were two long steam tables
and somebody had stacked up against them those trellis
gates, with artificial leaves stuck on them, that they use to
fence a dance band off from the floor. The only light was the
blue-white light of three fluorescent tubes slotted in the ceiling.

We heard nothing but a howling jungle of cries and
obscenities and saw a turmoil of arms and fearful faces and
flying limbs, and two enormous backs—of Roosevelt Grier,

the football player, and Rafer Johnson, the Olympic champion—piling onto a pair of jeans or chinos on a steam table.
There was a head on the floor streaming blood, and somebody
put a Kennedy boater under it, and the blood trickled down
the sides like chocolate sauce on an iced cake. There were
splashes of flash bulbs, and infernal heat, and the button eyes
of Ethel Kennedy turned to cinders. She was wrestling or slap-
ping a young man and he was saying, "Listen, lady, I'm hurt,
too." And then she was on her knees cradling him briefly, and
in another little pool of light on the greasy floor was a huddle
of clothes and staring out of it the face of Bobby Kennedy,
like the stone face of a child's effigy on a cathedral tomb.

I had, and have, no idea of the stretch of time, or any
immediate sense of the event itself. Everybody has a vulner-
able organ that reacts to shock, and mine is the stomach. My
lips were like emery paper and I was feeling very sick and
hollow. I pattered back into the creamy-green genteel dining
room. And only then did I hear somebody yell, "Kennedy's
shot, they shot him." I heard a girl nearby moan, "No, no,
not again!" And while I was thinking, "That was in Dallas,"
a dark woman suddenly bounded to a table and beat it and
howled like a wolf, "Goddam stinking country! No! No! No!
No! No! No! No!" Another woman attacked the bright television screen and the image of the placid commentators, who
had not yet got the news. My companion was fingering a
cigarette package like a paralytic. I sat her down and went
back in again. Everybody wanted to make space and air,
but everybody also wanted to see the worst. By now, the
baying and the moaning had carried over into the ballroom,
and it sounded like a great hospital bombed and in panic.

It may have been a minute or twenty minutes later when
a squad of cops bristling with shotguns burst toward us

through the swinging doors of the pantry with their bundle
of the black curly head and the jeans, and the tight, small
behind, and the limp head, and a face totally dazed.

Well, the next morning, when I saw and heard the
Pope in his gentle, faltering English, I still could not believe
that he was talking about the squalid, appalling scene in a
hotel pantry that I had been a part of and would always be
a part of.

I don't doubt that such an experience is a trauma. And
because of it, and five days later, I still cannot rise to the
editorial pages and the general lamentations about a sick
society. I for one do not feel like an accessory to a crime.
And I reject, almost as a frivolous obscenity, the notion of
collective guilt, the idea that I or the American people killed
John Fitzgerald Kennedy and Martin Luther King and Robert
Francis Kennedy. I don't believe, either, that *you* conceived
Hitler, and that in some deep unfathomable sense all Europe
was responsible for the extermination of six million Jews.
With Edmund Burke, I don't know how you can indict a
whole nation. To me, this now roaringly fashionable theme
is a great folly. It is difficult to resist, because it provides
emergency resuscitation to one's self-esteem. It deflects the
search for a villain to some big corporate culprit. It offers
cheap reassurance, cut-rate wisdom, but is really a way of
opting out of the human situation: a situation that includes
pity for the dead Kennedys and the living, compassion for
Sirhan Sirhan, and sympathy for the American nation at a
time when the vicious side of its frontier tradition—to which
it has owed its vigor and variety—is surging up again, for
reasons that no one has accurately diagnosed.

I said as much as this to a young friend. And he replied,
"Me too. I don't feel implicated in the murder of John or

Bobby Kennedy. But when Martin Luther King is killed, the only people who know that you and I are not like the killers are you and I."

It is a tremendous sentence and exposes the present danger to America and its public order. The more people talk about collective guilt, the more they will feel it. For after three hundred years of subjection and lively prejudice, any desperate black man or deluded outcast is likely to act as if it were true: that the American people, and not their derelicts, are the villains.

EPILOGUE

41

VIETNAM

There was once a British ambassador to this country, a good man now dead, who—like most of his predecessors, with the blinding exception of Lord Bryce—had much trouble understanding the difference between a parliamentary system and a federal system. He could not understand why the Cabinet didn't sit in Congress, nor why the legislature and the executive were completely separate. No one, I'm afraid, had explained to him the Founding Fathers' pressing fear of a military dictatorship, of a king with a private army, and the precautions they took to frustrate it by setting up the President and the Congress as natural enemies. Or you can say that they set up the President as the chief executive of the state and then provided for a permanent pack of watchdogs to check his every move. The ambassador wrote down in his journal this conclusion: "This leaves the President's press conference as a poor substitute for the regular cross-examination of ministers at question-time in the House of Commons."

Well, the President's press conference does seem to be the obvious counterpart. It is obvious but it is wrong. And many an American Cabinet officer could wish it wasn't. For occasional exposure in the House of Commons to a rasping question or even a guffaw is not to be compared, as a form of executive torture, to an all-day inquisition by a standing committee of Congress. The Congressional inquiry, I'd say, is the nerve system of what Americans like to call "the democratic process." And nowhere is it seen to more terrifying effect than in the cross-examination of a Secretary of State by the Senate Foreign Relations Committee. This committee has the power to reject ambassadors and treaties proposed by the President.

In the spring of 1968, then, it was anxious to recall the President to his constitutional duty to seek the "advice and consent of the Senate" on a war that had got away from both of them: the undeclared war in Vietnam. So the Secretary of State, called as the President's understudy, was subjected to the third degree by the representatives of the people. If that sounds a little lurid or sentimental, let me remind you of the cast of characters that sat like a court of judges there and challenged Secretary Rusk from ten in the morning to six thirty one day, and from nine to two the next.

The lives and labors of these men may not represent (as advertising executives like to say about their wives) a "cross section of the American people." But they made up an impressive sample of the variety of the millions who chose them. There was a farmer from Vermont, a mining engineer from Montana, a Rhodes scholar from Arkansas, the schoolteacher son of a hardware merchant from South Dakota, an electric-products manufacturer from Missouri, a stockman from Kansas. The mining engineer wound up as a professor of Latin American and Far Eastern history. The electric-products man was a former Secretary of the Air. The schoolteacher was also a famous fisherman. There were six lawyers, not too many to reflect the preponderance of lawyers who sit in Congress and who do, after all, make the laws. None of these men had been in the Senate for less than twelve years; the farmer had been there twenty-eight years and two others for twenty-four years. Five of them were veterans of the First War. One saw action in the Second in Burma and China. Another was a survivor of the Normandy invasion. Two of them had, and have, enough ordinary vanity not to give their ages in the *Congressional Directory*. If you think of them in this variety you will be less inclined to imagine a cartoonist's Star Chamber of Neanderthal men bearing the tag "Senate Committee."

Secretary Rusk had resisted this call for two years. But there was a well-substantiated rumor that General Westmoreland wanted another two hundred thousand troops. And suddenly the world expressed its distrust of American policy by losing its confidence in the dollar. So the Secretary yielded and agreed to go before the committee and talk about the administration's request for foreign aid. But the committee had brought him in to expound and defend the administration's policy on Vietnam. The excuse for ignoring the main theme being that you can't guess how much money will be left over for any other dependent country until you've gauged the expense and the probable scale of the war in Vietnam. For two days Secretary Rusk was questioned and quizzed and lectured to and pleaded with by a committee whose old ratio of hawks to doves was significantly shrinking. The role of Chairman Fulbright as a scold and ironist could now be presumed. So could the ringing patriotism of Senator Mundt of South Dakota and the troubled curiosity of young Senator Church of Idaho and the holy wrath of Senator Wayne Morse of Oregon, God's favorite maverick.

But at these sessions only Fulbright and Morse stayed with the usual script. The others were sufficiently disturbed to think aloud with more honesty and eloquence than they had shown before. And all of them maintained an unfailing gravity and courtesy such as men do when they are scared, when they are losing an attitude and acquiring an anxiety. Nothing was more startling than Senator Mundt's forlorn suspicion that elections in South Vietnam were not alone worth the ensnaring of half a million Americans into the continental bog of Southeast Asia. And a bugle sounding the retreat is not more ominous than the confession of Senator Symington, a resolute hawk, that he was now a prey to misgiving. Senator Symington had been saying for years that the war had better be won or written off, since the day was coming when the United States would have to weigh the cost of it in gold that wasn't there. He has always been indulged by his colleagues and friends as a man riding a comical hobbyhorse. This time, he had the sad satisfaction of being taken seriously.

We have not talked lately about Vietnam, whereas once we talked about little else, because everything that could be said has been said. Families, friends, and the workers at the same bench either ran with their own kind or resigned themselves, as so many bad marriages do, to a kind of despairing truce. But now we were measuring, with quite a new sort of alarm, the eleven and a half billion dollars in the Treasury that covered our stock of gold against the twenty-six billion a year that was being spent on Vietnam. And, at last, the American casualties in Vietnam surpassed those of Korea: a turn which, I suggested a year ago, would be the hardest test of the people's tolerance of the war.

So we were shaking ourselves out of the stupor and the truce, and starting all over again with the fundamental questions. How had it come about? Was it indeed a crusade or a vast miscalculation? Would Asia crumble to Communism if South Vietnam fell? Was it the wrong war in the wrong place, or the right war in the wrong place? Was the United States the only man in the boat rowing in time?

A hundred books and a thousand editorial writers have recited and disputed the political origins of the war and enlarged on the human tragedy of its conduct. What matters, or will come to matter to most people, I think, is not any new balance we can strike in the old argument; but the realization that America, which has seldom lost a war, is not invincible; and the very late discovery that an elephant can trumpet and shake the earth but not the self-possession of the ants who hold it. So when I say how did it come about, I am not thinking of splitting the hair between the SEATO treaty's pledge to resist "aggression" and the American protocol that stipulated "Communist aggression." I mean, how did the American people move from their early indifference or complacency to the recognition of a nightmare?

Well, the war crept up on us with no more menace than a zephyr. South Vietnam was only one of many strange place names that joined the noble roll call of countries which America, in the early glow of its world power, swore to protect and defend. If Russia, that atomic monolith, could be scared off Iran and Greece and Turkey and foiled in western Europe, it never crossed our minds that we couldn't intimidate Asian Communists who fought with sticks and stones. Certainly it would have been churlish to deny these brave little countries the handful of American "technicians" they needed to train their armies. (We presumed, without doing much detective work, that—as with Belgium and Finland at other times—the democratic credentials of Thailand, Pakistan, Laos, Cambodia, Vietnam, and the other signatories could be taken for granted.) In 1962, we moved troops into the Mekong Delta and the Pathet Lao withdrew. And that took care of Laos.

Johnson came in, and for a year or more the shadow of

Vietnam failed to darken the bright procession of legislation he drove through the Eighty-ninth Congress. It dawned on us very slowly that the American technicians were turning into American soldiers. Then we admitted that the men were off to the rice paddies and not the desks and hospitals behind the lines. The draft felt the chill, and the college boys, and the Vietniks were born. It was not with most of them a conscientious objection to war itself. Most, I think, would have admitted that Hitler had to be stopped and that Korea, the first United Nations war, was a good war. But they were baffled by the morality of this war, which killed more civilians than soldiers and devastated the land we were sworn to protect: a war in which there were no attacks at dawn, no discernible lines, and few human restraints either of rules or of weapons. "Napalm" and "fragmentation bombs" came into the language and sickened us, though our own "strategic bombing" of Dresden in the Second War had been worse than Hiroshima, and millions of women and children had been routed from their homes in Europe too. War, the administration could only remind us, was hell. So we piled up the forces and piled on the force and dropped more bombs than all the bombs dropped in Europe and Africa in the Second War. The American forces rose from thirty thousand to fifty, then to a hundred thousand and then to half a million. And the latest word was that perhaps seven hundred thousand might in truth fulfill the promises of the generals, whose estimates of when and how the turn might come had dreadfully paralleled the expert predictions of the French generals before them.

These and many other doubts and disasters were aired and tossed before Dean Rusk. The administration's position had something of the straightforward grandeur of Bach, if only Bach had been the tune that were called for. The theme was that the war in Asia was a continuation of the European struggle, first against Hitler, then against the Russians. The United States was pledged to resist aggression against free nations. If one pledge was betrayed, then the other wards and dependents would panic and succumb to Communism. The countries of Southeast Asia are a stack of dominoes and if one falls so will they all.

Down the years, the administration has offered us many warning historical examples of what happens to a strong power which yields to an aggressor bit by bit. The favorite analogy is Munich, and it has been reinforced by the old tag about nations that know no history being doomed to repeat it.

But many people have looked at this analogy and rejected it, as they have rejected, also, the analogy of Korea, where there was a clear aggression, so defined by all the sitting members of the United Nations Security Council. The New Left has a bad-tempered analogy of its own in the white man's treatment of the Indians in this country: the determination to obliterate him for his own good and resettle him on permanently protected "enclaves" of bare land on which no white man could exist. I myself keep thinking of Napoleon's disastrous adventure in Haiti. The ideology and the excuse for this overseas expedition were quite different from ours. On the contrary, Napoleon moved to denounce and destroy the extension of self-government to the natives. But strategically, the adventure so far from home has a lesson for us. To put down the native peoples he dispatched an expedition of seven warships and forty-five thousand of his crack soldiers; which, at the time, must have seemed every bit as formidable as our half million and their bombers. But there was a native general, Christophe, who revived a tactic used originally by the Tunisians against the Arabs and later known as a "scorched earth" policy. More successful still was his practice of "guerrilla warfare," so called. Not all the armament and skill of the most modern army in Europe could suppress these roving guerrillas, who were friends by day and enemies by night, who never stood and made a front, who could live on the forage of the fields, and take yellow fever or leave it, who pounded prepared positions and dissolved into the earth. A ragged native population whipped the best of France. It was enough to turn Napoleon against any more campaigns at four thousand miles and to decide him against conquering North America; with the happy result, for us, that he sold the huge reaches of the Louisiana Territory to Jefferson for fifteen million dollars.

These analogies are dangerous to press, because you are always faced with a situation in which what is new hurts more than what is familiar. Still, I think that the view of the United States as Napoleon in Haiti is better than the view of Ho Chi Minh as Hitler in Europe.

There is one awful possibility that was put to me, when the war was only beginning to warm up, by the late Pandit Nehru. It is that a Western power, finding itself deep in Asia, might simply refuse to believe, as the Romans did, that its Roman might could possibly be disabled by a primitive people. "You see," said this bland Indian, "the trouble with Westerners is, they hate to lose face." It was too early in the game to reflect that a Texan might hate it more than anybody.

Yet, it seems to me that anyone who ridicules the domino theory is obliged to say how and why it is wrong, and to suggest some better way of, as Dean Rusk put it, "organizing the peace" either through the United Nations or through some alliance that can guarantee preponderant power. Preponderant power—that has always been the true deterrent, in spite of the Christian rhetoric that breathed so piously through the preamble to the Treaty of Westphalia (1648) and through the preamble to the Charter of the United Nations (1945). All these favorable balances of power have expressed that power through their willingness to use their ultimate weapon. With the British it was the navy, and it was through their navy that they could patrol the seven seas, put down wars in Asia, confine all big wars to Europe, and backstop for landbound allies. Today the United States is the world's greatest power only through its nuclear power. But, what is never acknowledged, the universal taboo against the use of this power disarms America at a blow and leaves it a large and rich but far from omnipotent power, capable of fighting one or two unconventional wars with conventional weapons.

This, it seems to me, is the real American position in the world today and the reason why its best aims are frustrated. The United States has one hundred and thirty-two military bases abroad and solemn treaty "commitments" to come to the aid of forty-three nations if they are attacked or, what is more likely these days, disrupted from within. The earnest and gentle Senator Church put his finger on this Achilles heel by asking the Secretary if the great conflict was not between "commitment and capacity." In other words, America may be right, but is she able?

How did it come about that this country, led successively by a soldier, then by an alert foreign affairs student, and then by the shrewdest of politicians, committed itself to play St. George to forty-three dragons? We must go back, I think, to what I called the "early glow" of American world power, in the early 1950's. That is when the pledges were given, and when the cost of them was never counted. The Communists, not to mention the nationalists, and the millions of Asians who simply want to see the white men leave their continent for good, had not attempted a test of American power. As late as the day of Kennedy's inauguration, the United States was still flexing and rippling its muscles for lack of exercise. And on that day, the President delivered himself of a sentence, magnificent as rhetoric, appalling as policy. Secretary Rusk, very much moved, recited it to the committee as the touchstone of America's resolve: "Let every nation know, whether it wishes us well or ill, that we shall pay any price, bear any burden, meet any hardship, support any friend, oppose any foe to assure the survival and the success of liberty."

This is fine to read but fatal to act on. It may be the wish of a strong nation to do this, but in reality it will not support *any* friend or fight *any* foe, or support the burden, say, of a civil war in its own land, in order to rush to the aid of forty-three friends and fight forty-three foes. Vietnam, I fear, is the price of the Kennedy Inaugural.

Alfred Alistair Cooke was born, of Anglo-Irish parentage, in Manchester, England, on November 20, 1908. After schooling in the north of England he took First Class honors in English at Cambridge University and became a Scholar of Jesus College. Elected to a Commonwealth Fellowship, he did graduate work for two years at Yale and Harvard and returned to England in 1934 to become the BBC's film critic. After doing many BBC programs on the literature, life, and folk song of the United States, he covered the Abdication crisis of Edward VIII for NBC and returned here to be a commentator for that network. Subsequently he joined the London *Times* as a special correspondent on American affairs; in 1945 he was appointed the United Nations correspondent of *The Guardian* of England (then the *Manchester Guardian*), and since 1948 he has been *The Guardian's* chief American correspondent.

For nine years Mr. Cooke was the MC of the television program *Omnibus*. He is the author of *Douglas Fairbanks: The Making of a Screen Character; A Generation on Trial: U.S.A. v. Alger Hiss; One Man's America; Christmas Eve; A Commencement Address;* and *Around the World in Fifty Years* (done for the fiftieth anniversary of the World Book Encyclopedia); he is the editor of two anthologies, *Garbo and the Night Watchmen* and *The Vintage Mencken*. He lists his hobbies in *Who's Who* as "golf, music, photography, chess, beachcombing, and the American West." He is married to Jane White, the painter, has two children, and lives in New York City.

A NOTE ON THE TYPE

The text of this book is set in Monticello, a Linotype revival of the original Binny & Ronaldson Roman No. 1, cut by Archibald Binny and cast in 1796 by that Philadelphia type foundry. The face was named Monticello in honor of its use in the monumental fifty-volume *Papers of Thomas Jefferson*, published by Princeton University Press. Monticello is a transitional type design, embodying certain features of Bulmer and Baskerville, but it is a distinguished face in its own right. Composed, printed and bound by Kingsport Press, Inc., Kingsport, Tenn. Typography and binding design by Golda Fishbein.